AFRO-NOSTALGIA

THE NEW BLACK STUDIES SERIES

Edited by Darlene Clark Hine and Dwight A. McBride

A list of books in the series appears at the end of this book.

AFRO-NOSTALGIA

FEELING GOOD
IN CONTEMPORARY
BLACK CULTURE

Badia Ahad-Legardy

**UNIVERSITY OF
ILLINOIS PRESS**
Urbana, Chicago, and Springfield

Publication of this book was supported by funding from the
Office of Research Services at Loyola University Chicago.
© 2021 by the Board of Trustees
of the University of Illinois
All rights reserved
Manufactured in the United States of America
1 2 3 4 5 C P 5 4 3 2 1
♾ This book is printed on acid-free paper.

Library of Congress Control Number: 2020950322
ISBN 978-0-252-04366-6 (hardcover)
ISBN 978-0-252-08566-6 (paperback)
ISBN 978-0-252-05255-2 (e-book)

This book is dedicated to my mother, Anna Lowe (1953–2007), who taught me that even in the most of troubling times, there always exists a space for joy.

Contents

Acknowledgments

In November 2018, I had the pleasure of moderating a panel at the American Studies Association conference on the topic of everyday utopias and black happiness. A common thread in our discussion was the relative absence of these narratives within academia and popular culture—scholar Bianca Williams shared that people often experienced something akin to cognitive dissonance when she mentioned working on a book about black women and happiness; Tricia Hersey, artist, activist, and founder of *The Nap Ministry*, had to arrange her own photo shoot because there were so few stock photos of black people at rest and leisure. Though we were at a professional meeting, the room of a dozen or so people became a space of testimony and healing; by the end, I overheard Tricia taking addresses from attendees to send them a special tea made of chamomile and mugwort that would help them rest.

This book is my own contribution to highlighting spaces of pleasure and happiness in the lives of black folks. Selfishly, it was born out of my own desire to find a way through the ongoing grief I experienced around the deaths of my mother and grandmother, the deaths of black lives taken too soon, the social and political violence by which we're subsumed on social media, and the daily indignities we endure. Everyone who had a hand in bringing this book to life has been a source of light for me as I endeavored to construct an archive of black joy.

I could not have asked for a better hand to guide this project than that of my editor, Dawn Durante. When I first approached her to discuss this project, Dawn immediately understood the value of this project even in its earliest (and roughest) stages. I deeply appreciate your timeliness, your professionalism, and your transparency throughout this process. Thank you for being a champion of this book, and for believing in me. You are the kind of editor with whom every writer hopes to work.

Also, thank you to the anonymous readers of this manuscript for the time you took to read this book in full and to offer sharp insight and feedback. Your thoughtful comments, questions, and intellectual breadth and wisdom made the revision process more difficult than I could have imagined and, consequently, made this book better than I could have envisioned.

Malcolm Gladwell once said that unless you have had the experience of someone fine-tuning your sentences, you really haven't written. Thank you to Joshua Boydstun, Sarah Grey, and Katie Tweed for your keen eye and helpful suggestions. You have helped define for me what it means to be a writer.

This book simply would not be without the intellectual community of which I am privileged to be a part. A special thank you to Suzanne Bost, Elizabeth Fenton, Naomi Greyser, Jeffrey Glover, Habiba Ibrahim, and Krista Thompson. I am so grateful to you for reading portions of this book and offering comments that elevated it. I deeply appreciate the tough questions and the pushes to further clarify, complicate, and consider. This book is what it is because of your compassionate criticism and encouragement.

I would also like to thank the National Center for Faculty Development and Diversity (NCFDD) for instilling within me, at a very early stage in my career, the virtues of daily writing and building accountability structures for my writing practice. Without this discipline, writing this book without a sabbatical or research leave, while teaching a full course load and performing administrative duties, would have been nearly unachievable. Thank you to Julie Artis, Kimberly Blockett, Joy Gaston Gayles, Rachel McLaren, Anthony Ocampo, and Rosemarie Roberts for sharing your friendship and for normalizing daily rewards, taking weekends off, and prioritizing self-care. Thank you to the team at NCFDD, especially Kerry Ann Rockquemore, for allowing me so many wonderful opportunities to do the undervalued but important work of faculty development, and for creating the space for me to test new possibilities for myself, personally and professionally.

How fortunate I am to have found a special group of women—my academic girlfriends—with whom I can converse about everything from social theory to social media. Our brunches, lunches, dinners, midday conversations/venting sessions/therapy, goal-setting, and random "you got this" text messages have kept me sane and grounded. Despite the reality of often being "the only one" in far too many professional environments, because of you I have never felt alone in this journey. Thank you, Michelle Boyd, Lorena Garcia, Helen Jun, and Mindi Thompson. I cannot imagine going through this academic life without your loving support.

A special thank you to those with whom I've been in conversation over the past few years about scholarly and artistic life and work, and whose friendship and collegiality has been both invaluable and inspiring: Stephanie Batiste, Michelle Commander, Gavriel Cutipa-Zorn, Roderick Ferguson, Krista Franklin, Avery Gordon, Glenn Hendler, Tricia Hersey, Allyson Hobbs, Jennifer James, E. Patrick Johnson, Amanda Lewis, Aida Levy-Hussen, Dwight A. McBride, Jonathan Metzl, Koritha Mitchell, Natalie Moore, Walton Muyumba, Mark Anthony Neal, Oiyan Poon, Kyla Wazana Tompkins, Rhonda Wheatley, Amanda Williams, and Bianca Williams.

I would also like to thank my colleagues at Loyola University Chicago for their ongoing friendship and support: Twyla Blackmond-Larnell, Melissa Bradshaw, Pamela Caughie, David Chinitz, Sacha Coupet, Jack Cragwall, Helena Dagadu, Noni Gaylord-Harden, James Knapp, Priyanka Jacob, Paul Jay, Harveen Mann, Frederick Staidum, and Joyce Wexler. A special thank you to the Loyola University Chicago Office of Research Services for providing institutional support to assist with the publication of this manuscript, and to librarian extraordinaire, Niamh McGuighan, for offering research assistance and fair use expertise.

Put simply, family is everything. I could not ask for better in-laws than Byron and Willie Legardy and Jennifer and Charles Williams, who are always present to celebrate the small victories and huge accomplishments. I am grateful to my aunt, Romi, for reminding me to prioritize my health and well-being and for loving me since before I came into this world; my sister, Muneerah, whose friendship is one of my greatest gifts—your unconditional love and pragmatism are virtues from which I am fortunate to benefit; and my step/dad, Michael, for always being there, for offering your wisdom, and for showing me how to accept people as they are and love them anyway.

Lauren and Nathan Jr.—because of you I have become a better person. Your love has changed me mostly by motivating me to be the best version of myself. Keep shining, kiddos, the world is yours.

Last, but certainly not least, thank you to my husband, Nathan, for your patience, for your love, and for your gift of the space I needed to explore my ideas and to be alone with this book. I am grateful to have found a partner with whom I have so much in common, especially a love of leisure. You are my North Star.

Introduction
Ten Thousand Recollections

Afro-Nostalgia and Contemporary Black Aesthetics

In a recent NPR interview, novelist Zadie Smith commented that "histori-cal nostalgia" was a sentiment not "available" to black people: "I can't go back to the fifties because life in the fifties for me is not pretty, nor is it pretty in 1320 or 1460 or 1580 or 1820 or even 1960 in this country, very frankly."[1] For some Americans, evoking "the fifties" telegraphs a social and political era of white hegemony and power signified by *Leave It to Beaver*, social conservatism, and the suburban boom. Conversely, for many black Americans, 1950s America triggers black-and-white images of state-sanctioned violence and repression—kitchenette buildings, *Amos 'n' Andy*, and the innumerable indignities of Jim Crow. Smith's comment reveals much about the way we regard historical nostalgia in contemporary American culture—as a "pretty" form of memory and one that is largely unavailable to black folks. Historical nostalgia, with respect to African American memory, is rarely (if ever) invoked, precisely because narratives of black subjugation and disenfranchisement do not easily mesh with the romantic wistfulness generally associated with nostalgia. The conventional idea of nostalgia as a longing to return or homesickness for any era in American history, for black people, is generally read as counterintuitive at best and traitorous at worst.

As Smith's comments suggest, the privilege of historical nostalgia is more readily available to white people. This easy access to historical nos-talgia became the focal point of recent controversies surrounding the monuments of Civil War "heroes." In a 2011 piece in the *Atlantic*, Kevin

M. Levin argued against anti-Confederate monument activists, asserting that the more recent monument to African American tennis legend and activist Arthur Ashe, for example, "only works because it stands on the same street as Jefferson Davis, Robert E. Lee, and Stonewall Jackson."[2] Defenders of Confederate symbols share their refusal to grapple with the persistent, evolutionary effects of racial oppression. Symbols of the Confederacy serve as stark reminders of slavery's enduring past but also as reminders that US law and policy supported and enacted the abuses suffered by millions of black persons. These monuments represent a false racial reconciliation, suggesting that white Americans today can safely memorialize dead Confederate soldiers because race is no longer an issue of contention.[3] In essence, the monuments embody white national unity at the expense of confronting slavery's ongoing legacy. Levin wrote a follow-up piece, published six years later, titled "Why I Changed My Mind about Confederate Monuments." Levin noted that even after the murders of the Emanuel Nine in Charleston, South Carolina, in 2015, he "held firm to [his initial] view of the monuments." However, during a trip to Prague, he "noticed almost immediately the concrete foundations and empty pedestals where monuments to communist leaders once stood." It was then that Levin's views began to shift; he realized that the "removal of monuments to Stalin and Lenin lifted the weight of the memory of oppression, allowing the Czech people to begin to imagine a new direction for their nation."[4] Only in Europe did Levin learn how to grapple with the symbolic loss of white supremacist emblems and, I would argue, his nostalgic attachment to them. Levin's nostalgia was cured vis-à-vis identification with white Europeans. Such a view exemplifies how historical nostalgia is expressed in an American context—as a uniquely white phenomenon.

For African Americans, the broad unavailability of historical nostalgia comes out of centuries of racial violence, from which no period can be culled to inspire good feelings in the present. As early as the eighteenth century there existed a biomedical belief that African-descended people did not maintain the psychological capacity to experience nostalgia. As Cristobal Silva points out, "The repression of nostalgia as a diagnostic category for African slaves reveals fundamental differences in the way that eighteenth-century army and plantation medicine understood displaced European and African bodies." According to Silva, "slaves appeared to be immune to nostalgia."[5] The interior lives, much less the wistful memories, of black people would never emerge as a legitimate or fruitful object of study for white scientists (and politicians) in early America because African-descended people were thought to possess none. As a result, there is a missing archive of the positive historical scenes and memories from which the African-descended could draw, as well as a history of racist and wrongheaded theories about the psychic and intellectual capacity of black people.

Pretty Memories and Historical Pleasures

When Thomas Jefferson wrote his infamous *Notes on the State of Virginia* in 1781, he deemed black people categorically inferior to white people, organizing his thoughts across the areas of intellect, reason, and emotion. Notably, Jefferson conceded that there were two faculties—memory and misery—that black people held in abundance, writing that "in memory they are equal to the whites" and that "among the blacks is Misery enough, God knows."[6] Jefferson warns his fellow white brethren that the *"ten thousand recollections, by the blacks, of the injuries they have sustained . . . will divide us into parties, and produce convulsions which will probably never end but in the extermination of the one or the other race."*[7] While Jefferson cannot admit that his African and African-descended slaves have rich and complex interior lives, he does acknowledge—if only by implication—that they possess enough pain to suffer trauma and resentment. I turn to Jefferson because his example demonstrates how trauma has remained a largely uncontested and seemingly natural framework for interpreting black memory for well over three centuries. Such a framing leaves little space to apprehend other modalities of memory operative in African American culture, historically and presently.

In *Afro-Nostalgia: Feeling Good in Contemporary Black Culture*, I argue that "pretty" modes of memory are also the province of the African-descended. Black memory is not limited to traumatic resonances of the past, nor are they constituted only through or in relation to histories of violence. I consider afro-nostalgia a lens through which we can conceptualize the desires of the African-descended to discern and devise romantic recollections of the past in the service of complicating the traumatic as a singular black historical through line. The scholarship that examines the manifest suffering of African-descended people from the time of slavery through its enduring afterlife is crucial; for obvious reasons, we cannot contend with African American history without acknowledging the violent conditions that make black folks'

"Americanness" possible. Yet I argue that nostalgia presents another—more sanguine—aspect of black subjectivity that is equally worthy of intellectual pursuit, particularly given the historical presumption that nostalgia is a sentimental form of memory from which black folks were once thought to be "immune."

Despite the prevalence of the study of nostalgia across a range of academic fields, including psychology, sociology, history, and cultural and memory studies, there remains a lack of attention to the fraught relationship between blackness and nostalgia—specifically the state of well-being and happiness prevalent in contemporary theories of nostalgia—or even, more broadly, between blackness and well-being. While we may write off the notion of black folks' "immunity" from nostalgia as old, racist science, little scholarly or public discourse addresses nostalgia as a critical site of black memory. Furthermore, the focus on black Americans' exile from nostalgia, though politically exigent, has limited the range and complexity that we afford black affect in the present. In writing about the response to her research on black women and happiness, for example, Bianca Williams remarked that she was often met with "a puzzled look, as if these concepts are an oxymoron."[8] I put forth afro-nostalgia as a framework in which to analyze the seemingly dissonant concepts of historical memory, blackness, affect, joy, and thriving.

Afro-Nostalgia thus makes two important interventions. The first is within the field of African American studies, in which nostalgia is often interpreted as the memorial province of the black elite. As I will discuss later, the concept of nostalgia in the field of black studies has borne a dangerous suggestion: that attempts to recall a more sublime past necessarily enacts historical revision or erasure. The second intervention is within the fields of memory studies and psychological studies, two spaces in which the concept of nostalgia has enjoyed a spirited and healthy renaissance. Recent psychological studies show that nostalgia "promotes psychological health and well-being" and "gives people a sense of hope and optimism for the future."[10] Bringing these two fields into conversation with African American studies, I extend concepts of African American historical memory beyond the scope of the traumatic. At the same time, I argue that underscoring the racialized aspects of historical memory problematizes psychology's universalizing thesis that nostalgic memory seamlessly produces happiness or positive emotions. Eliding the pervasive presence of historical trauma in the individual and collective lives of African Americans complicates, at best, recent psychological imperatives to advance nostalgia as a race-neutral mode of positive memory. The most egregious consequence of this critical void in both African American and psychological studies is that an affective sentiment so intimately connected to feelings of emotional wellness remains disconnected from the lives of black people.[11] The goal of *Afro-Nostalgia*, then, is to unfold the capacious ways that historical nostalgia is fully operative in contemporary black cultural life as a means of historical pleasure.

I consider how recent African American artists have deployed nostalgia as a practice of emotional and historical reclamation, making accessible those sites of affect and sites of history generally deemed inaccessible to black people. My use of the term *affect* refers not to an isolated condition of feeling or sentiment but to evocations and expressions of emotion that bridge the relation between art and politics. Following affect theorists, I read the role of affect as a free-floating feeling that is rooted not just in the individual person but in institutions, places, objects, performances, or groups of people.[12] While there are few moments in the history of the West for which black people can be "historically nostalgic," I find that for the artists in this book, nostalgia emerges as a search for something indeterminate, defined against demands for precise historical subjectivity. The creativity enabled by nostalgia's indeterminacy is central to black nostalgic gestures, which are less about recovering lost pasts than about evoking ambient associations through food, clothes, and music. More riffing than citing, black nostalgia's suggestions, indeterminacies, flavors, and fleeting moments constitute a broader contemporary black aesthetic that works to break blackness out of a narrowly constructed frame of traumatic history.

In her 1921 essay "Nostalgia," Harlem Renaissance author and intellectual Jessie Fauset distinguished the nostalgia of African Americans from that of European immigrants to the United States. She deemed nostalgia, as experienced by African Americans, to be a "spiritual nostalgia": "He has been away so long from that mysterious fatherland of his that like all the other descendants of voluntary and involuntary immigrants of the seventeenth century,—Puritan, pioneer, adventurer, indentured servant,—he feels himself American."[13] The misidentification of *feeling* as opposed to *being* American is, perhaps, nostalgia's greatest cruelty for the African-descended. As Brent Hayes Edwards notes, Fauset identifies nostalgia as it is experienced by black subjects as a psychic state of "perpetual unfulfillment, a 'sadness without an object.'"[14] Fauset's formulation of nostalgia replicates for the "American Negro" the sense of malaise found in nostalgia's earliest iterations. By contrast, the projects in my archive grapple with this lack of an identifiable homeland through strategic methods of invention and the production of alternative historicities. Nostalgia, in the contemporary black imagination, functions as a psychic and emotional vessel onto which historical desires are cast. Nostalgia consistently shows up as a dominant feature of contemporary African American expressive culture, although it has been considered a privileged emotion that is absent from black narratives due to the lack of an identifiable homeland or, in racist views, to a lack of sentience. The disaggregation of nostalgic memory from black being results in a misguided and monolithic understanding of nostalgia as a form of memory attributed to white people and deployed by white people as a weapon of racial terror.

Working as agents and archivists, contemporary African American artists deploy nostalgic memory to reframe traumatic relationships to black historical narratives as well as to disrupt both white supremacist and black neoliberal narratives that have claimed that nostalgic past as their own. To demonstrate how nostalgia is invoked in a broader black cultural context, I turn to a range of aesthetic registers—visual art, performance, documentary film, literature, and the culinary arts. In contemporary black artists' attention to the historical past, *Afro-Nostalgia* locates recollections of black redemption, triumph over white supremacy, and resistance to state-sanctioned violence and repression.

Key moments loom large in black cultural memory and, by extension, black cultural production, including the slave rebellion led by Nat Turner in 1831, the Selma to Montgomery march over the (in)famous Edmund Pettus Bridge in 1965, the Watts rebellion in 1965, Tommie Smith and John Carlos's Black Power salute at the 1968 Olympics, and the election of Barack Obama in 2008. Re-creations of these celebratory moments in black history function as source material for a number of contemporary black artists. These artists embrace the inventive scope of nostalgic memory to reconcile a traumatic black past with the creative recollection of pleasure and joy. As Alastair Bonnett has noted, "We are used to imagining nostalgic longing as akin to reverie, a moment of drooping repose . . . but it seems it is also a moment of creativity."[15] In this book, I examine contemporary black artists as they draw on and imaginatively produce memories of "minor" victories and small rebellions within the black historical past. In doing so, I suggest that we read black nostalgia as "structures of feeling" (to invoke Raymond Williams).

Williams's "cultural hypothesis"—specifically his concept of the "residual" as opposed to the "archaic"—is important here. As Williams points out, the archaic is "that which is wholly recognized as an element of the past, to be observed, to be examined, or even on occasion to be consciously 'revived.'" Conversely, the residual has been "effectively formed in the past, but it is still active in the cultural process, not only and often not at all as an element of the past, but as an effective element of the present."[16] Though Williams is invested in the machinations of social class, his conception enlivens normative notions of historical eras as fixed, rendering them both active in and relevant to our understanding of present, lived experience. This perspective offers a lens through which to interpret and unearth redemptive aspects of the black historical past that inspire "good feelings" in the present. Afro-nostalgia evokes such moments of joy and pleasure even while reckoning with a history mired and memorialized in the traumatic. The realm of art creates space and time for the real and the imaginary, the past and the present, to collude to manifest a living memory that, in the case of black nostalgia, evokes sentiments of pain and pleasure, mourning and celebration.

Reading afro-nostalgia as an evocation of good feeling through romantic recollections of the past does not mean that this brand of nostalgia emerges in opposition to traumatic memory. The relationship between nostalgia and trauma is not a binary one; they are, instead, conceptual cousins. While trauma recalls a harmful past and nostalgia recalls a blissful one, both affective states materialize within what Ann Cvetkovich describes as "public cultures of memory." These public cultures engender "questions about what emotional responses constitute a reparative relation to the past and whether it is ever possible to complete the work of mourning, particularly while social suffering is ongoing." Cvetkovich turns to critical race studies and queer theories that read "unfinished mourning" as "productive rather than pathological."[17] This is to say that within oppressed subcultures, including black and/or queer spaces, traumatic pasts are refigured as transformative sites of healing.[18] This process is exemplified in what Aida Levy-Hussen describes as a "hermeneutic of therapeutic reading."[19] Levy-Hussen explains that interactions with fictional narratives of slavery, for example, offer readers the "promise" that "the act of reading will compel a difficult, emotional, and productive psychic labor; it will deliver you to a new and self-revelatory state of consciousness with both personal and political implications."[20] The "transformative pain" that readers willingly undergo to reap the benefits of self-continuity as a therapeutic praxis also forms the backbone of contemporary nostalgic endeavors. The concept of afro-nostalgia aligns with the therapeutic imperatives mapped out by Cvetkovich and Levy-Hussen, yet the archive I've compiled in this book turns to aesthetic projects that are less invested in the repetition and re-representation of historical pain for the potential of psychic resolution. Instead, I identify an aesthetic turn to romantic recall in the work of black artists and writers. They find within the past a space in which to intensify glints of a redemptive black history.

Though the productive capacity of traumatic recall has been well argued, I propose that nostalgic forms of "return" are an equally productive means to contend with the pain of both the past and the present. I suggest that, as an aesthetic mode, nostalgia animates the reparative impulse that drives a return to the black historical past. Nostalgia delivers the therapeutic intervention that traumatic repetition promises within the space of historical and cultural memory. When nostalgia is considered in this light, the concept becomes more than a benign or regressive category of memory but rather a cultural practice that reframes, and at times repairs, traumatic historical memories in the affective lives of contemporary black subjects.

We find the coexistence of reparation (psychic and social) and trauma at the heart of Christina Sharpe's "wake work," for example, which "imagines new ways to live in the wake of slavery, in slavery's afterlives, to survive (and more) the afterlife of property."[21] In considering Sharpe's "and more" as a way of living and of being that exceeds mere survival, I offer nostalgia as an often overlooked contender to help heal historical pain. Saidiya Hartman, Hortense Spillers, and Christina Sharpe aptly chronicle the multifold ways that the trauma of the transatlantic slave trade has been transmitted generationally, living in and through black bodies in the now. The concepts of "return" and "homeland" (and even "remedy") take on more capacious iterations in my analysis, and I interpret afro-nostalgia as a complement to the dominant discourse of black trauma. Afro-nostalgia, I show, expresses a desire to lace the gaps of historical memory with pleasure-inducing affect—not by rewriting the past but by embracing nostalgia's imaginative capacity to rehabilitate the black historical past and refashion the present. Contemporary black subjects reckon with the trauma of the historical past vis-à-vis pleasure-seeking and pleasure-making acts of *anamnesis* (bringing to the present an object or person from the past).

Tricia Hersey's interactive art installation *The Nap Ministry* demonstrates how afro-nostalgia works as an aesthetic mode that imaginatively recalls traumatic black pasts as an act of healing in the now. The aim of Hersey's project is to recoup the leisure, rest, and "dream states" stolen from enslaved African Americans forced to labor twenty (or more) hours a day. Her installations vary. Some take place in the cotton fields of Georgia, where viewers watch Hersey pick cotton for hours, mimicking the labor demanded of her ancestors; others function as napping pop-ups, in which mundane spaces within urban centers are transformed into rest havens for collective napping experiences. Hersey refers to her projects as "reparations" for the exhaustive labor required of her ancestors and encourages other black subjects to engage in "collective napping" as an act of resistance to late-market capitalism and white supremacy. Naps, for Hersey, reclaim the "DREAM SPACE" that slaves were denied. The act of rest provides "a healing portal" in which we can "dream, imagine, invent, plan, hope and communicate with our ancestors."[22] Recalling the exhaustion of enslaved African Americans, Hersey and her fellow nappers enact the wished-for slumber of their ancestors, translating the pain of the past into a dream state in the present. The reparative nature of Hersey's project functions as a double entendre in which napping operates as both respite from and resistance to ongoing structural and institutional demands on black folks' labor, a claiming of what we are owed on behalf of our ancestors' free and incessant work. We might locate *The Nap Ministry*'s mission within a broader black feminist imperative to form a politics of pleasure in which the black body is focalized beyond the scope of trauma and terror. Hersey's rest is reparation for her ancestors' pain: their labor is present in the installation, as signified by the cotton bolls strewn on her mattress. Their labor inspires her rest, her healing. Enacting what Joan Morgan refers to as "pleasure politics," Hersey's project exemplifies "the complex, messy, sticky, and even joyous negotiations of agency and desire that are irrevocably twinned with our pain."[23]

The inextricability of black pleasure and black pain emerges in *The Nap Ministry* as an afro-nostalgic endeavor, in its self-conscious solicitation of historical memory to foster good feelings in the present. Hersey's project differs from conventional interpretations of nostalgia as sentimentalizing the past. Skeptics might regard black nostalgia as being problematically antihistorical or as whitewashing history, yet Hersey's artwork stages a collective public grappling with historical violence. In many ways, Hersey's work is a black historiography that complements normative history's rote recitation of the archive of New World slavery; that is, she opens up space to grapple with history as part of its telling and recording. Indeed, Hersey recruits black historical (re)memories of slavery to remedy the traumatic past through invoking emancipatory pleasures. The art of black nostalgia conjures black historical moments as forms of restorative self-continuity in which the pain of the past gets imagined and subsequently reenacted and grappled with in the present through creative acts of pleasure-making. These artistic forms of black memory-making perform a therapeutic function for contemporary black subjects seeking to reconcile traumatic black history and its afterlife.

Afro-Nostalgia celebrates the complexities of contemporary black aesthetic practices, like Hersey's, that deploy nostalgia as "a technique" that is "used to 'warm up' and give vitality to a bleak present, and is thus evidence of the creative ways in which people can establish temporal agency."[24] In other words, wistful remembrances of the past allow us to garner hope and "feel good" in the present. Nostalgia is not always an unconscious form of remembrance; it also functions as a form of memory work that can be called on and self-induced for the purpose of feeling good in the now. This book takes black writers and artists seriously as historical interlocutors and theorists who raise important questions about the promises and limitations of historical returns, and the risks and rewards of historical (re)creation and affective embodiment. Conventional interpretations of nostalgia in psychoanalysis presume that the nostalgic seeks to construct a more advantageous history to counteract "a bleak present."[25] The lack of an "available" nostalgic past, to return to Zadie Smith's remarks, can have the effect of recycling black memory work within the field of trauma—or, as I argue, elicit from contemporary black subjects a creative impulse to recast the black historical past as an act of self-fulfillment and self-preservation. Critical scholarship in black, queer, and affect studies has pointed to the conundrum of living with historical traumas that resonate in the everyday. But if "racial trauma" acts as both a "site of unresolved suffering and an object of reparative desire,"[26] then we might consider black nostalgic acts in contemporary African American culture as enabling and animating the means by which subjects contend with this simultaneity.

Nostalgic Origins

While nostalgia shows up within contemporary culture as a feel-good sentiment, the belief that nostalgia could produce happiness did not emerge until the early 1920s. In the late seventeenth century, nostalgia was considered a medical condition, a "cerebral disease" brought on by homesickness. The term *nostalgia* is credited to a Swiss medical doctor, Johannes Hofer, who in 1688 described the effects of this malady as confusion between past and present, listlessness, and a disheveled appearance, among other damaging symptoms. In Hofer's assessment, nostalgia resulted from "continuous vibrations of animal spirits through those fibers of the middle brain in which impressed traces of ideas of the Fatherland still cling."[27] While the nostalgic's symptoms could be abated with opium, leeches, or purging, according to Hofer, "nostalgia admits no remedy other than a return to the homeland."[28] Hofer thought nostalgia was a "disorder of the imagination," given that those "suffering from it fantasized about home, leaving no psychological space for thoughts about the present world."[29] This early proscription of nostalgia corresponds to contemporary critiques that argue that nostalgia possesses no productive or political purchase because it fosters escapism rather than an active engagement or reckoning with either the past or the present. Given nostalgia's symptomology, it would seem that Africans extracted from the western coast of the continent would be the demographic thought to suffer most from its ailments. Yet white Americans likened those black bodies to the livestock within the plantation landscape and therefore regarded them as lacking the sentience to produce feelings strong enough to manifest nostalgia (though, curiously, in 1898 psychologist Linus Kline argued that animals experienced nostalgia, as evidenced by the fact that, for example, a "cow will make her escape for pasture and return home, at a distance of several miles, at every opportunity").[30] We might also surmise that eighteenth-century white Americans held such a negative view of Africa that they could not imagine it as a home worth being missed. Given the dearth of analyses on nostalgia in relation to African American people or historical memory, it would seem as though nostalgia was a disease that black people just did not catch.

There were, however, a few notable exceptions to the insistence that Africans and the African-descended could not suffer from nostalgia. After witnessing a line of chained slaves walking through the streets of Washington, DC, physician Jesse Torrey Jr. was so appalled by the sight that in 1817 he was moved to write a pamphlet titled *A Portraiture of Domestic Slavery in the United States: With Reflections on Restoring the Moral Rights of the Slave, without Impairing the Legal Privileges of the Possessor; and A Project of a Colonial Asylum for Free Persons of Colour: Including Memoirs of Facts on the Interior Traffic in Slaves and on KIDNAPPING.* For Torrey, the bondage of black people was not sufficiently immoral to repudiate, yet the ill treatment of enslaved persons and the "theft" of free black people warranted a book-length argument calling for the recognition of their humanity. Torrey draws on his medical expertise to recount the psychological injuries that enslaved people suffered as a result of their abuse, focusing on the mental stress caused by the separation of families. The pamphlet offers several anecdotes of the practice of selling members of a family to different slave owners, including one instance of a woman who jumped from a window after being sold away from her husband (figure 1).

In reciting the circumstances behind this enslaved woman's attempted suicide, Torrey invokes both Section 2 of Pennsylvania's Act for the Gradual Abolition of Slavery and Charles Darwin's account of nostalgia. Citing the act's proclamation that "the condition of those persons who have heretofore been denominated negro and mulatto slaves . . . has cast them into the deepest afflictions by an unnatural separation of husband and wife from each other and from their children—an injury the greatness of which can only be conceived by supposing that we were in the same unhappy case,"[31] Torrey condemns the common practice of familial separation and invites his white readers to envision the impact such a separation would have within their own families. In doing so, Torrey highlights the act's refutation of the Jeffersonian claim that the griefs of black people were "transient,"[32] and asserts that the practice of family separation was an affront to the moral and religious values of a civil(ized) society. As the title of Torrey's pamphlet makes clear, the practice of slavery was permissible because it was operating within the legal bounds of the US government. Yet the abuses committed within the context of this legal institution violated the supposed family values of the republic, and, for Torrey, these values transcended one's free/unfree status.

Torrey was invested in rethinking nostalgia in light of these misconceptions about the capacity of black people to feel. Making explicit reference to Darwin's assessment of nostalgia as an "unconquerable desire of returning to one's native country . . . in which the patients become so insane as to throw themselves into the sea, mistaking it for green fields and meadows,"[33] he draws a rich parallel between homesick European soldiers and the condition of enslaved African Americans. The image of the black slave woman leaping from a building resonates not only with Darwin's picture of Swiss soldiers throwing themselves into the sea but with those individuals sometimes referred to as flying Africans—those would-never-be slaves who jumped from their slave ships en route to an unknown yet feared space and fate. The mythology of those Africans whose suicides

"—but I did not want to go, and
I jump'd out of the window.—"

Designed and Published by J. Torrey Jun. Philad.ᵗ 1817.

1. Woman jumping from a building. Engraving by A[lexander] Rider. From
Jesse Torrey Jr., *A Portraiture of Domestic Slavery in the United States* . . .
(Philadelphia: published by the author; John Bioren, printer, 1817).

were recast as "flights" back to their homeland offers the most potent example of eighteenth- and nineteenth-century conceptions of nostalgia as a mental disease. Even some Africans who completed their journeys to the West "took a look around at the landscape and their imprisoned selves, and ascended into flight, 'stealing away' across the Atlantic back to their homelands."[34] Alexander Rider's illustration of the "flying" black slave woman also recalls (and predates) the fate of Jane Eyre's character Bertha (the "madwoman in the attic"), whose Creole ancestry and West Indian homeland are cited as the seat and cause of her insanity. Given Bertha's racial roots, we might also read her perceived madness and ultimate suicide as a manifestation of nostalgia for that "fiery West Indian" homeland from which she was taken. While their griefs are not explicitly named as nostalgic, each instance carries with it the symptomology of the disease: the unbearable grief of a lost place that can never be recovered, impossible "flights" of return, and, importantly, refusal to abide by the governing social order. As historian Terri L. Snyder has noted, "in the eighteenth-century Caribbean and in South America slave self-destruction was increasingly viewed as a symptom of *pining* rather than as a result of a stubborn temperament."[35] Prevailing scientific thought assumed that enslaved persons who "manifested medical nostalgia killed themselves through outright refusals: they would not eat or move and by these actions they deliberately courted death."[36] Though at the time these acts were seen as pathological, we now understand them as acts of resistance. These refusals reveal a great deal about eighteenth-century interpretations of black interiority and the manifest forms of violence, psychic and otherwise, that enslaved persons endured within that peculiar institution.

Following Torrey's analysis of the ill effects of nostalgia on the enslaved African American population, Marmaduke Blake Sampson, financial editor and chair of the British Homeopathic Society, outlined in an 1845 letter to Daniel Webster a comprehensive plan by which slavery could be effectively abolished in the United States through a systematic process of repatriation to Africa. The key imperative of this letter appeared to be Sampson's support of American colonization efforts to resettle slaves in the newly formed colony of Liberia. Such a correspondence would have been well received by Webster, who was a prominent member of the American Colonization Society. Sampson provided extensive psychological evidence to support his argument that Africans and the African-descended should be returned to Africa due to the devasting effects of nostalgia. He surmised that "whether it be regarded as arising from a primary faculty of the mind, or merely as a result of association, the fact is unquestionable, that the emotion itself is common to human nature, and especially, that it exercises an imperative sway over the negro race."[37] Contrary to the then-popular belief that nostalgia was primarily an affliction of European soldiers, Sampson refigures nostalgia as a raw emotion experienced keenly and devastatingly by black people, noting that "cases of death from nostalgia" were found "even amongst the aborigines of Van Diemen's Land."[38] Reporting that "one of the strongest propensities of [the black man's] nature . . . is his attachment to home or country," Sampson argues that "this feeling, innate in all men, has long been observed to display itself with singular force in the character of the negro."[39]

By the mid-nineteenth century, medical practitioners argued that black folks, globally (from African Americans to "aborigines"), suffered from nostalgia more acutely than *any* other race, in contrast to eighteenth-century plantation science's claims that enslaved black people were immune from nostalgia.[40] While Sampson shares with his medical predecessor, Jesse Torrey, a belief in the debilitating effects of nostalgia on the enslaved black populace, Torrey argued against resettlement efforts, claiming that "such projects are most certainly impracticable . . . because their completion would require the voluntary estrangement of its legal holders."[41] Torrey believed that enslaved black people would want to return to Africa; however, he knew that their "owners" would never abide by such a demand. Sampson could thus use as evidence the realization of Liberia, an American colony in Africa, established a mere four years after Torrey published *Portraiture*. Both Torrey and Sampson held relatively conservative views concerning the abolition of slavery: neither forcefully renounced the institution per se, and they contrasted with established Garrisonian abolitionists, who saw repatriation efforts as antithetical to the project of emancipation. I mention Torrey and Sampson as evidence that there was some debate within social and medical discourses around whether black people were sentient enough to experience nostalgia and, if they were, how such recognition figured into larger political debates concerning the problem of slavery. Torrey's and Sampson's arguments offer a compelling view of the creative ways in which nostalgia framed nineteenth-century debates about whether the African and African-descended would be integrated within the fabric of the nation, or whether instead their nostalgia warranted recolonization back to the continent of Africa. In addition, their writings emphasize nostalgia's place in discussions about embodiment, sensation, mental health, the human, and, importantly, the role that nostalgia played in broader debates about the future of the nation.

Within the past few decades, historical scholarship has unearthed the egregious abuses that enslaved persons suffered as experimental biological objects in the name of medical science,[42] yet evidence about the enslaved as objects of psychological study remains scarce. The most prevalent analyses are those of Dr. Samuel Cartwright, who coined the medical term *drapeto-mania*, described as a "disease of the mind" that apparently caused run-away slaves "to abscond." Cartwright was also responsible for establishing the diagnoses for what he termed *dysaesthesia aethiopica*, also referred to as "rascality," which was said to be a mental illness "peculiar to negroes" but "much more prevalent among free negroes living in clusters among themselves," in which their freedom and mobility resulted in "the liberty to be idle, to wallow in filth, and to indulge in improper food and drinks."[43] As in Jefferson's theory, the slave psyche emerges as a point of fascination only to highlight the extent of black people's perceived inferiority and, by extension, to normalize white psychic life. Like most scientific analyses of the black body, such insights generally served only to support racist socio-political agendas. The black subject's ability to experience nostalgia was yet another example of this kind of scientific rationale. As Susan J. Matt has explained, "In the antebellum years, southern whites had vociferously denied that African Americans experienced pain or homesickness when they were sold and forced to leave home and family behind." This perspec-tive was reversed immediately following the Civil War, when "southern whites claimed that blacks experienced a surfeit of homesickness and a deficit of ambition."[44]

Despite its legitimacy as a medical condition for almost two centuries, by the late nineteenth century, nostalgia was no longer considered a medi-cal affliction. By the early twentieth century, "nostalgia was not so much discarded as psychoanalysed."[45] By then nostalgia signified not the loss of a home long gone but a desire for a time long past, or for "any object that symbolized aspects of their past that [people] missed."[46] Nostalgia's symptoms were made even more acute by virtue of the fact that there was no cure for a disease that could be remedied only via time travel. As Linda Hutcheon puts it, "Time, unlike space, cannot be returned to—ever; time is irreversible," and thus "nostalgia becomes the reaction to that sad fact."[47] The study of nostalgia developed alongside the burgeoning field of psychology in the early twentieth century. By that time, nostalgia was largely considered the province of psychologists rather than of medical doctors. It was precisely when the "broader consideration of nostalgia as pleasure mixed with pain began to emerge, [that] the view of nostalgia as a mental illness started to lose ground."[48] As nostalgia increasingly became an object of psychological study throughout the twentieth century, it became associated with the production of good feelings.

The Risks of Nostalgic Remembrance

Despite the recuperation of nostalgia as an act of memory that could produce happiness, recent psychological studies have also suggested that "nostalgic remembering may tend to exacerbate patterns of negative thinking resulting in less positive affective outcomes."[49] Presently, nostalgia is interpreted within psychological and cultural spheres as a byproduct of feeling dislocated, temporally or spatially. This analysis coincides with nostalgia's interpretation in humanistic spheres as a sentiment that conveys "a failure to cope with change, a defeatist attitude to the present and future, and a kind of retreat into an idealized past."[50] Across psychology and sociology, as well as literary and cultural studies, negative thoughts associated with nostalgia are often read as a form of maladaptive coping that translate into impotent or regressive politics. This pattern was on full display in the 2016 presidential campaign but also operates within black social and political spaces. Nostalgia as a regressive politics shows up in what Michelle Boyd calls "Jim Crow nostalgia," which references a black conservative desire that "celebrates the image of insular black communities in segregated spaces during a time when racial boundaries were less frequently crossed in work and social life."[51] Rolland Murray similarly argues that the black "bourgeois managerial class" has historically used "the heyday of segregation and civil rights activism to produce a more coherent model of black community."[52] Black nostalgic desires to return to a moment of racial segregation embrace this period of "violent, repressive, and state-sanctioned racism" as "a haven from the uncertainty, disappointment, and inadequacy of the contemporary period," emphasizing the narrative reimagining of the segregation era as an affective mode of communal identification.[53]

This same nostalgic imperative formed the ethos of restoration development projects across the United States in the early 1990s, including the Bronzeville community in Chicago and Harlem in New York, that promised a return to "better times." The dangers of Jim Crow nostalgia formed the moral and satirical center of Mat Johnson's novel *Hunting in Harlem* (2003), in which the project to restore Harlem to its former status as a mecca for African Americans turns deadly for the community's "undesirable" residents. In order to realize his dream of a modern Harlem Renaissance, Congressman Cyrus Marks, founder of Horizon Realty, hires three ex-convicts as part of a "Second Chance Program" to facilitate his vision of a new "old" Harlem. The novel's "Terrible Tenth" represents "the drug dealers, the thugs, thieves, and rapists, those that abuse their children directly and through neglect, the ones who have no respect for others, civilization, society," whom the novel's protagonist, Cedric Snowden, must make "disappear."[54] Segregation-era nostalgia lies at the heart of the deadly impulses that drive Marks to restore Harlem to its former glory. The time of structural and legal violence is recalled poetically in his speech to Second Chance Program participants: "It was far from perfect, but we had our own doctors, our own services, our own stores. There was money here, circulating. Then desegregation came, and everyone who could afford to leave did."[55] *Hunting in Harlem* exemplifies the worst aspects of nostalgic memory; it also draws a direct correlation between black nostalgic memory and class status. More pointedly, Jim Crow nostalgia enacts Avishai Margalit's claim that nostalgia is particularly dangerous because it displaces "disturbing thoughts about the past and retains only the good ones."[56] Nostalgia's inherent dangers, then, lie in both its selectiveness and its false imaginative framing of memory to fuel particular political agendas.[57]

In Johnson's novel and across social-science discourses, nostalgic memory appears to be widely available to black elites whose economic advantages undermine racial solidarity. Houston A. Baker Jr. rehearses this problematic in his classic theory of public memory, offering an incisive critique of nostalgia as a "purposive construction of a past filled with golden virtues, golden men and sterling events."[58] Linking nostalgia to the province of "black conservative modernity," Baker sees little room for nostalgia to do anything other than provide "an exclusively middle-class beautification of history designed to erase the revolution, pray blessings upon the heads of white people and give a rousing cheer for free enterprise individualism."[59] Boyd, Murray, and Baker offer a glimpse into how nostalgia has been established in black scholarly and artistic discourses largely as a condition that afflicts black elites. The regressive impulses of nostalgia benefit those who can point to the "golden days" of the segregation era from the comfortable perch of a privileged class position. In these cases, nostalgia requires a special brand of repression in which the violence of that era and its attendant traumatic effects are obscured by romantic illusions of a historical past in which black folks were legally forced to stick together. Jim Crow nostalgia functions as a historical fantasy that signals the failures of integration and the unfulfilled promises of the civil rights movement.

Yet the concept of afro-nostalgia that I put forth differs from black conservative nostalgia in that the aesthetic projects I examine maintain a reparative impulse, are invested in historical continuity (not historical erasure), and focus on the evocation of individual and communal acts of affective pleasure. For example, as I argue in chapter 2, comedian Dave Chappelle's 2004 block party in Brooklyn, New York, emerges as a response to the black public sphere's fragmentation after desegregation; the block party is an attempt, albeit symbolic, to repair the "erosion of black communal networks" occasioned by the post–civil rights era.[60] In contrast to black conservative nostalgia's exclusionary impulses, the afro-nostalgic project of Chappelle's block party—and his 2005 film *Block Party*, which chronicles the event—is an attempt to reclaim a sense of communal solidarity and identification by recalling, explicitly, the 1972 Wattstax festival in Los Angeles. The black cultural productions in *Afro-Nostalgia* provide a redemptive opening to the past in ways that have been elided or thought inconceivable in public and critical discourses.

Taken together, these instances of white and black conservative nostalgia suggest that the wistful sentimentality that nostalgic memory furnishes is often catalyzed by more pressing and sinister desires for racial and class hegemony. The "happiness" that nostalgic memory invokes in these contexts is contingent on editing and erasure, and ultimately serves as an "invitation to brutality."[61] What these examples also show is nostalgia's power to shape and wield politically and socially conservative forces in the twenty-first century. Hutcheon has previously argued that "despite very strong reservations (based in part on personality limitations), I do know that I should never underestimate the power of nostalgia, especially its visceral physicality and emotional impact."[62] There is no denying that the nostalgic ethos of "Make America Great Again," as one narrative of white racist nostalgia, has sparked a spate of white violence in the form of regressive racial, economic, and environmental policies and a renewed spike in racial hate crimes. With this development, we might regard white and black nostalgia as mutual expressions of conservative historical memory that make people *feel* good but *do* bad things in the service of "self-preservation." Perhaps the most twisted manifestation of this phenomenon is highlighted in Jonathan Metzl's *Dying of Whiteness*, in which a white man named Trevor with a severe case of hepatitis C refuses to support or register for Obamacare, claiming he "would rather die."[63] As Metzl explains, people like Trevor "were dying in various overt or invisible ways as a result of political beliefs or systems linked to the defense of white 'ways of life.'"[64] In this instance, the affective desire to return the United States to a fantastical space of hegemonic whiteness trumps (pun intended) not only the conditions of one's livelihood but life itself. In cases such as this, nostalgia feels good—even if it kills you.

Looking Back to Feel Good

One of the concerns that motivates this project is whether the power of nostalgia works in only one direction, specifically toward conserving and consolidating power, including the sorts of power wielded by the political right. If we acknowledge that nostalgia maintains "visceral physicality and emotional impact," is its power the exclusive province of social conservatives? In other words, can the power of nostalgia be harnessed to shape a present (and a future) for black folks on the margins, for black artists, for black lives?

A 2016 psychological study published in the journal *Emotion* examines "how nostalgia fosters self-continuity," defined as "the sense that one's past is interwoven with one's present." The authors find that "nostalgia-induced self-continuity . . . confers eudaimonic well-being, operationalized as subjective vitality (i.e., a feeling of aliveness and energy)."[65] Other studies have shown that nostalgia promotes "enhanced social connectedness, social competence and satisfaction, continuity of self, enhanced self-esteem, and social-emotional coping, goal-directed strategies and positive reframing"[66] and that "engaging in nostalgic remembering increases positive affect and positive self-regard, heightens interpersonal connectivity and results in a higher sense of personal meaning."[67] The positive emotions generated by nostalgic memories, real or imagined, encourage a feeling of connection between the past and the present and a general sense of social connectedness and felicity. Certainly, American marketers have long known about the power of nostalgia's feel-good tendencies. Put simply, nostalgia animates good feelings (physiological) and feeling good (emotional). While the social and political climate of the contemporary present may make nostalgia's feel-good emotions appear suspect and frivolous, embracing nostalgia as a therapeutic praxis may be one of many alternatives to such realities. *Afro-Nostalgia* provides intellectual and affective ground from which to imagine new ways of black being, black doing, and black feeling that enable flourishing under adverse social and political circumstances.

The legacy of trauma has functioned as a dominant site of "self-continuity" for African Americans, fostering a communal sense of loss and suffering. But there is another underexamined and complementary African American legacy to unearth. The artistic works examined in this book produce a public archive, a *moodscape* of an alternative black historical past that, through nostalgia, engenders a sense of community, continuity, and reparation for black futures.

Afro-Nostalgia is invested in historical memory as a matter of recovery and redemption. Afro-nostalgia functions as a form of memory work in the service of creating a public affective archive not generally assigned to black subjects. I want to trouble the generalized sentiment that nostalgia's response to such transhistorical suffering is impotent at best and traitorous at worst. If Hutcheon suggests that the "aesthetics of nostalgia" may be the enmeshing of an "idealized history" and "dissatisfaction with the present,"[68] the artists in this project contend with this "dissatisfaction" by refracting historical moments in ways that allow an emotional reprieve and, quite possibly, a way forward. The power of nostalgia is often read as purely emotional or sentimental at its most saccharine and twee, but the force of nostalgia has the potential to translate into more public and communal forms of cultural production and social engagement. Afro-nostalgia satisfies reparative desires, providing an opening in which to contend with the past as a matter of reckoning, regeneration, and reclamation. Afro-nostalgia engages the past in ways that exemplify political and emotional ambivalences, where the "good feelings" inspired by pleasant memories/imaginaries are entangled with state-sanctioned repression and violence. From Tricia Hersey's *The Nap Ministry*, which juxtaposes the remembrance of slave labor with the restful slumber of the present-day African-descended; to the "wondrous thing," the artistic masterpiece that Alice creates from the memory of her experience as a slave on the Townsend plantation in Edward P. Jones's *The Known World*; to the vegan creations of chef Bryant Terry, who looks to the limited diets of his slave ancestors and the Black Power culinary politics of the 1970s to fashion a method of healthful eating for contemporary black diasporic subjects, afro-nostalgia consistently enmeshes historical pleasure and pain. This book recognizes a range of contemporary African American cultural productions—from black performance to black culinary endeavors—that employ nostalgia as a vessel that brings together promise of racial redemption and romantic reclamation of the historical past. My interest and investment in the artistic productions I have chosen to examine fundamentally rests on the contradictory ways they take up nostalgia as a transgressive reappropriation of black memory and an expression of cathartic historical desire.

In the four content chapters of this book, nostalgia is deployed in the following ways: as a mode of historical redress, as a disruption of "white nostalgia," as a means of cultivating well-being, and as a strategy of cultural reclamation. While each chapter addresses a different aspect of African American cultural practice (literature, visual art, music, and culinary art), collectively they converge around nostalgia as providing not only a holistic approach to reckoning with the pain of the past but also new pathways for memory that enable feeling good in the present. The range of the aesthetic endeavors and social acts outlined in this book forge, in a complementary fashion, a spectrum of aesthetic interventions that bring us closer to understanding the dynamism and artistry of black historical memory.

The first chapter, "(Nostalgic) RETRIBUTION: The Affective Power of the Petty in Contemporary Narratives of Slavery," reads contemporary creative re-creations of slavery as emblematic of the nostalgic desire for racial retribution. Contemporary slave narratives already proffer a vast archive that extends well beyond the historical record to include ways of feeling and being that cannot quite be captured within official documentation. This field has been richly examined by scholars of African American literature and culture as a source of insight into the formation of post-modern subjectivity (Arlene Keizer), as a therapeutic hermeneutic (Aida Levy-Hussen), as a reflection of the social politics of the 1960s to 1980s (Ashraf Rushdy), and as mnemonic restitution (Salamishah Tillet). I reflect on and expand this generative list by reading the return to the slave past as illustrative of a contemporary retributive desire. The nostalgic "longing to return" is less to re-live the experience of slavery than to redress the multivalent indignities and injustices it enacted. The creative clapbacks of Azie Dungey's fictional character Lizzie Mae in the web series *Ask a Slave*, the figuration of "crazy" Alice in Edward P. Jones's novel *The Known World*, and the Confederate-slaying images of Harriet Tubman found in popular fan art and James McBride's novel *The Good Lord Bird* form a collective body of twenty-first-century creative endeavors that recover and reenact the slave past as a practice of literary historical reckoning. As with Hersey's *The Nap Ministry*, in which black folks rest as an act of reparation for our ancestors' labor, nostalgic reckoning emerges in contemporary narratives of slavery as a form of historical recompense that challenges and resists white nostalgia about the "romance" of the antebellum era and the sentiment of reconciliation that the Civil War conventionally evokes. The acts of refusal and rebellion that were not readily available to our slave ancestors are realized as acts of black nostalgic remembrance, in which good feelings are made possible through imagining rebellious ripostes to antebellum-era brutalities. Violence and healing, keen historicity and anachronism interanimate these texts, underscoring the creative ways nostalgia gets deployed to craft alternative narratives of the black historical past.

While the first chapter examines how afro-nostalgia is used to disrupt the "magnolia myth" and exact historical revenge, the second chapter, "(Nostalgic) RESTORATION: Utopian Pasts and Political Futures in the Music of Black Lives Matter," poses an explicit challenge to white nostalgia's systematic erasure of blackness from the historical record and its willful dismissal of historical black pain and present-day trauma. This chapter also shares with the previous one an investment in critically reframing conventional white nostalgic narratives that erase and debase black bodies and experience. I introduce the concept of *restorative black nostalgia* to argue that reimaginings of black freedom emerge in contemporary black protest music and musical performance through the production of new "anthems" of black resistance created vis-à-vis the sonic collapse of the Black Power era and the "idealized pastness" of white music. I locate within Black Lives Matter–inspired music and performance an explicit extension of the Black Power movement's capacity to, as Shana Redmond argues, remix "the modalities of the state in order to foster alternative exercises and experiences of freedom and justice."[69] Restorative black nostalgia operates simultaneously as an extension of the Black Power musical aesthetic and as a disruption of white nostalgic sound. This analysis looks first at Lauryn Hill's musical response to the police killing of Michael Brown in Ferguson, Missouri. Hill's "Black Rage" masterfully samples the classic song "My Favorite Things," made famous by Julie Andrews in *The Sound of Music*, a process that exemplifies the project of restorative black nostalgia by stripping the classic version of its sentimental nostalgic resonances and displacing them with a chronicle of black suffering. Hill's song refuses the sweet, innocent recollections of the original, instead transforming that nostalgic object into an anthem of modern-day black protest. I then return to the previous decade, in which Lauryn Hill reunited with the Fugees, to discuss the restorative nostalgic imperatives of Dave Chappelle's *Block Party* (2005) as a precursor to more recent black popular musical performances. In these performances and others, I advance restorative black nostalgia as drawing on the legacy of an exigent counterdiscourse to an emergent white nostalgia, in which contemporary black anthems provide a radical ethos within popular politics and social movements.

While the first two chapters pose a direct challenge to white nostalgic memory as a way to redress white physical, psychological, and social violence, chapter 3, "(Nostalgic) REGENERATION: Absent Archives and Historical Pleasures in Contemporary Black Visual Culture," examines artists who deploy nostalgia as a mode of psychic healing. To this end, I examine the visual art of April Banks, Krista Franklin, and Rhonda Wheatley, who all, in ways that are equally disparate and compelling, deploy nostalgia as a balm for the present. Wheatley's "hybrid devices" and "power objects" claim to transport "users" through space and time. Her *African Diasporic Ancestral Memory Transmutation Device*, for example, "quells effects of trauma passed down genetically from ancestors," allowing the user the capacity to remember and heal from generational trauma induced by the transatlantic slave trade. Similarly, April Banks's photographic project *Make. Believe.* invites the audience to embrace the voids of history. For black people this means imagining a past in the absence of slavery. I introduce the concept of *regenerative nostalgia* as a method these artists deploy to cope with the inevitable losses and injuries that attend historical racial trauma. I invoke the term *regeneration* because its connotations are both medical ("formation of new tissue or cells; the natural replacement or repair of a lost or damaged part, organ, etc.") and spiritual ("to be spiritually reborn").[70] Regenerative nostalgia privileges healing and revitalization rather than the repetition of pain, rendering this brand of nostalgia both sentimental and dynamic. While nostalgia is often considered a crippling form of memory that does little more than satiate, regenerative nostalgia encourages the sentimental recall of historical memory as a way to heal from the pain of the past. For these artists, the past does not always lead back to the path of slavery or Jim Crow; instead, these aesthetic recollections imagine new black pasts and new black futures. A host of contemporary black literary works, particularly afro-futurist texts, invent alternative histories (and universes) that displace or replace the traumas of black history, yet I find that contemporary African American visual culture provides a productive space to explore the phenomenon of regenerative nostalgia because they take seriously the therapeutic connotations of regeneration. The artists in this chapter capture nostalgia's tendencies to foster good feelings in the present, and in doing so provide an opening to fundamentally reconceive the black historical past in ways that promote psychological and emotional well-being.

The therapeutic benefits of afro-nostalgia I outlined in chapter 3 extend into the book's last chapter, "(Nostalgic) RECLAMATION: Recipes for Radicalism and the Politics of Soul (Food)." In chapter 3, creative nostalgic recollections sought to inspire psychological reparation. This chapter examines the oeuvre of two popular chefs, Marcus Samuelsson and Bryant Terry, who endeavor to make visible the African origins of American cuisine and, in Terry's case, foreground the healthful benefits of reclaiming these origins. In unearthing the Africanness of the American culinary landscape, Samuelsson and Terry advance a dietary politic that is linked to the articulation of a post-black identity, one that recasts American culinary culture within a contemporary afro-diasporic framework. Through the deployment of what I refer to as a *post-black culinary praxis*, Terry's and Samuelsson's aesthetic projects seek to reclaim and reinvent Africanist cuisine as part and parcel of the American culinary landscape. In doing so, they challenge the universalizing whiteness of American food culture and the national food media. Erasing blackness from the American culinary scene has resulted in multiple forms of food oppression, including—but not limited to—the predominance of fast-food establishments and liquor stores in low-income black communities, a lack of access to healthy and fresh foods, and the prevalence of food-related death and disease among African Americans.[71] Reconnecting black people to their culinary roots emerges in these endeavors, I argue, as a memory project that engages a range of black historical nostalgias (for Africa, for the Harlem Renaissance, for the Black Power movement). Both chefs build upon earlier conceptual linkages between racial consciousness and food practices, like the culinary concepts of Elijah Muhammad (*How to Eat to Live*) and Dick Gregory (*Dick Gregory's Natural Diet for Folks Who Eat: Cookin' with Mother Nature*)—both of whom inspire the culinary projects of Bryant Terry, in particular.

The book's postscript, "A Future for Black Nostalgia," broadens the previous chapter's discussion of Africa as a locus of contemporary black nostalgic memory. Here, however, I focus on fantastical representations of the African past, specifically in the Marvel comic series *Black Panther* as written by Ta-Nehisi Coates, to highlight afro-nostalgia's function as simultaneously a feature of the imagination and a way to claim the authority of black historical memory. In my discussion of the Djalia—the spiritual purgatory of Wakanda—I cohere much of the book's previous discussions around the value of nostalgia in black contexts as a productive counterpoint to traumatic memory by offering another, more euphoric dimension of the afterlife of slavery.

My orientation to the aesthetic projects in this book is as a scholar trained in literary studies, particularly in the practice of close reading. As has long been argued, close reading is an ethical praxis in which one interacts with the object of study (the novel, the poem, the play, etc.) as "it is" rather than as we think it should be or expect it to be.[72] Since the publication of Jane Gallop's oft-cited essay "The Ethics of Reading" (2000), the process of close reading has been considered an accepted mode of interpretation across a range of intellectual fields. Cultural studies, in particular, is a field that has relied heavily on "textual analysis of one kind or another, applying techniques of close reading to a broad range of cultural phenomena."[73] This book's analyses of black performance and music, and of visual and culinary art, are animated, rather than limited, by the method of textual analysis. However, in addition to close reading methods, my interpretation of the artistic productions are informed by a broader historical context. The methodologies of close reading and historicism I deploy are part and parcel of the interdisciplinary fields of cultural studies and African American studies. My primary aim is to demonstrate the importance of nostalgic memory in contemporary African American culture, of which literature, visual art, performance, and food are a part, and to underscore how nostalgic memory operates in these spaces as a historical and cultural phenomenon.

Each artistic medium that I examine, from the performative to the culinary, advances nostalgia and its attendant affects (happiness, wanderlust, fulfillment, bliss) as modes of interiority from which black people have been considered "immune," particularly in the historical past. When (or if) we concede that historical nostalgia is simply "unavailable" to black folks, we also concede that black affective life is static and bounded by time and by history. This is a dangerous concession. Most urgently, privileging black misery reproduces the narrative that black affect is limited to the traumatic. While historical nostalgia in its more conventional form leaves little in the way of romantic recall for the African-descended, *Afro-Nostalgia* calls for its own redemptive remembrances, rooted in the imaginative landscape of the historical and the pleasure-seeking desires of the present.

1
(Nostalgic) RETRIBUTION

The Power of the Petty
in Contemporary Narratives of Slavery

I loved history as a child, until some clear-eyed young Negro
pointed out, quite rightly, that there was no place in the
American past I could go and be free.
—Sherley Anne Williams, *Dessa Rose*

We have never been free, but we have been being free.
—Joshua Chambers-Letson, *After the Party: A Manifesto for
Queer of Color Life*

In Herman Melville's short story "Benito Cereno" (1855), the slave Babo
orchestrates a revolt on the ship where he is initially loaded as cargo. The
entire narrative is told from the perspective of Captain Delano, who arrives
on the ship, which appears to be in distress, to aid the sailors—including
the ship's captain, the titular Benito Cereno. Unbeknownst to Delano,
the ship has been besieged by Babo and the other enslaved people on
board. What appears to Delano as "the strange vanity of a faithful slave"
(so impressive that at one point, Delano offers to buy Babo) is actually a
performance intended to disguise the fact that a slave revolt is in progress.
Because Delano occupies the entire narrative voice, the perceived victim
of the story is the captive Benito Cereno, who must remain steadfast in the
face of the murderous Babo and "all the negroes, though not in the first
place knowing to the design of revolt, when it was accomplished, approved
it."[1] The story is a visceral allegory whose interpretation shifts along with

history's view of the triangular trade. Though the nineteenth-century tale paints Delano (and even Cereno) in a heroic light, for a modern-day reader, it is Babo who wins sympathy and admiration.

In this new context, the narrative takes on a celebrated trope in the African American imagination: the rebellious slave. For Melville, Babo is a threat and a warning to the reader, a reminder that slaves are not inherently docile beings but rather Nat Turners lying in wait. As historian Greg Grandin puts it: "Aside from its sheer audacity, what is most fascinating about the ruse is how it exposed a larger falsehood, in which the whole ideological edifice of slavery rested: the idea that slaves were loyal and simple-minded people who had no independent lives or thoughts or, if they did have an interior self, that it too was property. . . . The West Africans used talents their masters said they didn't have (reason and discipline) to give the lie to the stereotypes of what they were said to be (dimwitted and faithful)."[2] Figures like Turner, Harriet Tubman, and Sojourner Truth play prominently in the African American memory of slavery because they disrupt dominant historical and popular cultural constructions of black servitude. Like Frederick Douglass's storied fight against Mr. Covey, which freed the future statesman—if only psychologically—from the bonds of slavery, the very idea of the enslaved forcefully exerting their humanity is powerful and, for a contemporary audience, nostalgic.

What a bitter past to yearn for.

Yet for contemporary black writers, the lure of the untold, unknown, and unknowable narratives of slavery in the United States proves a difficult theme to ignore. Recuperating the once-silent "Babos" of American history has been a central aim of recent African American fiction, arguably its most defining. These forays into the historical consciousness of the antebellum era register as both historical re-creation and reprisal, or what I refer to here as *nostalgic retribution*. The (re)memory of slavery in these texts carries with it a desire for redemptive justice for the formerly enslaved that gets deployed at the level of content and form.

The connection between the concepts of retribution and nostalgia is somewhat counterintuitive because they manifest opposing sentiments: nostalgia with positive affect or "good feelings," and retribution with scorn and contempt. Yet both concepts are inspired by a sense of the past as unfinished and the present as unfulfilled. In an African American context, this historical irresolution and contemporary desolation can take the form of collective trauma, calls for reparations, and the production of contemporary novels of slavery, for example. This last provides a lens through which we might interpret nostalgia's utility as a critical medium for black psychic reconciliation with the antebellum past. If we consider nostalgia's conventional definition as "a sentimental longing or wistful affection for the past, typically for a period or place with happy personal associations,"[3] then African American recollections of slavery do not inhere. As a set, the artists and writers in this chapter re-create the Civil War era and reinsert themselves (or their characters) into this past, not as subjugated victims but as rebellious agents. Their wish is not to return to the slave past but to resituate black subjects within that past as defiant, emancipated (psychically if not physically), and complex actors.

The concept of nostalgic retribution advances extant scholarship in African American studies that attends to the possibilities and even the ethics of such reparations. Most notably, Saidiya Hartman poses the problem of reparation vis-à-vis narration: "how does one recuperate lives entangled with and impossible to differentiate from the terrible utterances that condemned them to death, the account books that identified them as units of value, the invoices that claimed them as property, and the banal chronicles that stripped them of human features?"[4] I do not seek to rehearse here the series of impossibilities that trouble the project of recuperation as Hartman has previously and expertly navigated that difficult terrain. Instead, I turn to those works that attempt this feat by giving in to nostalgia's romantic impulses to retrieve from that history a rhetoric of resistance and refusal that cannot, and likely will never, be found in the archive. As Hartman writes, "Loss gives rise to longing, and in these circumstances, it would not be far-fetched to consider stories as a form of compensation or even as reparations, perhaps the only kind we will ever receive."[5] The stories in this chapter elucidate the concept of nostalgic retribution in that they are driven by a historical yearning for restitution and seek to "write a romance that exceed[s] the fictions of history."[6] The imperatives of longing and romance constitute the nostalgic frame of the contemporary recollections of slavery examined in this chapter.

Contemporary Aesthetics of Slavery

The trope of the rebellious slave subjects as those who stand in courageous defiance against the system that subjugates them has been ongoing in black diasporic cultural productions since the 1960s. Arlene Keizer mentions that the "rebel slave came to symbolize black agency within the slave system" during the Black Arts movement, in particular, and that the "black slave in rebellion against white domination is the prototype for black resistant subjectivity."[7] Black artists have attempted to "correct" or repair the historical record in diverse ways, from radically imagining slave rebellions to making visible the emotional lives of enslaved subjects in their narratives. Recent artistic representations of slavery as a corrective have taken multiple forms, from the contemporary novel to the Hollywood film. The re-creation of the slave past has been most widely pursued in literary texts; subsequently, the field of literary studies has witnessed the formation of a distinct subgenre dedicated to the study of contemporary novels about slavery.

The term *neo-slave narratives* originated in Bernard Bell's *The Afro-American Novel and Its Tradition* (1987), in which Bell broadly refers to these works as "modern narratives of escape from bondage to freedom."[8] Ashraf Rushdy's formative study *Neo-Slave Narratives* (1999) extends Bell's analysis by linking the advent of the neo–slave narrative to debates over the representation of slavery that emerged in intellectual, social, and historical discourses in the 1960s. Rushdy argues that black writers became especially invested in the neo–slave narrative as a way to consider the meaning of "contemporary racial identity after Black Power,"[9] and he focuses on novels that "assume the form, adopt the conventions, and take on the first-person voice of the antebellum slave narrative."[10]

Since the publication of Bell's and Rushdy's texts, a healthy discourse has emerged concerning "contemporary narratives of slavery," a term offered by Keizer that seeks to "cast a wider interpretive net" to account for those novels that "move so far beyond the traditional [slave] narratives that their works are not bound by that frame of reference."[11] Keizer, in particular, reads contemporary novels of slavery "alongside established theories of subjectivity" by turning to psychoanalysis, performance theory, and postmodern theory to examine "the multiple and often contradictory processes through which human beings in the modern and postmodern worlds come to identify themselves."[12] For Keizer, these processes of subject formation vis-à-vis contemporary narratives of slavery are enacted through *postmemory*—Marianne Hirsch's concept that describes the means by which succeeding generations process the "cultural or collective trauma" of their ancestors through "projection, investment, and creation."[13] Keizer extends this concept beyond Hirsch's intended subjects (descendants of Holocaust survivors) to account for the methods that African American and Afro-Caribbean subjects employ to grapple with an unknowable yet ever-present past. The logic of postmemory is, in many respects, quite similar to that of nostalgia, in that both forms of memory are made possible largely through imagination and "creation." However, I would distinguish these concepts by highlighting nostalgia's investment in the romantic return to the past as well as its deployment as a conscious form of recollection invoked precisely to allow some form of positive affect. Contrary to the seventeenth-century diagnosis of nostalgia as an illness, nostalgic returns to the past, in this case, inspire feel-good sentiments in the present.

Though scholars of this subgenre tend to consider recent narratives of slavery as cathartic, Madhu Dubey has argued that speculative fictions of slavery, in particular, point to "the uncertain prospects confronting black racial politics in the post–Civil Rights period."[14] Similarly, Aida Levy-Hussen's study of contemporary novels of slavery suggests that this body of work is an "articulation of collective racial grief" that "consists simultaneously in the unresolved trauma of the slave past and the political, civic, and psychic dismantling of the modern Civil Rights Movement."[15] Rather than offering a mode of reconciliation with the slave past, these narratives reflect a sense of disillusionment with the social and political realities of black lives in the now and the foreseeable future. I sympathize with Dubey's and Levy-Hussen's assessments of these texts as pointing to an ongoing racialized pain and trauma experienced by modern-day black subjects. Yet, I also see within contemporary aesthetic productions of slavery an attempt to navigate this history alongside the framework of the traumatic. Even if these narratives express the "uncertain prospects" of black lives in the post–civil rights era, such articulations do not foreclose the desire for resolve or—better still—redemption. Clearly, when we talk about slavery, the traumatic is ever present. The project of returning to the traumatic past of slavery is undertaken not solely to express "racial grief," but to imagine and to create what Caroline Rody refers to as "a kind of historical sublime."[16] Rody interprets black women's historical fiction, in particular, as an "imaginative reclamation of an ancestral past."[17] The historical sublime produced through reclamation meshes with my own interpretation of nostalgic retribution as a desire to represent a historical self outside of subjugation and as a form of reprisal.

What nostalgia offers to this body of scholarship is an analytic for contending with the contradictions of the slave past, contradictions that Dionne Brand names "a horror and a romance."[18] In writing about the "Door of No Return"—the literal and figurative threshold between slavery and freedom—Brand explains that "the horror is of course three or four hundred years of slavery, its shadow was and is colonialism and racism." But on the other side of that door is the "romance," where "some of us reinvent these origins as a golden past of serenity, grandeur, equality—as one living in a state of dread invents its opposite for sustenance." The horror has invited a wealth of critical interventions and interpretations, but far less has been written about the romance that lies "beyond the door."[19] In reckoning with this contradiction, nostalgia can proffer a framework for considering the diverse ways that black cultural producers attempt to recapture and reimagine the era of slavery beyond the scope of the traumatic, not solely to provide "sustenance" but also to satisfy the desire for reparation. I also acknowledge here Angelyn Mitchell's concept of the *liberatory narrative*, which is "primarily concerned with the nature of freedom—of affranchisement—for those who were formerly enslaved."[20] Mitchell's study focuses on historical novels of slavery written by black women that are largely concerned with "the protagonist's conception and articulation of herself as a free, autonomous, self-authorized self."[21] Yet Mitchell's attempt to apprehend the liberatory imperatives of these works aligns with my interest in the ways that a traumatic past is imaginatively recalled in the service of historical redemption. In a similar fashion, Salamishah Tillet's concept of *mnemonic restitution* identifies the contemporary black subject's desire for historical recompense. Tillet refers to mnemonic restitution as a "rhetoric of redress" that "challenge[s] the purposeful and 'polite' national amnesia around slavery."[22] While mnemonic restitution primarily confers honor in the form of "slavery museums, formal apologies, historic commissions, and the public accounting of private corporations and institutions that benefited from slavery," nostalgic retribution imagines justice through affective acts of resistance. For instance, Michelle Obama's now-famous expression "When they go low, we go high" exemplifies the expectation for black folks to retain an exceeding sense of grace and dignity in the face of injustice. The trope of the "magical Negro," an extension of the ever-noble Uncle Tom, illustrates this phenomenon vividly: in this role, black folks are represented as largely unaffected by their subjugation, privileging instead an elevated spiritual and moral selfhood.

This chapter investigates the opposite posture by underscoring the affective power of the petty,[23] a power that is made possible through nostalgic sojourns to a slave past. This method of redress offers little toward immediate or material social change; instead the rhetoric of nostalgic retribution functions as "payback," specifically in the "form of the symbolic reordering of the social and political hierarchy."[24] Akin to Tavia Nyong'o's deployment of "critical shade,"[25] the goal of nostalgic retribution is not reconciliation or forgiveness or social transformation but the (smug) satisfaction that attends the want of revenge and reparation enacted by contemporary black subjects as recompense for their own (historical) pain and for that of their ancestors.

Nostalgic Retributions

The concepts of nostalgia and retribution assume that the past that we recruit is *more* desirable than the present moment. This premise is a key feature of white nostalgia or what Svetlana Boym describes as *restorative nostalgia*, a form of memory that "does not think of itself as nostalgia, but rather as truth and tradition."[26] About an hour before I sat at my desk to revise this chapter, several hundred white men and women descended on the campus of the University of Virginia with burning tiki torches to protest the removal of Confederate monuments. How timely. Their longing (and revenge) took the form of a public spectacle of white pride that resulted in both injury and death. White nostalgia is animated by a feeling that a once glorious past is fast receding or will be entirely lost (as the events in Charlottesville attest). Those who seek to preserve this past often do so through violent means.

If the recompense associated with white nostalgia is motivated by the fear of an endangered white-supremacist past, what might nostalgic retribution look like for black folks who do not find many occasions to commemorate the antebellum moment? For black people the evocation of nostalgia is not for a better moment in historical time, as Williams's epigraph makes clear. While all nostalgic memory is arguably a feature of the imaginary, the artists I discuss in this chapter desire not to relive the past as it "once was" but rather to reframe the moment of slavery through the emancipated voice of the contemporary black subject.

While the sojourns to the historical past in contemporary novels of slavery often serve as a corrective, there are a number of scholars who reject such re-memories. For them, historical interventions of this kind become a "ventriloquized call of a pained and unappeased racial past." These scholars assert that the "experiential authority of the past's 'true' victims is usurped by contemporary discourse that presumes to speak in their place, on behalf of modern resentments and desires."[28] Rather than view these "ventriloquized" voices as dubious, I read such "modern resentments and desires" as precisely what constitute the nostalgic imaginary in contemporary narratives of slavery. The act of taking on the voice of the formerly enslaved expresses a longing to reimagine the justice denied to that past's "'true' victims," as well as to satisfy the contemporary desire for reparation.

Nostalgic retribution is not simply a matter of recovering past pain or returning to the traumatic moment. It is neither consumptive nor self-indulgent. Nostalgic retribution is a historical desire for retribution and reconciliation of a traumatic moment that remains extant. Nostalgic retribution does not account for the violent resistance we associate with "divine retribution" for the sin of slavery, but consists in conversational rejoinders, ridicule, and feigned madness—justice on an entirely different register than the kinds of retributive justice that so occupied nineteenth-century writers on the subject. Nostalgic retribution is a proximity-seeking affect deployed by contemporary black artists who retroactively anticipate and enact a future of justice, even if it only exists at the level of the symbolic. Nostalgic retribution in contemporary black fiction is enacted at the levels of the authorial and the textual; black authorial subjects and the subjects of black texts dismantle and challenge the logic of white supremacy by renarrating the slave past through a nostalgic lens. The "longing" or "yearning" attendant in nostalgic retribution manifests as a desire for reparation, particularly at the psychic level. In contrast to Babo's famous silence at the end of "Benito Cereno," these figures are reimagined historical subjects who *do* speak, and the affective mode of their speaking is key to how they disrupt and dismantle received historical narratives. I consider such acts of retribution nostalgic because they enmesh a series of affective sentiments like pleasure, longing, satisfaction, and desire that are distinct from other iterations of memory (postmemory, for example) as a contemporary phenomenon. African Americans have reframed the atrocities committed on them in diverse ways and have found "comfort," as Brand puts it, in the realm of the aesthetic.

Nostalgic retribution in contemporary texts that take slavery as its theme serves as a form of historical recompense and, significantly, as a disruption that challenges white nostalgia for the romanticized antebellum era and the sentiments of reconciliation that the Civil War was meant to instantiate. Whereas Tillet's mnemonic restitution takes the form of memorials and formal apologies, the language of nostalgic retribution manifests in "clapbacks," subversions, "shade," attitude, and other displays of verbal and nonverbal contempt. Nostalgic retribution is made possible vis-à-vis the liberated voice of the modern black subject; it is a past that could only be possible through a contemporary subjectivity that imagines itself as the emancipated interlocutor of the slave subject.

Sherley Anne Williams's novel *Dessa Rose* (1986) exemplifies this phenomenon in an exchange between Dessa, a runaway slave who has been captured, and Adam Nehemiah, a white writer attempting to extract from Dessa the details of a failed rebellion coordinated by Dessa and her friends. When asked why she and the other slaves plotted to kill white men, Dessa responds, "I kill white mens . . . Cause I can."[29] While such a reaction may have been articulated by nineteenth-century slave subjects, it is more feasibly imagined by Williams as an appropriate response to a vile figure like Nehemiah. Dessa's voice in this scene registers more as the wished-for historical retribution of a modern-day black subject than as an attempt to authentically represent an enslaved woman in the nineteenth century. Despite Dessa's bondage, she uses the leverage she has—firsthand information—to resist Nehemiah. Rather than answer his questions, she responds "with a flick of her eyes—almost as though he had been a bothersome fly and her eyes a horse's tail flicking him away."[30] Though Dessa takes part in a violent and physical resistance to slavery, the conversation with Nehemiah dramatizes her affective resistance to his authority. Dessa's cooperation would allow Nehemiah, a white historian, to produce a text that would inform American historiographic understandings of slave uprisings well into the twenty-first century. Thus, Dessa (and Williams) literally disrupts the historical narrative. The artists in this study invoke nostalgia as an interventionist strategy to unsettle received historical narratives and enact their own forms of textual and psychic recompense. While Dessa's slave status is a fact with which Williams has to contend, how Dessa enacts agency within and despite that condition expresses the author's desire for redress or, as Williams articulates in the epigraph, a place in the past where she can "be free."

Contemporary audiences have been relatively accepting of imaginative reinterpretations of slavery and the antebellum South, but one image has been consistently met with vehement opposition: that of the "happy" slave. In January 2016, Scholastic Books decided not to move forward with its children's book *A Birthday Cake for George Washington*, which told the story of the first president's celebrated cook, Hercules. The text was widely criticized for representing slaves as joyfully performing their duties. In an extensive response to her critics, the book's author, Ramin Ganeshram, argued:

> I know these facts from the nearly four years of research I did with the aid
> of historians, largely, at the National Park Service's President's House site
> in Philadelphia, where my story is set. We know from first-hand accounts
> that Hercules was famous in his day as a towering culinarian—admired and
> in-charge, despite his bondage. . . . In a modern sense, many of us don't like
> to consider this, fearing that if we deviate from the narrative of constant
> cruelty we diminish the horror of slavery. But if we chose to only focus on
> those who fit that singular viewpoint, we run the risk of erasing those, like
> Chef Hercules, who were remarkable, talented, and resourceful enough to
> use any and every skill to their own advantage.[31]

One could argue that Ganeshram's imperative was nostalgic: she re-created the history of Hercules and his servitude under George Washington as relatively pleasant despite his and his family's unfree status.[32] However, such a reading would typify nostalgia in its most dangerous form; narratives that portray slaves as virtually unbothered by their condition are as damaging as those that fail to "deviate from the narrative of constant cruelty." These too-rosy narratives are also intellectually dishonest, as evidenced by the fact that Hercules escaped.[33] Unlike *A Birthday Cake for George Washington*, this chapter is interested not in reconciliatory representations of slavery but in the contemporary black aesthetic investment in reprisal—primarily in the form of affective resistance—and the ways that such acts of retribution are made possible through the deployment of nostalgic memory.

This chapter focuses on three artistic works that demonstrate nostalgic retribution as a cultural frame: Azie Dungey's web series *Ask a Slave* (2013), Edward P. Jones's novel *The Known World* (2003), and James McBride's novel *The Good Lord Bird* (2013). In these works, nostalgia is invoked not as a wistful longing for a time now passed but as a way for these artists and writers to implant actors and characters into that history to elicit decidedly modern forms of redress. All three works collapse the past and the present, invoking a radicalized voice of defiance to undermine contemporary nostalgic (and largely misinformed) ideas about the Civil War era and the lives of the enslaved therein.

Time-Traveling Black Girls

Actress Azie Dungey has "played every black woman of note that ever lived."[34] She cites Harriet Tubman and Diane Nash among those esteemed women. Most of Dungey's acting jobs have been as a character interpreter at historical sites like Mount Vernon, the home of George Washington, and she refers to herself as "the time-traveling black girl." Dungey's time travel involves the conflation of the eighteenth and twenty-first centuries in difficult, yet important, ways:

> Studying American history and the lives of these women, while virtually living in their heads and experiences each day, made me feel like I was in some sort of twisted time warp. This was also the time of Barack Obama's first term in [the] White House and his subsequent run for a second term. I ask you to remember the racial tension that was all around. We had people saying that the President would be planting watermelons on the White House lawn. Emails were forwarded proclaiming that this was the beginning of a race war and the end of the country as we know it. People bought guns. (A lot of guns.) A scientist reported the evolutionary explanation as to why black women were the least attractive of all the races. The Oprah Show ended. It was mass chaos. And in the midst of all this, I was playing a slave. Everyday, I was literally playing a slave. . . . Talking to 100s of people a day about what it was like to be black in 18th Century America. And then returning to the 21st Century and reflecting on what had and had not changed.[35]

Dungey's web series *Ask a Slave* is the creative manifestation of her experience enacting historical "scripts" while also contending with the emotional and psychic dilemmas that attend blackness in the contemporary moment. As Lisa Woolfork points out, "for black interpreters . . . a crucial shift from the context of freedom to that of assumed bondage is implicit in the chore of performing history in the first person."[36] Indeed, Dungey recalls her former roommate reminding her that she had been "horribly miserable" during the time she worked at Mount Vernon playing the role of Caroline Branham, George and Martha Washington's housemaid/slave.[37] And when asked by interviewer Amy M. Tyson, "What do you wish could happen at sites where interpreters are hired to portray slaves or interpret slavery? What do you think could improve their experience?" Dungey (half-jokingly) responds, "PTSD support."[38] While Dungey acknowledges that Lizzie Mae was created to articulate what Caroline could not, it seems plausible that Lizzie Mae's creation was also inspired by Dungey's own inability to speak as a twenty-first-century agent during her employ at Mount Vernon.[39] In her interview with Tyson, Dungey alludes to prioritizing the comfort of the tourists above her own impulses to respond to their racism and ignorance. She comments that she sometimes "felt like [she] was an imposition in their minds," and that "sometimes it would be really awkward, so [she] had to make them feel comfortable."[40] In another instance, Dungey refused to play the role of Charlotte, another slave at Mount Vernon, because "every story I read about Charlotte makes her come across as upset or angry or abrasive, and I just felt like I couldn't really do that to the visitors."[41] While Dungey may have felt contractually obligated to perform the role of Caroline in a way that would meet the expectations of visitors at Mount Vernon, she releases that sense of responsibility and expectation in *Ask a Slave*.

Dungey's project can be interpreted as an attempt to reconcile a psychological divide but also to reestablish the framework of authenticity that reenactment demands. Rather than remain historically true to the fact of black subservience that slavery reenactors are asked to perform, Dungey offers the uncomfortable truths of both white supremacy and black interiority in *Ask a Slave*.

The series features Dungey in the role of Lizzie Mae, an amalgam of many black women Dungey played in her role as a character interpreter at Mount Vernon. According to the biographical page dedicated to Lizzie Mae, she is a fictional character who "would have been one of 316 slaves that worked and lived on George Washington's five farms." Lizzie Mae's biography also notes that she "would have worked very long hours, starting at about 4 in the morning and leaving the mansion at about 9 at night." Lizzie Mae was, according to the site, "a house servant" who would have had "very little time to herself and family, and almost no privacy."[42] Dungey implants Lizzie Mae into a historical narrative in which she is primarily associated with labor devoid of pleasure, personhood, interiority, or voice.

In creating the character, Dungey writes, she hoped "to honor the memory of those people who struggled and survived through their uncanny intelligence, their strength, their love, and . . . laughter."[43] Like many writers of contemporary narratives of slavery, she seeks to paint slave subjectivities with a sense of dynamism often denied in conventional historical representations. However, Lizzie Mae's "sass" reflects Dungey's own historical ambitions for slave subjects who were forced to perform subservience for their own survival. We might consider Dungey's project within the broader imperatives of what Soyica Colbert calls *reconstruction*, which "names acts of narration and staging that emerge through reparative reading." In Colbert's assessment, the act of reconstruction is a theatrical mode of narrative repair constituted by a "mode of reading" and a "mode of invention."[44] There exists a degree of overlap between the concepts of reconstruction and nostalgic retribution; both are invested in the project of reparation. Yet, nostalgic retribution is distinguishable by its focus on the affective desires of contemporary black subjects to avenge past injuries and, in doing so, invoke the "good feelings" that nostalgic returns to the past enable. *Ask a Slave* was initiated by Dungey's desire not only to reconcile the dissonance between eighteenth- and twenty-first-century black subjectivities but also to embolden a historically silenced figure with a resistant voice.

The structure of *Ask a Slave* follows the popular "Ask an Expert" format commonly associated with radio programs and television talk shows, establishing the series' satirical frame. The character Lizzie Mae is positioned comfortably in a room reminiscent of a nineteenth-century parlor, where she sarcastically addresses the questions of Mount Vernon's tourists. Each of the series' thirteen episodes lasts approximately four minutes and consists entirely of the question-and-answer format. Lizzie Mae's position as authority is an overt response to slave bodies that are often talked about or projected on. Cora, the protagonist of Colson Whitehead's *The Underground Railroad* (2016), expresses as much when she is called on to "play" a slave as part of a museum exhibition entitled *Typical Day on the Plantation*: "She had numerous suspicions about the accuracy of the African and ship scenes but was an authority in this room. She shared her critique."[45] In a similar vein, Lizzie Mae offers up her own critique with each answer primarily through an underlying tone that betrays the ignorance and insensitivity of the question and, by extension, the questioner. The opening epigraph for each episode reveals that the content reflects real interactions Dungey had with visitors during her work at historical sites; the epigraph also states that she has changed the names of the visitors to "protect the guilty." Dungey does not treat her subjects as "innocent" or their questions as merely ignorant. She reads her "visitors" as complicit within an existing and long-standing lineage of white supremacy and treats them accordingly; their failure to know Lizzie Mae's truth is met with the condescension and sarcasm that it deserves.

It is the function of satire here as well that propels Dungey's project. In his influential study of African American satire, Darryl Dickson-Carr writes that "irony may be a muted expression of anger and aggression toward an authority and a sign of contempt for those unable or unwilling to pick up the clues the speaker/writer lays out for his irony to be understood."[46] Lizzie Mae is aware of the insincerity of her visitors' claim to want to learn about the "truth" of her slave experience, their underlying desire to confirm their own misconceptions about the era. For example, in one episode, a visitor remarks that her job at the clothing store Forever 21 is like slavery.[47] This comment exemplifies the kind of willful ignorance and racial insensitivity that Dungey's project aims to highlight. The comparison of one's experience in retail to eighteenth-century chattel slavery registers as absurd, yet it provides the justification for Dungey's deployment of satire in her responses, which are largely dismissals of the questions and the questioners. In another episode, a visitor named Samantha Dillon asks Lizzie Mae, "Where do your children go to school?"—to which Lizzie Mae responds with a guttural laugh. It is a laugh that reads squarely as nonverbal contempt laced with condescension, mockery, and fatigue. The distinctive laugh-as-response coincides with Sigmund Freud's articulation of the joke as a release of repressed feelings of aggression. For Freud, jokes are a way to save psychic energy; the energy used to repress hostile feelings is released in laughter.[48] While working at Mount Vernon, Dungey felt compelled to privilege the comfort of the site's guests to the exclusion of her own sentiments of anger and disgust. An enslaved woman like Lizzie Mae would likewise—though to a greater degree—also not have been able to freely articulate her feelings about her circumstances. The "joke" of *Ask a Slave* emerges as a psychically emancipatory experience for Dungey and as reparation for the slave woman who was forced to repress her emotions for fear of bodily harm or death.

Although Dungey inserts the figure of Lizzie Mae into eighteenth-century American history in order to speak back to white authority, the white authority in each episode aligns not with Lizzie Mae's temporal existence but with ours in the present. Lizzie Mae does not challenge eighteenth-century racial assumptions so much as bring to light the spectrum of twenty-first-century shades of racism that emerge in encounters with the past. Another visitor, Peter Mencken, tells Lizzie Mae that slavery isn't "that bad" because slaves received "free room and board" for their labor.[49] To this, Lizzie Mae snaps, "Oh no, this mother****er did not come up in here talking about *** . . ." The rest of scene is bleeped out as Lizzie Mae utters nothing but expletives in response to this visitor's comment. The episode then cuts sharply to a test pattern. When Lizzie Mae reappears on the screen, she is composed and asks, "I'm sorry, what was the question?" The slippage between past and present, Lizzie Mae and Azie Dungey, response and retribution, is what constitutes the project of *Ask a Slave*. This anachronistic reversion to twenty-first-century vernacular also reflects a black feminist narratology that manifests in "the stories we create, in riddles and proverbs, in the play with language."[50] The slippage allows Dungey to reckon with the simultaneous intersection and dissonance between historical and contemporary forms of racist rhetoric. Dungey's break from character and the blanking of the screen manifest as a temporary moment of chaos in which Dungey could not sustain the performance of the past. The temporal break represents an emotional and psychic collapse in which the veneer of eighteenth-century "civility" in the face of racial indignities could not withstand the twenty-first century impulse to "cuss out" the visitor as a means of enacting justice—both for Lizzie Mae and for Dungey. John Ernest's invocation of chaos theory is an appropriate lens through which to read Dungey's break, given Ernest's attention to chaos as a critical mode of representing racial history.[51] As Ernest explains, "the racial system can be characterized as a system rich in feedback, regularly folding in on itself as various eruptions resituate the racial landscape or redirect the cultural current."[52] The "feedback" or changing sameness of racial temporality that Ernest describes is characteristic of the imperatives (and dangers) implicit in Dungey's time-traveling project. The unspeakability of Dungey's response can also be considered a disruption of the neatly recursive space-time continuum on which her performance is grounded. Dungey's "eruption" resituates not only the racial landscape she recalls but the temporal landscape as well, through the abrupt "redirection" of the "cultural current" from the past to the present, to unrepresentable/unaccounted-for time (signaled by the test pattern), and back to the past again. The "justice" embedded in Dungey's representation of Lizzie Mae resonates well beyond the imperatives of her project to assign an interiority and a dignity to Lizzie Mae; it extends to the rhetoric of retribution that a nonlinear mode of time travel makes possible.

Dungey's critique does not focus squarely on contemporary modes of white racism. An African American visitor, Gerald Johnson, accusingly poses the question, "We were kings and queens in Africa—how could you allow yourself to be a slave?" In response to Johnson's question, Lizzie Mae responds sarcastically, "Every crow thinks he's the blackest."[53] While it may be the case that visitors of these historical sites want to learn more about eighteenth- and nineteenth-century US history, everyone comes to these spaces with their own remembrances, many of which reflect their own nostalgia for that particular past, whether it is a vision of Africa as a place where black people were "kings and queens" or one that proves broader cultural assumptions about the benevolence of the nation's first president. As Jessyka Finley has argued, "Romantic narratives of slavery as a benevolent and/or harmless institution are reworked, and Lizzie Mae uses her satirical responses to dissect and divest them of their endurance."[54] Finley's assessment thus begs the question: what remains of the old nostalgic narratives of the slave past after they are destabilized by these refigured slave subjects?

In Dungey's work, the project of reclamation takes place at the level of the affective and the textual. The retroactive black interventionist project, in this case, reclaims the voice of the "Babos" and the "Lizzie Maes" and disrupts, even effaces, white nostalgic remembrances of the pre-emancipation era. Those old nostalgic narratives remain, but they do not possess the same historiographic primacy they once did. Now they must stand alongside these voices of alterity.

What *Ask a Slave* also reveals is that while the audience participates in and even generates the dialogue, their questions are meant to validate their existing beliefs and, often, to diminish the brutality of slavery. Most guests wonder whether slavery was "that bad," seek to establish that the Washingtons were "good people," or deracialize slavery by claiming that white people "were slaves too." Lizzie Mae is an afterthought. For them, her fictional character is less a site of knowledge about slavery than a prop on which a nescient audience relies to shore up often nostalgic fantasies about the Civil War era and its attendant "heroes." Also notable is how the visitors project an antebellum framework onto a revolutionary-era figure. For example, one visitor asks, "What does George Washington think of Abraham Lincoln freeing all of his slaves?"[55] In the white-supremacist idyll, the antebellum era has swallowed all preceding eras, including the revolutionary one. The questions posed to Lizzie Mae reflect not nationalist concerns but racial ones. Dungey exposes her audience's endeavor to render invisible the trauma inflicted on the black body in their effort to retain romantic remembrances of the nation's founding fathers; as Finley notes, "it seems that no one cares to listen to the vast contingent of black people who remain alienated, misrepresented, and marginalized today."[56] Even within a framework as explicit as "asking a slave," there exists a general tendency to obscure or ameliorate the slave experience so as not to disrupt existing (re)memories of white Southern benevolence in the antebellum moment, a tendency that bears a clear connection to white complicity with existing systems of social and institutional racism.

The series is premised on disrupting historical assumptions about slavery through the mouthpiece of an eighteenth-century black woman who would not have had the ability to openly and explicitly critique the social and political environment in which she existed. Dungey's rhetorical retribution takes place largely in the form of signifyin', an Africanist mode of discourse designed to challenge white authority and produce new meanings. De facto limitations on free speech notwithstanding, black folks in the twenty-first century ostensibly have the privilege to speak freely. Dungey's work becomes even more relevant because of her own psychic quandary of simultaneously playing a slave and contending with twenty-first-century racism. *Ask a Slave* functions as retribution, given that "the seductive qualities of time travel as described by many Civil War reenactors [are] based on a particular fantasy and nostalgic longing, largely unavailable or inapplicable to blacks who might reenact slavery."[57] Not only is the romance of the South unavailable to black people because of their role as slaves, but the nostalgic longing for the antebellum moment is largely made possible through the willful erasure of black slavery altogether. As Amy M. Tyson writes of George Washington and Mount Vernon, "The mythology surrounding the ethos of *the* Founding Father seemed to blind some visitors from even seeing the history of slavery as meaningful to the site."[58]

Ask a Slave emerges as Dungey's own form of "time travel" and instantiates a brand of nostalgia that *is* available and applicable to African Americans. The fantasy created in the web series functions as Dungey's "wish" for Lizzie Mae, for the slave who would have worked from four in the morning to nine at night in the service of the First Family. Eschewing reenactment's demands of historical authenticity, *Ask a Slave* offers an alternative authenticity that reflects, perhaps more accurately, how a slave woman in the nineteenth century would have preferred to respond to her conditions. Yet the ventriloquized endeavor is explicit and unapologetic in its desire to return to that historical moment with the mission of retributive (rhetorical and affective) justice. Dungey makes a redemptive effort to reclaim the voice of Lizzie Mae but also to reclaim her own subjectivity, since her reenactment experience reproduced its own set of silences and prohibitions. Nostalgia's imperatives of proximity-seeking and self-continuity play out in *Ask a Slave* as Dungey's project of historical reclamation.

In Lisa Woolfork's study of black slavery reenactors in Colonial Williamsburg, she recalls a moment in which a slave reenactor, Cate, "would answer any opening questions with few words and in a tone that discouraged further conversation."[59] Woolfork recounts Cate's tour as an anomaly in Colonial Williamsburg, where most black reenactors aimed to make guests comfortable by engaging them in a kind and welcoming manner. Because Cate registered as unfriendly and even "surly," white visitors were often "offended by the visage of black anger and resentment they observed."[60] Indeed, "Cate's character, in its controversial, unapologetic, and unaccommodating stance, was an attempt to represent the inner life of slavery through a subtle representation of the emotional consequences of bondage."[61] Similarly, Dungey plays on white fragility through her refusal to prioritize the comfort of the questioners and, in doing so, destabilizes their expectations of the black slave body (and mind) as well as their own historical assumptions around the romance of the South.[62] Like Dessa's "flick" of the eyes, Cate and Dungey reject the white revisionist project(ions) of history and offer, instead, pointed rhetorical gestures and not-so-subtle rebukes to this dishonest memorializing. Moreover, Cate and Dungey fail to validate and reinforce the visitors' white nostalgic recollections by assuaging their white guilt. Part of what establishes and reproduces white nostalgic projects is that they work to resolve white unease about the present moment, whether that unease stems from disaffection or shame. Instead of contributing to the sense of reconciliation and reaffirmation that white nostalgics seek at these sites, Cate and Dungey upend that narrative project in their refusal to confirm it. In this way, both actors shift the dynamics of racial power in which, even in contemporary reenactments, black subjects are expected to appropriately play their (historically accurate) subordinate roles. These visitors venture to historical sites ostensibly to learn about what they believe to be historical circumstances. Performative recreations of slavery reflect a desire to deny a unilateral white gaze as well as a unilateral white historical narrative. In the role of Lizzie Mae, Dungey can enact a nostalgia of retribution that allows for revisiting eighteenth-century America, not with the romantic sentiment we generally associate with nostalgic feelings, but as a radical wish to return to the past on new terms defined and enacted by the contemporary black subject.

A Future Well Lived

If there is a hero in Edward P. Jones's novel *The Known World*, it is the novel's most enigmatic character, Alice Night. Most critics interpret the narrative in terms of its revision of and challenge to conventional narratives of slavery by focusing on the implications of black ownership of slaves. Yet scant attention has been paid to Alice, who emerges as the book's most subversive figure and the character for whom the logic of retribution most readily applies. In the beginning of the novel, Alice is distinguishable by the fact that her perceived mental illness allows her a range of enhanced freedoms that include wandering far outside the parameters of the plantation and cursing at white patrollers. While plantation lore attributes Alice's mental illness to having been kicked in the head by a mule, the novel's proleptic narrator immediately calls into question the veracity of this tale: "No one questioned her because her story was so vivid, so sad—another slave without freedom and now she had a mind so addled she wandered at night like a cow without a bell. No one knew enough about the place she had come from to know that her former master was terrified of mules and would not have them on his place, had even banished pictures and books about mules from his little world."[63]

The narrative surrounding Alice's supposed disability is one of many examples in the novel in which powerful stories readily become undisputed truths. *The Known World* is punctuated with scenes where Alice's deviance from plantation norms is ascribed to her assumed disability. These moments often portray Alice lurking at night, spying on the overseer, Moses, while he pleasures himself in the woods, and cursing at the patrollers' horses. These instances also function as an explicit disavowal of the disciplined practices enforced by the condition of slavery. As the narrative explains,

> Alice, the woman without a mind who had watched Moses be with himself in the woods, had been Henry and Caldonia's property for some six months the night he died. From the first week, Alice had started going about the land in the night, singing and talking to herself and doing things that sometimes made the hair on the backs of the slave patrollers' necks stand up. She spit at and slapped their horses for saying untrue things about her to her neighbors, especially to Elias's youngest, "a little bitty boy" she told the patrollers she planned to marry after the harvest. She grabbed the patrollers' crotches and begged them to dance away with her because her intended was forever pretending he didn't know who she was. She called the white men by made-up names and gave them the day and time God would take them to heaven, would drag each and every member of their families across the sky and toss them into hell with no more thought than a woman dropping strawberries into a cup of cream.[64]

Alice resists her condition by performing madness and leveling her own form of retribution in her day-to-day encounters with the authority figures empowered to surveil and control her. Yet Alice is able to elude punishment for a number of reasons; her "insanity" is equated with harmlessness ("Alice was nothing to worry about, Henry said to the patrollers, coming down the steps in his nightclothes and helping Alice up from the ground"), indifference ("the patrollers got used to seeing Alice wander about and she became just another fixture in the patrollers' night, worthy of no more attention than a hooting owl or a rabbit hopping across the road"), and superstition ("the patrollers heard from other white people that a crazy Negro slave in the night was akin to a two-headed chicken, or a crowing hen. Bad luck").[65] The affective register here is different than that of Dungey's work with Lizzie Mae, who is more collected and sharper than her questioners, and who uses her verbal resources and withering contempt to reveal their ignorance. Jones's Alice can speak freely precisely because she is assumed *not* to have intellectual and psychic resources, even though that is later revealed to be untrue. Lizzie Mae is an all-too-knowing subject; Alice is a subject who adopts a rhetorical stance of unknowing.

In the novel's culminating moment, Moses implores Alice—after her years of servitude to the Townsend family—to take his wife and son and leave the plantation. Because Moses has taken up with Caldonia Townsend, the recently widowed mistress of the plantation, he believes that with his family gone he can achieve his goal of becoming the plantation's new master. The novel reveals that Alice and Moses have been careful observers of each other, and Moses's suspicion that Alice's mind may not be as "addled" as many believe proves true.[66] When Priscilla, Moses's wife, threatens to remain at the Townsends', not wanting to leave Moses behind, "Alice stepped up to her and slapped Priscilla twice." At this point, the narrative poses its own hypothetical question: "Who was this new woman, who was this Alice acting like this in the night?"[67] Her lucidity reads as a shock to the characters in the novel, though careful readers should—at this point—be aware that Alice's mental illness is feigned. Her seemingly aimless wandering in the night, we now know, was her mental mapping of the landscape toward freedom. To literalize Sarah Cervenak, "free black worlds become possible in wandering."[68]

We do not meet Alice again until Caldonia's brother, Calvin, discovers her art in a boardinghouse in Washington, DC. In the novel's penultimate scene, Calvin recounts his experience of finding this art—a mixed-media map of the Virginia county where the Townsend plantation resides—in a letter to Caldonia. It is, he describes,

> a grand piece of art that is part tapestry, part painting, and part clay struc-
> ture—all in one exquisite Creation, hanging silent and yet songful on the
> Eastern wall. It is, my dear Caldonia, a kind of map of life of the County of
> Manchester, Virginia. But a "map" is such a poor word for such a wondrous
> thing. It is a map of life made with every kind of art man has ever thought
> to represent himself. Yes, clay. Yes, paint. Yes, cloth. There are no people on
> this "map," just all the houses and barns and roads and cemeteries and wells
> in our Manchester. It is what God sees when He looks down on Manchester.
> At the bottom right-hand corner of this Creation there were but two stitched
> words, Alice Night.[69]

The map of the "Eastern wall" is largely described by the mixed media used to create it, clay, paint, and cloth—"every kind of art." The contrasting elements that constitute Alice's artistic piece reinforce and highlight one another, exposing parts of the past that would go unnoticed if viewed distinctly. When Calvin writes to Caldonia that "there are matters in my memory that I did not know were there until I saw them on that wall,"[70] he expresses the power of the tapestries to evoke memories of the past that were unknown or illegible to him given his privileged status as a slave-holder in Manchester. Calvin's response to Alice's tapestries is an explicit instance of nostalgic retribution, in which her memory of the Townsend plantation causes him to suffer with shame, both at his complicity in the institution and at the beauty Alice has fashioned of that space. Scholar Maria Seger notes that Alice's "maps" inspire "an emotional response in the viewer based on [their] ability to portray both omniscience and subjectivity through aesthetics."[71] But more than that, the "maps" re-create the world of Manchester County, not as it was, but as it might have been. In her interpretation of Alice and her "maps," Sarah Mahurin Mutter argues that Calvin's declaration of a "wondrous thing" refers not just to Alice's creations but to Alice as well.[72]

Here the novel makes a point about the role of aesthetics and the artist in representing the memory of the past. It is not a memory that belongs to governments or historians or the "winners" of wars; this memory is also the possession of the (formerly) dispossessed. Twice in Calvin's description he refers to the piece as a "map of life." Instructive here is the kind of life that Alice represents; in this work there are "no people," only the landscape, unspoiled by the machinations of humans and the hierarchies that they bring. I see Alice's "Creation" as nostalgic in its imperative to re-represent Manchester County less through the lens of experience. It reveals an idealized vision of humankind absent the atrocities wrought by that peculiar institution; indeed, her "map" is what God sees rather than what "Man" has made.

The second part of this "map," as Calvin explains, "may well be even more miraculous than the one of the County." He writes to Caldonia, "This one is about your home, Caldonia. It is your plantation, and again, it is what God sees when he looks down. There is nothing missing, not a cabin, not a barn, not a chicken, not a horse. Not a single person is missing. I suspect that if I were to count the blades of grass, the number would be correct as it was once when the creator of this work knew that world. And again, in the bottom right-hand corner are the stitched words 'Alice Night.'"[73] In this version of the map, Alice has portrayed the people of Manchester County. What is distinctive about this map is the way in which the people, the living and the dead, stand as equals in "God's" eyes.

As Calvin describes, "every single person is there, standing and waiting as if for a painter and his easel to come along and capture them in the glory of the day."[74] Calvin's description refers not only to the figures' stillness ("standing and waiting") but to them as aesthetic subjects; in this representation and in this moment their "earthly" roles as slaves and masters are immaterial to the beauty conveyed through God's (and the artist's) lens.

I have always been struck by Alice's rendering of Manchester County, particularly its beauty. There is something counterintuitive about Alice's aesthetic marvel, a work that is also an intricate representation of her former plantation. This is the site where families were broken, digits and ears were severed from the bodies of recalcitrant slaves, and black people owned other black people, which the novel portrays as no worse than white masters owning black people (though I would argue that it was). Alice's "map" is the inverse of the map of the "Known World" owned by Sheriff John Skiffington, a map that depicts "America." Despite purchasing it as a gift for his wife, Winifred, the sheriff keeps the "Known World" map hanging in his office because she thinks it "too hideous to be in her house."[75] But Alice's map depicts none of the "ugliness" of slavery; as Calvin reiterates, it is a representation of "what God sees." As Mutter writes, "Alice Night understands the significance of the art object's durability—when she sees Elias carving Tessie's doll, she counsels him, 'You just make it good, make it to last'—and her own acts of creation reflect this understanding."[76] Alice's artistry is an apparent inversion of Elias's, in that it attempts to portray the given world, the real world, rather than to improve on it by creating an alternative world. Conversely, Katherine Clay Bassard argues that Alice's map shows "an alternative way of seeing that is not confined to a 'map' or 'narrative' but is at once immanent and transcendent."[77] Bassard and Mutter exemplify opposing ends of the spectrum with respect to precisely what is depicted in Alice's maps (and how). Yet I read Alice's creations as the reflection of a past that never was. Such an approach could easily reflect the chaos and ugliness of the institution in which Alice and the other slaves were bound; instead, her works are set in the past but are not of it.

In her analysis of *The Known World*, scholar Regina Bradley assesses, "Jones' construction of powerful, independent black female characters like Alice Night (Walker), for example, provide black women the opportunity to move past slave women as strictly traumatic figures."[78] Alice is a character who experiences traumatic circumstances yet is not defined by them. Instead she uses her experiences to construct a vision of the past that reflects her current status as a free subject, one who can craft a narrative of plantation life that exceeds reality and serves as a reminder of her physical and psychic distance from that former life. Alice's genius no longer has to be hidden in the dark of the night but is now available for the world to see. Her robust liberation is its own form of retribution, especially compared to the emptiness suffered by Calvin, a queer man who now fears being outed, not for being queer but for being a former slaveholder. For both Alice and Calvin, the plantation remains an emotionally significant space; its memory reflects Alice's triumph and Calvin's shame. Nostalgia plays a counterintuitive role in each case: Alice's artwork recalls the slave past in a redemptive light, one in which Calvin yearns to forget (and to be forgiven). In the boardinghouse—a place where Calvin "labors" in an attempt to compensate for his slaveholding past ("trying to make myself as indispensable as possible and yet trying to stay out of the way, lest someone remember my history and they cast me out")—"all that is here is owned by Alice, Priscilla and all the people who work here, many of them, to be sure, runaways." That Calvin works while Alice and the formerly enslaved "own" alludes to the text's own investment in retribution, or at least karma (which is yet another brand of psychic reconciliation). Calvin's shame and guilt are his own form of suffering, and it is only through the grace of Alice and Priscilla that he is allowed to remain in the house, undetected.

The voice of the novel's proleptic narrator also carries with it a nostalgic view by simultaneously conveying the events of the past, present, and future. In one of the novel's numerous asides, readers learn that two of the slave children on the plantation—twins Caldonia and Henry—would "live to be eighty-eight years old."[79] According to the narrator, "Caldonia would die first, and though her brother Henry had a good and happy life with a good wife and many offspring with their offspring, he decided to follow his sister." In this instance, the reader learns that the siblings had once been "seized for two weeks by a paralyzing and feverish malady that the white doctor could not understand and so could not cure."[80] But the twins survive both a punishing illness and a punishing servitude, and the narrator—speaking after the twins' deaths—assure the reader that Caldonia and Henry led "good and happy" lives and, perhaps most importantly, left behind a "legacy" of "many offspring." This collapse of past, present, and future reads as a textual instantiation of nostalgic memory, particularly for the novel's enslaved figures, who have yet to experience or perhaps even envision the new life (and new world) to come. Mark Currie points to the import of prolepsis, noting that "by making an excursion into the future which is already in place, fiction can therefore instruct us in the kinds of significance acquired by an event when it is looked back upon in a moment of teleological retrospect."[81] There is something innately tender about the narrator's "recollection" that a slave girl, Delores, "would live to be ninety-five years old," or that Stamford, the slave most noted for chasing "young stuff," would go on "with his wife to found the Richmond Home for Colored Orphans," and that "the colored people in Richmond unofficially renamed a very long street" for him. We also learn that in "1987, after a renewed drive for renaming led by one of Delphie's great-granddaughters, the city of Richmond relented, and it put up new signs all along the way to prove that it was official."[82] The awareness of a future in which former enslaved persons experience longevity in the form of generations, state markers, and archives is significant. This future is a sign of karmic justice, especially when compared to the lives of masters who fade and disintegrate by the novel's end.

The proleptic narrator plays an instrumental role in refashioning nostalgia as more than mere sentiment; prolepses in *The Known World* signal a mode of retribution through an explicit engagement with the notion of legacy. Legacy is that which the novel's slaveholders are committed to preserving. When Henry Townsend dies, Maude reminds Caldonia, "The legacy is your future, Caldonia, and that can't wait. I wish it could, but no. All else can, but not legacy." The novel goes on to state, "For Maude, the legacy meant slaves and land, the foundation of wealth."[83] Thus, the novel's revelatory knowledge of the legacy of its slave figures functions as nostalgic retribution in that it allows the reader to see beyond the present circumstances of those enslaved on the Townsend plantation and bear witness to the multitude of "good and happy" lives that they were able to make possible for themselves and for generations thereafter. The Townsends, as well as other figures who were complicit in the slave trade, are left with nothing but their material wealth. The legacy that is Caldonia's future, for example, is meaningless, as the novel intimates that she is unable to bear children, and her brother, Calvin, is queer (and thus, presumably, will leave no heir) and comes to reject his inheritance. Fern Elston is also childless. Counsel Skiffington, arguably the text's worst villain, seems to escape death (barely), but he, too, is left without a family and penniless by the novel's end. I interpret the futures of the enslaved figures and the textual knowledge of their livelihoods in the aftermath of slavery as a retribution because, taken alongside the demise of the novel's slave owners, their longevity and "good lives" appear as an indemnification for the harms that they have suffered. The novel's enslaved figures achieve the very thing denied their oppressors—a legacy, a future—while those who support the system are forced to reckon with their degeneracy.

Consequently, the reader is privileged to possess knowledge of the life-span (and beyond) of the novel's enslaved figures. What prolepsis enables, then, is retribution. More significantly, prolepsis functions as retribution in its offsetting of the narrative's traumatic present to secure for the slaves a future of freedom. Alice's art even acts as a form of prolepsis by recall-ing the past in a light that anticipates a future of moral justice and social and spiritual equanimity. The nostalgic current of prolepsis, like Alice's artistic creations, can be read as an ethic and as an aesthetic; it produces knowledge of the future as a lens through which the legal, social, and moral violence within the novel is redressed. Because nostalgia is a remembering of the past not so much as it was but as we would want it to be, the act of nostalgic remembrance shares much with aesthetic creation. We might then consider the aesthetics of nostalgic memory in *The Known World* as a pleasure-inducing act that satiates the figures within the text as well as a readerly desire for redemption.

Trust Black Women

In James McBride's *The Good Lord Bird*, a novel that retells the story of the legendary John Brown through the eyes of a young black protago-nist, Henry "Onion" Shackleford, black women play a small but crucial role in reimagining the history of John Brown. Similar to Jones's Alice Night, formerly enslaved black women in *The Good Lord Bird* embody an emancipatory ethic that historically has been ascribed to men (such as Frederick Douglass, Nat Turner, and Gabriel Prosser). The narrative participates in reproducing the legacy of John Brown, but it also interrupts what could be described as the nostalgic history of John Brown, a history premised in the nostalgic recollection of Brown as a white-savior figure. While Brown's import is significant, his iconic status within American his-tory is bolstered by the repeated romanticization of *his* efforts to capture Harpers Ferry. The nostalgia for Brown manifests in the glorification of his divinely guided violence, which is deemed heroic, in part due to his maleness and his whiteness. Yet a figure like Dangerfield Newby, who fought alongside Brown and suffered a humiliating death as punishment for his participation in the failed insurrection, remains in the footnotes of the historical canon. I read *The Good Lord Bird* as the displacement of one brand of nostalgia for another, one in which Brown exists within a constellation of black radicals who formed a collective resistance to slavery in manifold ways. In McBride's novel, nostalgic retribution is evoked as a form of commemoration for African American subjects who are largely regarded as having been "freed" rather than as having been agents in their own liberation. Though they are only minor characters in *The Good Lord Bird*, Harriet Tubman and a fictional black woman named Sibonia play an important role in the novel's repositioning of John Brown from white savior to one among many radicals who sought to challenge the institution of slavery. The novel both appropriates and intercedes within the nostalgic lore associated with Brown by placing black women front and center in the nineteenth-century struggle for freedom.

When I teach *The Good Lord Bird* in my undergraduate classrooms, I always begin by sharing quotes about John Brown from famous writers and intellectuals from the nineteenth to the twenty-first centuries. I start with Henry David Thoreau's 1859 "A Plea for Captain John Brown": "Insane! A father and six sons, and one son-in-law, and several more men besides,—as many at least as twelve disciples,—all struck with insanity at once; while the sane tyrant holds with a firmer gripe than ever his four millions of slaves, and a thousand sane editors, his abettors, are saving their country and their bacon! Just as insane were his efforts in Kansas. Ask the tyrant who is his most dangerous foe, the sane man or the insane."[84] I conclude our discussion with a tweet from Cornel West in 2013: "Brother Edward Snowden is the John Brown of the national security state. He's the canary in the mine" (@CornelWest, June 28, 2013). Thoreau's defense of Brown is in response to the overwhelming perception that John Brown was a madman, an opinion that also forms the basis of Brown's characterization in *The Good Lord Bird*. However, as West's quote implies, African Americans' sentiments regarding Brown are far more sympathetic. In an oft-revisited remark to a reporter as to whether white people would be allowed to join the Organization of Afro-American Unity, Malcolm X famously responded, "If John Brown were still alive, we might accept him."[85] In the acknowledgments to *The Good Lord Bird*, McBride even expresses gratitude to those "who, over the years, have kept the memory of John Brown alive." The honorary blackness bestowed on Brown posthumously signals how the legacy of John Brown is bolstered by his violent response to the violence of the state.

The Good Lord Bird is, of course, McBride's own reimagining of a figure who has maintained a mythical status in the American consciousness since the mid-nineteenth century. Perceptions of John Brown have variously characterized him as a "prophet," "pawn," or "pariah."[86] McBride retells the story of Brown's fateful raid on Harpers Ferry through the eyes of Henry, a former slave who was approximately thirteen when John Brown took him from his master, Dutch Henry. However, this retelling of Brown's raid is further mediated, given that the story to which readers are privy is taken from "a series of interviews conducted in 1942" by Charles D. Higgins, a cook and "an amateur historian."[87] It was Higgins who "recorded the account of another elderly United Baptist congregation member, Henry 'the Onion' Shackleford, who claimed to have been the only Negro to survive the American outlaw John Brown's raid on Harpers Ferry, Va., in 1859."[88] As with most contemporary novels of slavery, *The Good Lord Bird* aims to challenge conventional historical truths by highlighting the inherit unreliability of historical narration and asserting the legitimacy of black oral histories within the national archive. Such novels disrupt historical narratives by staging interventions in the process of making history and producing archives. *The Good Lord Bird* can be considered a paradigmatic example of Linda Hutcheon's concept of *historiographic metafiction*, in which the novel is "self-consciously art 'within the archive' and that archive is both historical and literary."[89] The novel's impetus to intervene within the historical archive is, I argue, a nostalgic endeavor given the privileging of the enslaved figure as the one who recalls and produces memory in the narrative, specifically memory in the form of historical longing.

As "the only Negro to survive" the raid at Harpers Ferry, Henry becomes central in *The Good Lord Bird* as both an "author" and a participant. That Henry's story is of "national academic interest" also points to the enthusiastic endeavor to recover a black presence and a black voice within and throughout mainstream American historical narratives.[90] In referring to Henry's recollections as nostalgic, I do not mean to suggest that the protagonist romanticizes slavery (though he is not entirely critical of it) but that his remembrances of Brown's raid commemorate his burgeoning friendship with Brown. Importantly, his nostalgic recall also extends to the valorization of black people, women in particular, who similarly fought and died for their freedom—a fact that is all but absent from American historical consciousness. A key example of nostalgic retribution in the narrative is its depiction of black subjects as agents in their own freedom, which subverts the white-savior model attached to Civil War memory and, by extension, to figures like Abraham Lincoln and John Brown.

While the novel largely focuses on the events leading up to the Harpers Ferry raid, the inclusion of the fictional Henry animates the paradox that is John Brown by complicating Brown's relationship to black subjects, who are largely read as mere beneficiaries of Brown's benevolence and sacrifice. Though *The Good Lord Bird* is consistent in its reverence of Brown, it also complicates the hero worship and white-savior phenomenon attached to Brown's legacy. Perhaps ironically, nostalgic retribution is ascribed not to the heroics of John Brown but to Henry's impetus to convey the historical "truth" surrounding Brown's legacy. The narrative power ascribed to Henry serves as its own form of nostalgic retribution, critiquing Brown's white authority even as it extols his efforts to organize a slave rebellion. Importantly, the novel challenges the historical-nostalgic memory normally assigned to Brown and relocates it within a new nostalgic framework authored by the black slave subject. In this way, the text's nostalgic retribution appears as an interventionist desire to return to the past as an actor and an agent in history and, significantly, in one's own liberation. This is what also distinguishes *The Good Lord Bird* from the previous two projects discussed in this chapter: Henry's inclusion in the narrative as a character and as a narrator functions as an addendum, even a corrective, to the existing historical record. It is less about destabilizing neo-Confederate narratives than about destabilizing American radical nostalgia for a white antislavery leader.

In the opening pages of *The Good Lord Bird*, Henry recalls the rumors about "Old John Brown" that circulated around his master's place of business, which "served as a kind of post office, courthouse, rumor mill, and gin house for Missouri rebels." According to Henry, the story was that

> Old John Brown and his murderous sons planned to deaden every man, woman and child on the prairie. Old John Brown stole horses. Old John Brown raped women and hacked off heads. Old John Brown done this, and Old John Brown done that, and why, by God, by the time they was done with him, Old John Brown sounded like the most onerous, murderous, low-down son of a bitch you ever saw, and I resolved that if I ever was to run across him, why, by God, I would do him in myself, just on account of what he done or was gonna do to the good white people I knowed.[91]

The repetition of "Old John Brown" signals Brown's mythical status. In this scene, his reputation as an outlaw is so pervasive that it strikes fear even among those Brown aimed to liberate. As evidenced in the passage, McBride not only reconstructs the image of John Brown but offers readers a somewhat troubling image of the slave subject with the character of Henry. Upon being taken by John Brown, Henry spends the bulk of the narrative complaining about the squalid and scarce conditions of the camp and the attendant miseries of being an unwilling soldier in Brown's army. Henry's reluctance to fight for the freedom of enslaved black people under John Brown is not merely a function of Henry's inertia (though the narrative suggests this is partially true); it also reflects Brown's blindness to the power that his whiteness yields. After Brown rescues Henry from his master and declares him free, Henry admits, "I didn't make head nor tails of what he was saying, for I was to learn that Old John Brown could work the Lord into just about any aspect of his comings and goings in life. . . . That's one reason I weren't a believer. . . . But it weren't my place to argue with a white man, especially one who was my kidnapper, so I kept my lips closed."[92]

Despite Henry's acquiescence to John Brown, who bestows on him the nickname "Onion," he reveals to the reader the mask that he and other black folks are compelled to wear: "Back in them days white folks told niggers more than they told each other, for they knowed Negroes couldn't do nothing but say, 'Uh-huh,' and 'Ummmm,' and go on about their own troubled business. That made white folks subject to trickeration in my mind. Colored was always two steps ahead of white folks in that department, having thunk through every possibility of how to get along without being seen and making sure their lies match up with what white folks wanted. Your basic white man is a fool."[93] Henry's critique of Brown throughout the novel is largely framed as a critique of the self-centered nature of Brown's endeavor. This critique is also similar to Dungey's project, in which nostalgic retribution finds its point of entry in a white inability to account for racial dynamics and hierarchies. Brown "frees" slaves so that they may fight in his army; hence Henry's consistent references to Brown as his "kidnapper." As Henry states, "Nobody asked the Negro what he thunk about the whole business, by the way, nor the Indian, when I think of it, for neither of their thoughts didn't count, even though most of the squabbling was about them on the outside."[94] This sentiment emerges more explicitly in a later scene after Brown liberates another enslaved man, Bob. When Henry attempts to orient Bob to the machinations of daily life in Brown's army, Bob counters, "I ain't come here to read nobody's Bible and fight nobody's slavery. . . . I come to get myself out from under it. . . . [John Brown] didn't ask me if I wanted to be free. Course I come along 'cause I had to. But I thought he was gonna free me to the north. Nobody said nothing about fighting nobody." Henry is sympathetic to Bob's anger as he, too, felt that his recruitment into Brown's army was yet another form of forced servitude: "That was the thing. The Old Man done the same to me. He reckoned every colored wanted to fight for his freedom. It never occurred to him that they would feel any other way."[95]

Here Henry does not suggest that black people are not invested in their own freedom; instead, these moments buttress the larger argument—historically and presently—that black people have often been excluded from the very discourses that would dictate the terms and methods in which their freedom would be achieved. It is not that Henry and Bob do not want to be free, but that they would rather participate in the dialogue around what that freedom would look like and how it might be attained. These moments in the text problematize John Brown's "honorary black" status and highlight the problem of black exclusion from broader historical narratives. While Henry makes for an unlikely and unwilling hero in the narrative, his retelling of the days leading up to the Harpers Ferry raid allows for the existence and inclusion of black experience and interiority. The impressions of Brown (and of white people more generally) offered by Henry and Bob in the aforementioned scenes recenter black subjectivity in the conversation around slavery and offer a multivalent perspective on the iconic figuring of John Brown.

The Good Lord Bird further contextualizes Brown's legacy through the inclusion of African American fictional figures and fictional representations of black historical figures who also sacrificed their lives and fought for their own freedom, thus resituating Brown within a larger black freedom struggle rather than as part of a white abolitionist movement. At one point in the novel, Henry becomes reenslaved and is forced to work as a maid in Miss Abby's Pikesville Hotel, also a saloon and brothel, where he learns that there are "house slaves" who work in the saloon and as prostitutes in the brothel. It may also be worth mentioning here that for the better part of the novel, Henry is recognized as a girl. John Brown mistakenly identifies the protagonist as "she" upon meeting him, presumably because of feminine features. Henry fails to correct Brown, initially because he is terrified of his kidnapper, and later because his (mis)gendered status saves him from having to engage in fighting against slavery sympathizers. Despite what might be perceived as Henry's cowardly intentions, he expertly navigates the perils of being held captive, both in Brown's army and at Miss Abby's. Later, his perceived girlhood places him in a position to attempt to help Brown realize his plans to overtake Harpers Ferry. At Miss Abby's, Henry learns about the slaves who work in the "pen," which is a "penned-in area . . . where the colored set on crates, played cards, and had a little vegetable garden."[96] Behind the garden was "a hog pen, which opened right to the colored pen for easy tending of Miss Abby's hogs," the placement of the slaves' "home" constructed for the convenient care of Miss Abby's hogs. While the slave pen reads as a site of depravity, it also functions as a site of resistance. Specifically, the slaves congregating in the pen are doing much more than "playing cards" and "tending hogs": they are planning an insurrection. We learn that Sibonia (one of the women in the pen) and her sister are orchestrating a rebellion among the enslaved at Miss Abby's.

When asked to confess to her plot to murder the white citizens of Pikesville, including the reverend who ministers to Miss Abby's slaves, Sibonia remarks,

> Reverend, it was you and your wife who taught me that God is no respecter of persons; it was you and your missus who taught me that in His eyes we are all equal. I was a slave. My husband was a slave. My children was slaves. But they was sold. Every one of them. And after the last child was sold, I said, "I will strike a blow for freedom." I had a plan, Reverend. But I failed. I was betrayed. But I tell you now, if I had succeeded, I would have slain you and your wife first, to show them that followed me that I could sacrifice my love, as I ordered them to sacrifice their hates, to have justice for them. I would have been miserable for the rest of my life. I could not kill any human creature and feel any less. But in my heart, God tells me I was right.[97]

Sibonia's unapologetic admission that she is willing to kill others in order to obtain her freedom and that of others resonates with the rhetoric Brown uses to justify his own *divine violence*, a concept owed to Walter Benjamin and applied to Brown by Ted Smith. Benjamin, in his essay "Critique of Violence," distinguishes divine violence from what he describes as "mythic violence." For Benjamin, mythic violence is either law making or law preserving; in both instances, it works to maintain the social order and is thus part and parcel of the state apparatus. Divine violence, on the other hand, operates outside the bounds of the law, and the state more broadly; it is law destroying. Ted Smith clarifies that divine violence "operates not by the destruction of bodies but by the destruction of the systems of law or ethics that declare an action to be right or wrong."[98] As Smith explains, the "divine" aspect of violence does not "press theology into service as a justification for action but to open a gap of incommensurability between the law that would justify or condemn an action and the action itself."[99] Reading Brown within the framework of divine violence seems logical, particularly since Brown himself asserted that his actions were theologically motivated.

In the above scene, divine violence provides the grounds for Sibonia and her sister to plot rebellion. The text's inclusion of Sibonia—and her speech to the reverend in particular—works to reconstruct the memory of this historical moment in a way that privileges black agency. Importantly, it also recontextualizes the legacy of John Brown within a more expansive network of black resistance. Sibonia explains that her motivations are personal, institutional, and theological; she is moved to "strike a blow for freedom" because of the injuries she has suffered as a slave and because of a desire to serve as an example for others. McBride's creation of Sibonia indicates the kind of imaginative reparation that nostalgic retribution evokes. Her inclusion in the narrative memorializes her retroactively as a justice-seeking rebel who may not displace the American radical nostalgia for Brown but who certainly relocates him in a broader context of black revolutionary history in which he is evoked as a figure of valor, yes, but not a person above suspicion and critique. In the narrative, Sibonia serves not only as a model for Henry, who is largely defined by his aloofness to the politics of slavery, but also as a representation of the "forgotten heroes" who fought valiantly against the institution but are not represented in the national archive. The invention of Sibonia is nostalgic and necessary. Her inclusion in the text is exemplary of the concept of nostalgic retribution: she instantiates a disruption of historical memory by shifting our conventional "recall" of the momentous 1859 raid on Harpers Ferry to account for the missing black folks who stood and suffered with Brown. Sibonia is one of two characters the novel treats with unambiguous reverence; the other is "the General," Harriet Tubman.

When Tubman enters the narrative, she instructs Brown, "Your average Negro would rather run from slavery than fight it. You got to give 'em direct orders. With a direct, clear plan. With an exact time. And a fallback plan if the thing don't go. You can't deviate from your plan once it set. Start down the road and don't go sideways. If you deviate, your people will lose confidence and fail you. Take it from me." To this, Brown humbly responds, "Yes, General," and Henry notes it is the "first and only time [he] ever heard the Old Man capitulate to anyone, colored or white, or ever call anyone a general."[100] John Brown is generally read as the "captain" of his own army, guided only by his sense of justice and religious fervor, yet this scene places Brown within and even subordinate to Tubman's successful and prolonged freedom struggle. Harriet Tubman's character in the novel corresponds to a growing and rightful imperative in popular culture to place her within a broader and grander narrative of American history. There is also an imperative among African American visual artists to represent Tubman in a vein similar to that of John Brown, by pointing to her proclivity to wield a rifle and threaten to use it against anyone, including slaves along the Underground Railroad who contemplated turning back. These images perform a challenge to long-standing visual images of an elderly Tubman seated in a wheelchair; she appears relatively non-threatening, despite her life-risking and life-saving efforts. Tubman's fan art represents its own brand of nostalgia, not dissimilar from Sibonia but different from that expressed by Dungey and Jones. Tubman's recharacterization as a historical yet futuristic badass is indicative of a nostalgic desire to unsettle the consensus memory of Tubman as a grandmotherly figure whose encounters and enactments with racial violence are obscured to highlight the end result of her efforts: the runaway slaves complete their dangerous journey in the glorious North. These works are also expressive of nostalgic desires to instate in the archive narratives of violent resistance, eschewing the affective gestures and stances performed by figures like Lizzie Mae and Alice Night.

In the works I have examined, black women have manifested their comeuppance by making use of the stereotypes normally meant to malign them—affects like attitude, flippancy, craziness, anger, and bossiness. As I wrote this chapter, it became clear that black women's affective modes enable their capacity to compel revisions of large and ingrained revolutionary and Civil War–era historical narratives and their major figures. In these texts such affects figure as nostalgic rebukes of white power and authority, largely by undermining present-day white nostalgic fantasies and their attendant narratives of the Confederate past.

Though it is counterintuitive, we stand to gain by considering contemporary re-creations of slavery through the lens of nostalgia. Nostalgic retribution is part wish fulfillment and part restitution. It occurs at the levels of the authorial and the textual. These artists do more than give voice to the enslaved of the past: they underscore and dramatize the language of retribution as constitutive of slave subjectivity. Nostalgia is deployed to reframe the means by which the past is recalled in contemporary narratives of slavery, and it serves as the apparatus through which the rebellious slave is realized in the historical imagination. *Nostalgia* is a term capacious enough to account for the diverse modes of sentiment that entail returns to the historical past. Although nostalgia is often read as merely a romantic attempt to recapture a precious moment in time, nostalgic retribution encompasses a range of desires meant to assuage feelings of loss, trauma, and injury in the present. More importantly, it is an attempt to grapple with how we account for or reckon with an atrocity as widespread and long in duration as slavery.

Perhaps offering reimagined subjects as critical rejoinders to received historical narratives does not seem like a satisfactory or useful response to the critical injuries produced and reproduced by slavery. But I see this endeavor as an ethical one and, arguably, a reparative one. Instantiations of a retributive justice in the black literary imagination reflect present-day desires for reparation and remembrance. At base, nostalgia is a proxy for a wish left unfilled; its imagined continuity produces feelings of creativity, inspiration, and an "attainable future."[101] Thus, while I have spent the bulk of this chapter arguing against a traditional, sentimental definition of nostalgia, there is a sliver of the romantic in nostalgic retribution; it creates a vision of a past in which black subjects occupy a time, a space, and a justice that have been denied in history, in memory, and in the present. This vision is set against a contemporary white nostalgic desire for black erasure, from the historical archive and from American historical memory. Contemporary afro-nostalgic projects are inherently restorative in nature. In the case of this chapter, the project of restoration emerges through retributive acts that seek to center and make visible black bodies and interiorities that are absent from national memory. In the next chapter, I consider black restorative nostalgia more explicitly as a radical response (and perhaps an antidote) to the violent rhetoric of contemporary white nostalgia, which attempts to maintain its tradition of racial supremacy. Is it possible, then, that restorative nostalgia—a form of memory invoked by (white) nationalists to "conquer and spatialize time"—maintains an emancipatory ethos for those very (black) subjects it was meant to exclude?

2

(Nostalgic) RESTORATION

Utopian Pasts and Political Futures in the Music of Black Lives Matter

Nostalgia is a "disease," and I do believe that it's a disease that many white Americans have.
—Lynn Nottage, *Sweat*

The desire to return to a past that never existed is the hallmark of nostalgia. This sentiment is far from divorced from our political realities; in fact, nostalgia has come to define them. White nostalgia,[1] specifically, reflects the desire to return to an imagined past of unfettered white supremacy, primarily through rejecting, marginalizing, or erasing racialized Others through manifold forms of violence. The project of white nostalgics is one of "restoration" that champions an "antimodern myth-making of history by means of a return to national symbols and myths,"[2] hence the battle cry to "make America great *again*." As Tavia Nyong'o has plainly stated, "we undoubtedly live in an era of malignant imperialist nostalgia and white supremacist fantasy."[3] White nostalgics routinely deploy state, physical, and symbolic violence against perceived Others to satisfy their historical fantasies of origin and return.

This chapter considers forms of nostalgic restoration and return that are both available to and created by black people. Black restorative nostalgia returns to shining moments of black resistance signified by the long civil rights and Black Power movements to reinvoke the emancipatory affect captured in those historical moments. Black restorative nostalgia involves revivifying a black communal spirit of resistance and solidarity made through intentional intertextuality with the imagery, iconography, and sound of the civil rights and Black Power eras. These movements are being evoked at a social and political moment in which regressive social policies and the rolling back of political gains made during the civil rights era make it seem like we are being transported back to that moment in time. The response, particularly in black music, has been to establish continuity between the long civil rights and Black Power movements and the contemporary present to capture the emancipatory ethos of a civil rights era.

I argue that restorative nostalgia—as an immediate rejoinder to white nostalgic claims—can be psychically, if not materially, salient in the hands of black cultural workers. Critics of nostalgia argue that it impedes the possibility of radicalism because the longing and yearning that emerge from nostalgia are largely self-indulgent and antithetical to progressive politics.[4] Yet, artists in our post–Trayvon Martin civil rights moment deploy nostalgia as a means of engaging historical memory in order to define a new black cultural moment and, by extension, a new black political and social subject.[5] Considered in this light, key contemporary black popular music and musical performances illustrate how the concept of nostalgia can enable, rather than foreclose, the radical imagination.

Reading against critiques that nostalgia can only serve as a politically impotent brand of sentiment or a cudgel to advance racist political agendas, we find in contemporary black anthems a fertile space in which to test the limits of restorative nostalgia's capacity to serve modern-day black radicalism. I draw on Shana Redmond's definition of black anthems as "composed of a series of alternative performance practices developed and executed to counteract the violent exclusions and techniques of silencing contained within the governing structures of white supremacy."[6] Black anthems are restorative in nature in that they reinscribe black subjects within the spaces from which they have been marginalized and excluded. Part of the contemporary black project of restoration involves looking back to the black radical past as a site of inspiration and continuity. For Redmond, "the post–Civil Rights moment provides the framing for these politics that move through multiple media technologies and performances of collectivity and individuality, which are successful in part due to their significations on the past . . . the 'post' is literally attached to the movement(s) from which it is argued to have departed."[7] Such "significations on the past" are part and parcel of a black restorative nostalgic praxis, a praxis that is fundamentally invested in the restoration of black radicalism inspired by the long civil rights and Black Power movements. The Black Lives Matter movement, in particular, has inspired and come to be associated with a set of songs—anthems and musical performances—that constitute almost their own genus within contemporary songcraft. Pop-music publications like *Rolling Stone, Vibe, Paste,* and *Pitchfork* take turns compiling lists of the new protest songs augured by current tensions around policing and communities of color. These new black anthems enjoy high visibility and mainstream appeal. One way they connect to their audiences is through invoking these movements, especially at the level of the symbolic. Black restorative nostalgia appropriates the black radical past as an affective mode of resistance to white supremacy in the present. While nostalgic retribution, which I discuss in the previous chapter, serves as an act of rhetorical redress, black restorative nostalgia disrupts, resists, and challenges white nostalgic formations of history that marginalize and exclude. Black restorative nostalgia relocates black subjects within hegemonic and monolithic white historical frames by establishing a temporal continuity, primarily with the long civil rights movement, a "moment" that, as Jaquelyn Dowd Hall has argued, spans from the late 1930s through the 1970s.[8] This desired temporal continuity is exercised through affective and aesthetic means, showing up in a range of contemporary black cultural productions—particularly music and musical performance. The explicit intertextuality of contemporary black music with recent historical modes of black radicalism invites further examination of the "work" that nostalgia does to revive these movements' activist sentiments. In addition to repurposing the past to enable critical nostalgia, black restorative nostalgia also disrupts white nostalgic fantasies of racial hegemony and racial purity.

This analysis looks first at "Black Rage" (2014), Lauryn Hill's musical response to the police killings of black men and boys. There is a sophisticated enmeshing of temporality in "Black Rage," wherein Hill takes the collective black rage following the murder of Trayvon Martin (2012) and Michael Brown (2014), collapses it with the collective black rage following the murder of Malcolm X in 1965, and conveys this affect by disrupting the (white) nostalgic framing of "My Favorite Things." The chapter then rewinds about a decade to Dave Chappelle's "Block Party," a politically informed music festival hosted by comedian Dave Chappelle that featured about a dozen hip-hop and neo-soul artists, including Lauryn Hill and the Fugees. The film *Block Party*, which chronicles the 2004 concert, is deliberately modeled on a performance documentary of a 1972 benefit commemorating the Watts rebellion, which electrified Los Angeles and brought police brutality against African Americans to the forefront of the American consciousness. Finally, the analysis returns to the 2010s and the music of the Black Lives Matter moment, first to Beyoncé's 2016 performances at the Super Bowl and the Country Music Awards, and then to the Kendrick Lamar 2011 song "HiiiPoWeR." In such music, restorative black nostalgia—an exigent counterdiscourse to an emergent white nostalgia—continues to evolve alongside popular politics and social movements. I have chosen this set of "texts" because they exemplify black restorative nostalgia in their recruitment of historical radical black activist movements to address present-day forms of white supremacist violence. In addition, Hill's "Black Rage" and Beyoncé's performance at the 2016 Country Music Awards, in particular, deploy black restorative nostalgia by disrupting white nostalgic fantasies of racial hegemony and reinscribing blackness in aesthetic spaces coded as historically and unambiguously white.

When the Dogs Bite

After Michael Brown was killed by police officer Darren Wilson in 2014, R&B and hip-hop artist Lauryn Hill posted to social media a recording of an unreleased song, newly dedicated to activists in Ferguson, Missouri. Hill's "Black Rage" recruits white nostalgic affect in the service of a politicized call to action. The 1959 Rodgers and Hammerstein song "My Favorite Things" from the musical *The Sound of Music* serves as Hill's lyrical inspiration. Hill's version of "My Favorite Things" is a whimsical melody that challenges the nostalgic memories associated with the popular tune. Actress and singer Julie Andrews popularized the song in the 1965 film version of the musical. For most Americans, "My Favorite Things" is synonymous with wholesomeness, though the film grapples with its own nostalgic longing, for the Trapps' Austrian homeland, which is lost to Nazi forces. The song has been recorded by scores of artists since its 1959 release and was famously revised by jazz great John Coltrane, who in 1961 released a fourteen-minute version of the song. An unexpected parallel between *The Sound of Music* and "Black Rage" is the desire to escape fascism, and a refusal to be co-opted by an authoritarian government. Instead of pacifying one's sadness with thoughts of "raindrops on roses and whiskers on kittens," Hill doubles down on traumatic memories, referencing "blatant denial, squeezing economics, subsistence survival." Whereas the Rodgers and Hammerstein version is meant to create good feelings—invoking sentimental memory as a panacea to pain or sorrow—Hill dramatically shifts this meaning to produce the opposite affect, recalling the history of black subjugation to incite critical action. By way of example, the original chorus reads,

> When the dog bites
> When the bee stings
> When I'm feeling sad
> I simply remember my favorite things
> And then I don't feel so bad

Yet Hill employs the same melody and riffs on the original lyrics to convey the horrors of police brutality:

> When the dogs bite
> When the beatings
> When I'm feeling sad
> I simply remember all these kinds of things
> and then I don't fear so bad!

By enmeshing the twinned sentiments of trauma and nostalgia, Hill lays bare the need to reenvision a past in which "sad" feelings are easily resolved through the conjuring of gleeful memories of "raindrops on roses." Further, her seemingly innocuous revision of the line "When the dog bites" to "When the dogs bite" transforms the lyric from the individuated pain caused by, perhaps, the family pet to the use of dogs as weapons of racial terror. As Tyler Wall points out, "the figure of the dog—as flesh and symbol—has historically evoked the law's ability to make and unmake personhood in fundamentally racialized ways."[9] Hill both critiques and transforms the wistfulness normally associated with nostalgic memory by supplanting the original lyrics with episodes of racial violence, memories that cannot so easily be washed away with remembrances of one's "favorite things." In its simplest terms, we might refer to what Hill has accomplished as an act of intertextuality, or even sampling. Yet "Black Rage" evokes so as to purposefully upend the nostalgic memory of the 1959 song.

    "My Favorite Things" is a straightforward ode to sentimentality and suggests that the evocation of good feelings can and will displace melancholia. Hill's "Black Rage" distorts and confuses the nostalgic emotions brought on by the original verse and, instead, reopens the wounds of the past. As Kimberly K. Smith has noted, nostalgia "reflects long-standing debates about whose memories count, what kind of attachments and modes of life are valuable, and what kinds of harms are politically relevant."[10] This interpretation of nostalgia as an "ideologically charged construct"[11] lends greater clarity to the extent of Hill's innovation, specifically her impulse to invoke nostalgic memory to expose rather than to obscure, to feel more rather than to feel less. Hill's song negates the positive affective sentiments associated with "My Favorite Things" by bringing to the fore a less wistful affect, black rage. Hill poses an aesthetic and a political challenge to white nostalgia that is founded on the absence, marginalization, and erasure of blackness. Given the expansive range of musical selections from which Hill could have drawn, it is instructive that Hill appropriates "My Favorite Things," a song that so easily transports its listener to romanticized memories of idyllic childhoods, the holiday spirit, and a benign whiteness, as exemplified by the Trapp family and the film's geography (a small village in Salzburg). It is also notable that *The Sound of Music* was released in the United States on March 2, 1965, two weeks after the assassination of Malcolm X and five days prior to the historic march from Selma to Montgomery. We might then read Hill's act of appropriation as one that restores black history and black affect within the historical time of *The Sound of Music* and "My Favorite Things," and lays bare the racial contrast evident in teleporting back to that temporal moment. Hill's project is meant to restore blackness, particularly black affect, in temporal spaces in which it has been obscured, where it is least expected, and where it is often thought not to exist. Hill's "Black Rage" thus serves as part of a broader discourse of contemporary black protest music that seeks to inspire a transformational politics through the restyling of nostalgic memory.

Homecomings/Homegoings

In September 2004, ten years before Michael Brown's body was left for hours on the streets of Ferguson, comedian Dave Chappelle hosted an all-day hip-hop extravaganza in New York, possibly the most elaborate and culturally significant block party ever held in the Bedford-Stuyvesant community of Brooklyn. The event brought together powerhouse hip-hop and neo-soul artists like Jill Scott, Dead Prez, Mos Def, Kanye West, Talib Kweli, and the Fugees (with Lauryn Hill joining former bandmates Wyclef Jean and Pras Michel for the day). The concert was captured on film by independent director Michel Gondry, who at that time was known for quirky films and inventive music videos. The resulting concert documentary, *Block Party* (2005), is a bounty of black restorative nostalgic representation. It picks up on iconography of black historical memory meant to contest the logic of white nostalgic claims.

At the opening of *Block Party*, Chappelle states that he has chosen this particular group of artists because he believes "that they all have a personal message they try to get across and it's about more than just making money," thereby revealing his view of the relationship between art and commodity or, better, the dangers of the commodification of artistic production. Chappelle's decision to host a Brooklyn block party featuring artists for whom—at the time—neither commercial nor mainstream success had served as a motivating factor is important to his own vision of the past. In the trailer for *Block Party*, the film's performers are described as "distinguished not only by the caliber of their music but also by the strength and power that their art draws from keeping their creativity *pure* [italics added]. Offering moviegoers front-row seats at a unique entertainment and communal experience, *Dave Chappelle's Block Party* showcases how vital and vibrant music and humor can unite us and help transcend our turbulent times." The notion of "pure" creativity is somewhat troubling, given the event's homage to hip-hop and neo-soul, two genres that arose from the fusion of styles from various musical periods, but clearly artistic integrity and authenticity play a major role in *Block Party*. The artists seem to have been selected for their commitment to instrumentation and for what appears to be an allegiance to artistry as opposed to "entertainment." That Chappelle made the concert entirely free to the public seems in line with these artistic principles. Although one could argue that the documentary complicates Chappelle's relationship to commodity, the impetus of the venture appears not overly capitalistic. The film was released for limited screening in small theaters in select locations. This release strategy, a literal act of community building, highlights the film's endeavor to showcase a dimension of hip-hop that is rarely visible in commercial spaces. The performances in *Block Party* are largely collaborative, free of "bling," and infused with political rather than materialist sensibilities. The artists perform to live music and don styles that can be described as either Afrocentric or "urban prep." Notably absent is the aura of bravado, virtuosity, or pretense that tends to function as a fundamental part of hip-hop performance. The visual elements of the film lack any of the trappings or gloss of a high-budget film.

One of the most politically salient artists at Chappelle's block party is the hip-hop duo Dead Prez (stic.man and M-1). For Chappelle, groups like Dead Prez compose a largely unrecognized segment of hip-hop artists:

those whose music addresses issues like political activism, institutional racism, social justice, and corporate censorship. Dead Prez uses hip-hop as a vehicle for the expression of politically exigent concerns, particularly those emerging from M-1's involvement with the International People's Democratic Uhuru Movement.[12] Such political inclinations coincide with Chappelle's incisive humor, which encourages a rethinking of racial paradigms and hierarchies by pointing to their absurdities. Chappelle's use of the instrumental version of Dead Prez's "Hip-Hop" as the theme music for his former television series *Chappelle's Show* (2003–6) demonstrates the alignment of his comedic performance with Dead Prez's political imperatives: both conflate the boundaries of art and politics for a post-soul generation. The documentary spends a significant amount of time highlighting "Hip-Hop," which is Dead Prez's most recognized song. The chorus, "It's bigger than hip hop," signifies the group's belief that its music is more than mere entertainment. The song offers a message of warning and wisdom for budding hip-hop artists who believe that the music industry will provide them with financial freedom and commercial success. Dead Prez's advice to young hip-hop artists ("You would rather have a Lexus or justice, a dream or some substance?") calls for them to reject the commercialization of their music in favor of more intangible measures of success and achievement: justice, substance, and freedom. This call is reminiscent of an earlier age of hip-hop, the mid-1980s, which was typified by socially conscious artists like KRS-One, X-Clan, and Public Enemy.

Many performers in *Block Party* incorporate nostalgic symbols as a way to bridge a black historical past and present. Erykah Badu wears a sizeable afro wig, for example, that evokes and explodes Angela Davis's trademark style. In a particularly revealing moment of the film, Badu enters the stage wearing this hyperbolic afro wig and a plaid vest with a vintage Black Panther Party button on the lapel. During the song "Back in the Day," which revels in its own nostalgic longing for simpler times, the wind begins to unsettle Badu's wig. Anticipating that the wind will soon strip the wig from her head, she snatches it off, revealing a much shorter (and blonder) afro underneath. Clearly Badu's onstage gaffe is just that, but I disentangle what may be viewed as Badu's use of the afro wig as mere costume to suggest that it allegorizes the reframing of nostalgic icons and images as sites of both artistic and activist inspiration (which any of these artists deem mutually inextricable) and as locational markers from which to self-fashion a black subjectivity. In a simple chorus, "Back in the day when things were cool, All we needed was bop-bop, bop-bop, bop-ba-domp," Badu captures a bevy of unarticulated desires as she attempts to navigate the uncertain nature of her feelings about the past. Such inarticulation identifies, perhaps idealistically, the Black Power era as a less complex world, both socially and technologically. Despite the fact that the 1970s was an era of racial strife and struggle, neo-soul music like Badu's casts it as a more desirable historical moment, suggesting that it was also a time in which black folks were less spatially and economically alienated from one another. Even as Badu longs for a return to or a reclamation of a black revolutionary past, the chorus also reveals an afro-futurist sensibility that transcends the borders of black consciousness. In adopting a soul aesthetic along with the language of fantasy and futurity, Badu creates a virtual and utopian world that reclaims a black radical past and imagines alternative black futures through that reclamation. These aesthetic choices suggest that the possibility of a reformulated black community can only be imagined as a futuristic utopia, nostalgia can only be interpreted as a fantastical remembering of the past.

Chappelle's invocation of nostalgia allows for multiple and complex modes of black subjectivity that engage the black radical past as a point of departure rather than as the basis for identity. The intimacy of the block party format itself references childhood memories of neighbors coming together to restrict automobile access to their street so that residents could commune via playing games, grilling, and making private (albeit temporarily) a public space. In New York City, where the luxury of a yard is generally reserved for a privileged few, the block party fosters feelings of communal cohesion. It offers those who are enveloped within massive urban centers the brief luxury of spatial play, as well as a reaffirmation and reinstantiation of geographic belonging to a specific place within a place. Within the context of the block party, the vastness of the urban center is dramatically scaled down, generating a small-town feel and, by extension, a small-town sensibility among neighbors. Chappelle's *Block Party* attempts to reproduce the sense of community created by the traditional New York City block party by invoking a musical moment that harks back not only to the 1970s soul era but also to the late 1980s/early 1990s era of socially conscious hip-hop. The artists who perform in *Block Party*, including Chappelle, have attained economic success by virtue of their transnational reach, but the film resists any pretense of grandeur, instead constructing Chappelle's (re)imagined black community as one that is intensely local and inclusive.

The nostalgic reference and the return home figure prominently in Chappelle's reimagined vision of black community. These tropes are expressed both literally (a significant portion of the film takes place in

Chappelle's hometown of Dayton, Ohio) and figuratively (Brooklyn is the home of influential hip-hop artists Shawn "Jay-Z" Carter and Christopher "Notorious B.I.G." Wallace). As scholar-filmmaker John L. Jackson Jr. explains, the impulses of spatialization are inherent in hip-hop, which "demands of its fans and practitioners alike a geographical grounding for all identities—be that grounding neighborhood-specific, citywide, regional, national/istic, or even post-imperial. Whether debating hip-hop's origin stories or presentist impulses (i.e., distinguishing between where people are 'from' and where they are 'at'), mooring selves firmly to particular locations has become a way for hip-hop artists and fans to translate their individual experiences into culturally intelligible narratives."[13] Although physical geography plays a significant role in Chappelle's vision of community, specifically in his choice of Brooklyn as the site of his free concert, the community that takes part in the event encompasses local New Yorkers, Chappelle's invitees from Dayton, and busloads of twenty-something black folks from around the country who claim to have heard about the concert on the internet. In this sense, Chappelle's imagined community has less to do with spatial immediacy than it does with a sociocultural ethos that transcends both space and time. *Block Party* is a nostalgic sojourn meant to recapture a Black Power/Black Arts moment of cultural production and expression in the hope of creating the affect of a racial, cultural, and spatial proximity among contemporary black subjects.

By filling the gaps and fissures that naturally occur over the course of time, recognizable cultural motifs enable the project of an imagined historical continuity, and *Block Party* openly draws from—even re-creates—cultural precedents. When the documentary was released in 2005, many black cultural productions represented the post-soul generation's nostalgic longing for the social and cultural moment of Black Power. After the "dislocating effects of the Reagan revolution" and the lack of a coherent African American response, "the late 1960s and early 1970s looked like an attractive oasis," especially in young black circles.[14] The Richard Pryor T-shirt that Chappelle wears underneath his blazer signifies his recognition of the elder comedian's role in the narration of *Wattstax*, the 1973 film documenting the 1972 music festival of the same name, an event that commemorated the seventh anniversary of the Watts riots. For many critics, "the Wattstax film remains one of the finest examples of social commentary involving music on celluloid"[15] and is exemplary of what scholar Lars Lierow refers to as a "black cinematic aesthetic."[16]

Wattstax functions as more than a concert film; its imperative to examine the status of the Watts community and the conditions of urban black America seven years after the riots elevates the stakes of the documentary. It serves as an explicit yet nuanced call to action. The film does not go so far as to suggest that another riot is in order; in fact, it reflects on the riots' ineffectiveness in manifesting long-term change in the lives of Watts residents. The film "works" to the extent that it utilizes music to provide the sound track of black experience in this temporal moment to express the muddled sensations of love, rage, hate, pride, hurt, joy, and spirit—"the texture, taste, and sound of our soul"—that can only be conveyed through artistic channels. A visual anthem of the "Black is beautiful" ethos of the Black Power era, *Wattstax* both captures and produces a sense of black consciousness and black nationalism.

In addition to providing the sound track for the soul era, Stax Records serves as an exemplar of African American economic empowerment. Under the leadership of its president, Al Bell, the company worked to integrate the aesthetics of black consciousness into mainstream and corporate culture. Bell's commitment to African American political and social advancement became intensely visible in the production of *Wattstax*, for which he employed a predominately African American film crew. In addition, Bell hired Hollywood producer David L. Wolper and director Mel Stuart (who had recently worked together on *Willy Wonka and the Chocolate Factory* [1971]) to shoot the film. Stax Records financed a large portion of the event itself, and Bell was explicit about the multiple purposes of the concert, which were to "aid in [increasing] the visibility of black culture" and to serve as "a PR tool for Stax and its artists."[17] While critics have challenged Bell's assertion that *Wattstax* was an "all-black" production, given that it was, in part, "underwritten by white corporations, including Columbia Pictures, which bought the film rights, and Schlitz beer," I hesitate to think that the film itself was in some way compromised by its funding sources.[18] Perhaps any reluctance to problematize the production's uneasy relation between black artistry and corporate commercialism is a testament to the success of its performance of black authenticity.

As biographer and historian Rob Bowman points out, Bell was insistent about projecting a view of the Watts community that reflected the actual lives of its members. Despite Wolper Pictures' involvement in the film, Bell made certain that his vision and the film's portrayal of the Watts community remained under his creative control. His partnership contract with Wolper contained a clause stating that Stax Films maintained "the absolute right of prior approval of film or narration which is included in the Picture which relates to Black relationships and feelings; words or phrases having a special Black connotation; and, if the Picture has a narrator, approval of the narrator and the accuracy of the narration script as to the music contained in the Picture."[19] Bell's unusual contract clause offers some useful insight on his understanding of and commitment to black agency; in his unwillingness to give Wolper creative license to interpret black voices and black interiority, he signaled his own alignment with the broader impulses of the Black Power movement and the black aesthetic that emerged from that political era.

Larry Neal's foundational 1968 essay "The Black Arts Movement" declared that the primary role of the black artist was to "speak to the spiritual and cultural needs of Black people" by challenging "the contradictions arising out of the Black man's experience in the racist West."[20] While Neal was referring primarily to black literary culture, Lars Lierow has noted that both Neal and his fellow Black Arts arbiter Amiri Baraka were increasingly interested and invested in film and television as promising mediums to advance the message of black radicalism and black consciousness. Lierow asserts that the Black Power movement sought a place within television and film mediums to broaden the scope of black aestheticism, and that "it was during the Black Arts era that a serious black critical and theoretical discourse on film began to take shape, an influence barely acknowledged by scholarship on black cinema." Further, the Black Arts movement "motivated Black artists to pursue film projects in documentary, narrative, or artistic-experimental styles, through independent as well as commercial channels."[21] According to Lierow, "for Neal, the film industry's failure to represent and address meaningfully African Americans was ingrained in its system of cultural co-optation."[22] Both Neal and Baraka believed it important to teach "young people how to use film as a means of propagating ideas and fostering group consciousness."[23] Bell has stated that *Wattstax* was his "investment in a training program for Stax films to start preparing us for motion pictures as well as develop the talent base for doing video, because I knew at the time that video was coming."[24] Thus, Bell's *Wattstax* project was a seamless incorporation of Black Power/Black Arts imperatives. He used the film to advance a mode of black consciousness on screen, and he was invested in producing black cultural workers who could maintain greater agency over black representation behind the screen.

Along with showcasing the rich musical performances of the Staples Singers, the Bar-Kays, Rufus Thomas, and headliner Isaac Hayes, the film also provides a powerful view of the Watts community seven years after the riots. Framed by interviews with local residents and narrated by a young Richard Pryor, *Wattstax* paints a portrait of a community that remains imperiled by poverty and uncertainty but continues to regard the 1965 riots as both a foundation for communal cohesion and a mode of resistance to white authority and the status quo. Carla Thomas's song "Pick Up the Pieces," which she performed at Wattstax, exemplifies the spirit of the Watts community. On the surface, the song describes the repair of a romantic relationship, but it also provides an apt metaphor for the condition of Watts. The song's chorus, "Got to pick up the pieces, got to pick up the pieces, / And start all over, start all over," reflects the determination of Watts residents to rebuild their community. The residents' resilience displayed in the film is the expression of a resolved black consciousness; the concert begins with the black national anthem, "Lift Every Voice and Sing," which is then followed by Jesse Jackson Jr.'s rallying cry, "I Am—Somebody." In his opening remarks, Jackson tells the audience, "Our experience determines the texture, the taste, and the sound of our soul." The relationship Jackson articulates between experience and sound, specifically music, is central to the way *Wattstax* structures the relation between personal experience and musical performance. The film provides views of the various dimensions of life in Watts, including the barbershop, the church, and the street corner.

Wattstax is significant not only because it offers a visually stunning vignette of black Los Angeles in the 1970s, but also because it represents the black community as one that is formed by and through sociopolitical and economic struggle—and best expressed within the sphere of music. In one of the interviews, a young man expresses his sense of marginalization and figurative homelessness: "I ain't got a damn thing to fight for. I ain't got no country. I don't have no flag." Others convey similar feelings about their socioeconomic situation, their views on race and racial relations, the significance of religion in black communities, and gender dynamics. The viewer witnesses intimate barbershop and "stoop" scenes in which men describe the first moment they were called "n*****" as a process of coming into black consciousness even amid an intraracial politics of color. Some wonder aloud whether it will take another riot to solve the continued problems of poverty, unemployment, and despair in the Watts community. By highlighting important elements of the Watts community alongside musical performances, the documentary reveals the inextricability of the culture of soul music from the music of black culture. There is a clear relation between soul music and communal space and its attendant politics, values, and ideologies, emphasizing the extent to which the music reflects a larger social and communal dynamic.

Oddly, the live performances garnered lukewarm reviews, at best.[25] In an editorial written for the *Los Angeles Sentinel*, Emily F. Gibson wrote the following:

> What is there to celebrate? Are the conditions which gave rise to an unparalleled unleashing of tempers then any different than they are now? . . . Have [the Watts Summer Festivals] been instrumental in bringing about black unity for the purpose of strategizing the liberation? . . . The opportunists and demagogues who perpetuate the idea of the Watts Festival are as guilty of the crimes committed against black and poor as the most vicious racists, money hungry merchants, blood thirsty police, and panhandling politicians.[26]

Gibson's charge that *Wattstax* was but a mere distraction from the material problems facing the Watts community in the aftermath of the rebellion is a legitimate critique of the inefficacy of music festivals and artistic productions to exact social change. The current fascination with and adoration of *Wattstax*, which Gina Arnold admits is "now generally spoken of with reverence,"[27] is likely due to the privilege of hindsight. A twenty-first-century viewer has no expectation that *Wattstax* will "do" something in the form of social activism, yet in retrospect the documentary provides a necessary historical through line in which to situate black protest performance to reconcile a fractured black community. While the Wattstax concert may have failed to incite social change in its own time, the documentary serves as an idyllic nostalgic object in the present. The imperative of *Wattstax* to help rebuild the Watts community in the years following the Watts riots provides a critical framework for Chappelle's own endeavor to reconcile a twenty-first-century diaspora of black subjects made fragmented through contemporary forms of displacement including globalization and gentrification.

Picking up on black activist aesthetics made emblematic in *Wattstax*, *Block Party*'s director, Michel Gondry, deploys naturalistic techniques, only slightly more nuanced than home video or cinema verité. Even Chappelle's choice of Gondry as director speaks to his strategic decision to apply a stylized naturalism to the film's quality. Gondry's consciously understated production of the musical performances and interviews provides an air of realism that is the film's most explicit nod to *Wattstax*, showcasing Gondry's imitative ability to create a direct lineage to the 1973 film. Gondry and Chappelle's production incorporates a vision of black subjectivity similar to the one portrayed in *Wattstax*, even as Block Party is steeped in neo-black nationalist modalities, marking *Block Party* as both emblematic and constitutive of the post-soul moment it occupies.[28]

The documentary form is the most viable medium for fashioning and cohering subjects vested equally in post-soul iterations of black artistry and black subjectivity because, in the context of black cultural production, the documentary format "produces a concentrated spell-binding close-up on black voicings—on the subject or purveyor of a literate, black, mass-certified, public self-representation," voicings that "become metonymic for community."[29] The use of *Wattstax* as an inspiration for *Block Party* is both a textual and a politicizing strategy meant to engender a brand of communal collectivism and nationalism. Through references to *Wattstax*, Chappelle deploys nostalgia as a methodology to make possible the specific critiques of contemporary culture that he more often makes through comedic arts.

Of Chappelle's "comic discourse," Bambi Haggins notes "a sense of wary hopefulness, self-determination, and self-aware black pride."[30] His humor expresses the essence of the political sensibilities of the "post-soul intelligentsia," whom Mark Anthony Neal describes as "a generation of urban-bred black intellectuals born during the waning moments of the civil rights/Black Power movements, raised on the rhythms and harmonies of 1970s soul but having come to maturity during the mid- to late-1980s and embracing the oppositional possibilities of urban and hip-hop aesthetics, mass media, and popular culture as vehicles for mass social praxis."[31] The oppositional possibilities to which Neal refers are embodied in Chappelle's effort not only to make visible the black cultural particularity that uniquely defines post-soul artistic production but also to generate a new and renewed sense of black community that makes "mass social praxis" possible. Mass social praxis is an inherently vague concept, but in *Block Party* it takes shape in an idealized community constituted by a particular racial, cultural, and ethical positioning that attempts to undo the fragmentation of black communities since the civil rights era and the corporatization of black cultural expression.

Chappelle often villainizes mainstream media outlets, singling out radio for its failure to sufficiently air and publicize politically vocal musical acts. His decision to produce a documentary film suggests both a rejection of mass media culture and a deployment of that culture as a vehicle that enables certain modes of contact. Music, in both *Wattstax* and *Block Party*, encourages a collective politicism in which the audience becomes more than a community of listeners and viewers: audience members also become politically, socially, culturally, ethically, and technologically engaged subjects through the experience of seeing, knowing, feeling, dancing, and singing together. In *Block Party*, expressing the sociopolitical desires of a refigured black community grounded in the ethos and ethics of black consciousness requires that community members find identification, not just as racial subjects but also as political subjects invested in the practice and ideology of black consciousness.

Part and parcel of Chappelle's restoration project is an insistence on recapturing the ethos of the Black Power moment, which is imagined as an era when an inextricable black artistry and black radicalism operated outside the purview of white capitalism. Despite the fact that the film *Block Party* is, by its nature, a commercial endeavor, the event it captures on screen is emphatic about its disinterest in commodification. When hip-hop artist Mos Def (Yasiin Bey), formerly of the duo Black Star, performs "Umi Says," the refrain ("I want black people to be free, to be free") encourages a collective dynamism from the crowd and offers the obvious suggestion that despite the advances that black folks have achieved since desegregation, true "freedom" remains elusive. Even though Chappelle refers to his block party as the "concert I've always wanted to see," which suggests a personal investment more than a political one, the choice of venue, the selection of artists, and the documentary style of the film all work to encourage a more socially, politically, and culturally substantive moment than he admits. The film's nostalgic impulses ultimately work to create the aura, if not the reality, of a black historical past in which black community functioned singularly as a locus of black consciousness and black nationalism. The "hip-hop soul" sound that provides the film's content and score reflects not only black cultural production but the production of a twenty-first-century mode of black nationalism. In this and many respects, Chappelle's *Block Party* presents itself not only as an iteration of its predecessor, *Wattstax*, but as an extension of the political impulses of that urgent sociopolitical moment.

Nostalgic Formations

While *Block Party* captured what could be considered an early 2000s element of nostalgic consciousness in hip-hop, the second decade of the century could be remembered as the crucible for a new racial consciousness, forged from widespread awareness of racial and social injustices bolstered by the Black Lives Matter movement. This section examines the ways that the consummate cultural amalgamator Beyoncé deploys a black restorative nostalgia as a mode of social critique and trenchant black radicalism. The mainstream response to Beyoncé's now (in)famous 2016 Super Bowl performance, in which she and her background dancers rocked a style that can best be described as Black Panther chic, was mixed. Some critics celebrated the superstar's unapologetic tribute to the women of the Black Panther Party, and others appeared confused by her "sudden" racial revealing. Like most "crossover" African American pop stars, Beyoncé had become "race-less" in the public consciousness, what media vernacular describes as "transcendent." This transcendental labeling is but an exemplification of a colorblind ideology that frequently gets assigned to black exceptionals who have seemingly proved unthreatening to the racial status quo. Beyoncé's explicit homage to the Black Panther Party was an unambivalent affirmation, not only of her own blackness, but of the revolutionary politics of the Black Power movement. Beyoncé's song of choice, her February 2016 single "Formation"—in which she expresses her preference for "negro noses" and "afros"—leaves little space (or need) for a close reading. The stylist of the event, Marni Senofonte, explained that she absolutely drew on the radicalism of the Black Panthers as inspiration for the performance, and the fact that the Super Bowl was held in the Bay area (the birthplace of the Black Panther Party) only strengthened her resolve to use the Black Panthers as a reference point. I, like many other cultural critics, have invoked the term *homage* to describe the Super Bowl performance in which Beyoncé's dancers sported natural afros, black leather jackets, and black berets, the signature look of the Black Panther Party. Yet, the invocation of Black Power imagery in this moment should be read as more than just homage; it is a function of nostalgic memory. Even though Angela Davis herself has critiqued black pop culture's appropriation of the Black Power movement skeptically, referring to nostalgic iconography and fashion as "revolutionary glamour,"[32] nostalgic images do more than simply reflect (or distort) the pasts they invoke.

Though Davis fails to "get the fascination" with her afro, saying in 1994 that "it is both humiliating and humbling to discover that a single generation after the events that constructed me as a public personality, I am remembered as a hairdo,"[33] it is possible to read Beyoncé's Superbowl performance, in particular, as a brand of nostalgia that extends beyond mere image and iconography. As it is deployed in contemporary black performance, Black Power iconography is evolutionary as opposed to abstracted. Beyoncé's explicit allusions to Black Power imagery are nostalgic in the sense that they reference a specific moment in black revolutionary history as both a desired point of return and a call to action, seamlessly collapsing aesthetics and political imperatives. Several pop culture critics have noted that viewers who were historically unaware of the Black Panther Party would have regarded the Super Bowl performance as pure entertainment.

For viewers sympathetic to (and aware of) Beyoncé's wokeness—specifically the unapologetic blackness of "Formation"—and her financial support of the Black Lives Matter movement, Beyoncé's Super Bowl halftime
show harked back to a moment in American history in which racial pride
in the form of Black Power was public spectacle. Though many mainstream
viewers may have been unaware of the Black Panther/Black Power references, Beyoncé's Super Bowl performance and style consciously invoke
the collective memory of the Black Panthers through the deployment of
iconography meant to inspire nostalgia for a black radical past. "Formation" was the first single from Beyoncé's sixth album, *Lemonade* (2016), for
which she also created a sixty-five-minute film, dubbed a "visual album."
In creating the groundbreaking videography, Beyoncé was explicit in her
desire to convey "the historical impact of slavery on black love, and what
it has done to the black family."[34] For the "Formation" video, in particular,
director Melina Matsoukas "rented a museum in Pasadena and decorated
it to summon 'Gone with the Wind' and 'Twelve Years a Slave.'" Matsoukas
instructed her art director to "blackify" the museum by "hanging French
Renaissance–style portraits of black subjects" in order to invert the trope
of featuring white people in these roles of power and position and "turn
those images on their head."[35] Matsoukas's spatial styling is a form of black
restorative nostalgia as well, disrupting the romantic sentimentality often
associated with *Gone with the Wind* and the nostalgia it invokes for white
subjects who read the antebellum era through the lens of a lost southern
gentility. By inverting the racial logic of that scene, Matsoukas quite literally restores blackness within a historical frame in which it has been placed
under erasure, largely through the repetition of white nostalgic impulses.

I do not want to suggest that a musical performance at the Super Bowl
is a sufficient material response to twenty-first-century modes of white
supremacy, but rather that the performance evoked the affective spirit
of a black radical past for some, and a haunting memory for its critics.
Former mayor of New York City Rudy Giuliani called for law enforcement
nationwide to boycott Beyoncé's concert performances by refusing to offer
security.[36] Citing her tribute to the Black Panther Party, Giuliani recalled
the Black Panther Party's instruction that African Americans exercise their
Second Amendment rights and arm themselves against police who were
terrorizing their communities. Her performance rehashed the very same
media debates from the late 1960s, in which the Black Panther Party was
simultaneously and conversely represented as both modern-day Robin
Hoods and "all of white America's nightmares."[37] The right-wing response
to Beyoncé's aestheticization of radical nostalgic memory points to the

very efficacy of such a performance as a threat (real or perceived) to white hegemony, specifically the police state. Exemplifying the aims of transformational politics, Beyoncé's spectacle produced a sense of dissonance for many who thought Beyoncé to be a racially and culturally transcendent figure, and who were now forced to contend with her univocal racialized and politicized body.

Nine months after her Super Bowl performance, and in what might best be described as an act of celebrity trolling, Beyoncé performed "Daddy Lessons"—another song from the *Lemonade* album—in front of the overwhelmingly white audience of the 2016 Country Music Awards. This performance operated on multiple planes of nostalgia. Beyoncé shone on center stage in a bejeweled, floor-length, nearly transparent dress, with her hair fiercely straightened, invoking the spirit of 1970s country music star Crystal Gayle. With the long-maligned Dixie Chicks (now The Chicks) in tow, Beyoncé conjured up her country twang and sang, "With his right hand on his rifle, / He swore it on the Bible, / My daddy said shoot." The performance is a master class in knowing one's audience, its subversive nature marked not only by the very being of her blackness but by her disruption of country music's nostalgia for whiteness. In his discussion of the "white sound" of country music, Geoff Mann argues that "if country music sounds white, it is perhaps worth considering the possibility that something claiming the status of 'white culture,' something like a purportedly American whiteness—however historically baseless—is not *reflected* in country music, but is, rather, partially *produced* by it."[38] Mann deploys nostalgia as the critical lynchpin to link music to the development of a particular mode of racial subjectivity, asserting that "country music's nostalgia . . . provides the subject a cultural-political narrative that produces its own past, a past that is not only white but this kind of white."[39] To bolster his argument, Mann draws on John Mowitt's conception of "musical interpellation," which itself takes up an Althusserian-inspired theory that "music is not simply tendentious—that is expressive of some particular line (white supremacy, heterosexism, etc.)—but also ideological through and through."[40]

It is not my intent to merely exchange the kind of interpellation that Mann sees happening in the production of country music with the black nationalist underpinnings of hip-hop and R&B music, but rather to point to how Beyoncé's historical mining in both her Super Bowl and her Country Music Awards performances turns conventional modes of nostalgia on its head. Beyoncé's "Daddy Lessons" performance at the Country Music Awards was a stark reminder to the nearly all-white audience that the right to bear arms applies to black folks, and that black folks are "country" too. Beyoncé's refrain, "my Daddy said shoot," is not an implicit threat to white bodies; rather, she summons white nostalgia for "simpler times" (read: the imagined absence of blackness) vis-à-vis the sound of country music and reinscribes the black body at the center, thereby disrupting the fantasy of historical continuity and further feeding into the "anxiety" of right-wing restorative nostalgics. As scholar Inna Arzumanova notes, Beyoncé's "conjuring of black histories and black futures—and presumably the haunting it activates—also messes with neoliberal progressive temporalities to offer the kind of rendering of time that might begin to accommodate the diversity of black traditions and lives."[41] In this way, Beyoncé demonstrates that restorative nostalgia works both ways: as a right-wing longing for a past without the presence of the racial Other and, conversely, as a radical corrective to the white imagination by undoing such attempts at historical erasure.

Nostalgia for the fantasy of white purity that the sound of country music invites was met with a radical counterpoint not only in Beyoncé's lyrics and appearance but also in her delivery. As journalist Spencer Kornhaber has pointed out, Beyoncé and her musicians "were some of the only black people at a ceremony celebrating an art-form whose origins, as is well documented, were nowhere near entirely white."[42] Thus, Beyoncé's performance successfully interrupted the nostalgic illusions (delusions?) produced by country music and its attendant significations of an unadulterated whiteness. The idea that country music reflects and produces particular ways of being "white" certainly opens the door for a broader consideration of how contemporary protest music advances specific ways of being black that are founded on both the logic of black nationalism and the revision and disruption of white nostalgic forms of memory. Recent black protest performances pose a fundamental challenge to white nostalgic claims through their own nostalgic projects of restoration and reclamation.

In 2018, Beyoncé opened her groundbreaking performance at the Coachella music festival with the classic black national anthem, "Lift Every Voice and Sing," the same song that opened the 1972 Wattstax concert. Beyoncé's decision to invoke James Weldon Johnson and John Rosamond Johnson's 1899 song at the beginning of her show creates a seamless through line between the historical struggles and those of the contemporary present. As Shana Redmond notes, "to sing this song is to revive that past—but also to recognize, as the lyrics of the song reveal, that there is a hopeful future that might come of it."[43] Notably, most of the audience members in attendance were not African American; even Beyoncé conceded that "most of the young people on the stage and in the audience did not know the history of the black national anthem before Coachella."[44] In performing this song in that space, Beyoncé rejected not only the national anthem with which her audience—mostly young, white people—would be readily familiar, but also the sentiment of national unity the song is meant to represent. Instead, she invoked the collective nostalgia of 1970s-era schoolchildren, like myself, who grew up amid the Black Power era and who could wistfully recall each lyric and immediately be transported back to their childhood. Indeed, it was a fleeting nostalgia, a fear of losing her connection to the black historical past, that inspired her to perform Weldon's classic at Coachella: "In the show at the time I was working on a version of the anthem with these dark minor chords and stomps and belts and screams. After a few days of humming the anthem, I realized I had the melody wrong. . . . I was singing the wrong anthem."[45] The realization that she was singing "the wrong anthem" provided the impetus for her restoration of "Lift Every Voice and Sing" within her own nostalgic imagination and within the public imagination. Though the audience may not have been familiar with song, she believed that they got "the feeling." Beyoncé's nostalgic retreats to the civil rights and Black Power movements resonate throughout current activist struggles, invoking nostalgic memory as a way of consciously harking back to an inspirational legacy of racial uplift and radicalism.

Restorative Time

Contemporary black anthems allow for a reconsideration of nostalgia outside the context of whiteness, through the refashioning of (white) restorative nostalgia. Central to the efforts of restorative nostalgics is the drive to produce an idealized community or "home," yet (white) restorative nostalgics tend to form communities "based on exclusion more than affection, a union of those who are not with us, but against us."[46] The concept of an imagined or constructed symbolic community informs the black restorative enterprise as well. However, the communities these artists fashion are informed by "utopian, redemptive, insurgent power from below,"[47] meaning that they are constructed in response (resistance) to a sense of exclusion and invisibility from the broader social order. Rather than attempt to reforge a community so as to re-place oneself at the top of the social hierarchy, the black restorative project is invested in reinvigorating the affect of black radicalism in response to the continued devaluation of black lives.

The resurgence of black radicalism in our contemporary moment is evident in the Black Lives Matter movement, which has recently resurfaced in the wake of the deaths of George Floyd and Breonna Taylor at the hands of police officers. In this very moment (June 7, 2020, at 7:05 a.m.) my timeline is saturated with images of Black Lives Matter protests across the globe, with memes of Malcolm X, Audre Lorde, Ella Baker, and James Baldwin issuing prescient warnings from the past. There is not, as of yet, a protest song to capture where we are right now. Yet, the ethos of the first wave of the Black Lives Matter movement was captured in Kendrick Lamar's 2015 song "Alright," which serves as the movement's unofficial anthem. Its persistent refrain of resilience and hope in the midst of painfully challenging times for black people is emblematic of the utopian redemption narrative that relies heavily on black nostalgic memory. In her assessment of contemporary protest music, scholar and critic Daphne A. Brooks reaches to the past, invoking figures like Curtis Mayfield and Marvin Gaye as "soul activist" precursors to Lamar's sometimes contradictory blend of the "spiritual and the profane."[48] We should turn also to Lamar's 2011 debut single "HiiiPoWeR," whose title has functioned as a platform in Lamar's musical repertoire. The correlating music video features a fast-moving sequence of global resistance movements including the Arab Spring, then ongoing, interspersed with historical footage of Malcolm X, the Black Panther Party, Martin Luther King Jr., Huey P. Newton, and Nelson Mandela. The video, essentially a mash-up of transnational rebellions spanning the course of six decades, is not subtle in the historical lineage it maps out between the oppression (and resistance) of marginalized and racialized Others "then" and now. But "HiiiPoWeR" is more than just a glimpse to the historical past; it exemplifies black restorative nostalgia, in which political aspirations are enmeshed within figurative retreats to a black nationalist past. The video's dizzying array of figureheads from the Black Power moment alongside images of Lamar among a present-day crowd of "rebels" signals a desired historical continuity but also serves as a marker of Lamar's own political designation—one that hinges on a specific kind of radical remembrance. The lyrics of "HiiiPoWeR" further attest to this sense of political succession. Beginning with the verse, "Visions of Martin Luther staring at me, / Malcolm X put a hex on my future someone catch me, / I'm falling victim to a revolutionary song," Lamar conjures the ghosts of black radicalism. His succumbing to a "revolutionary song" reflects his political engagement as a "calling," rather than a consciously invoked memory like nostalgia. His use of the words "hex" and "victim" points to his unwillingness to act as a politically engaged or vested subject. His notion of HiiiPoWeR (the three i's stand for heart, honor, and respect)[49] reads more like a curse by which he is afflicted than a subject position he actively claims, and yet he nonetheless accepts his fate and positions himself within the lineage of Martin Luther King Jr., Malcolm X, and Huey P. Newton.

As with Beyoncé, Kendrick Lamar's lyrics reflect a political desire that can only be constructed through a figurative return to the mode and discourse of black nationalism. His advice to "build your own pyramids, write your own hieroglyphs" in "HiiiPoWeR" is a gleaning of the self-sufficient, agential logic of black nationalist discourse, rejecting Western conventions and aesthetics. The aestheticization of black nationalist culture enables a sense of continuity that is grounded in black consciousness and political progressiveness without resorting to the didacticism that often characterizes Black Power rhetoric. For both Beyoncé and Lamar, the summoning of the black radical past through nostalgic reference is meant to serve as a critical through line to our present moment. The notion of continuity and symbolic formation at the core of the concept of restorative nostalgia functions for each artist as a refutation of what Aida Levy-Hussen refers to as *traumatic time*, a "structure of narrative temporality . . . that defies chronological mapping and instead takes shape through repeated, affectively charged references to an original traumatic event"; it is "non-linear, dis-unified, and regenerated by the impossible desire for a redemptive return to the past."[50] Conversely, black restorative nostalgia is deeply invested in redemptive returns to the historical past through the imaginative process of invention and restoration. Black restorative nostalgia's insistence on continuity functions as a productive counterpoint to trauma's (and white nostalgia's) punishing circularity.

In *Block Party*, Dave Chappelle disrupts classic restorative nostalgia's regressive tendencies by conflating his personal or literal home (Dayton) with a cultural or artistic home (Brooklyn, which emerges as another fiction of Chappelle's imagination, given that hip-hop originated in the South Bronx), with yet another metaphorical home or point of origin (*Wattstax*). Similarly, the music of Lauryn Hill, Beyoncé, and Kendrick Lamar recenters the black body within the frame of white nostalgic memory and, in doing so, elucidates the emancipatory possibilities inherent in nostalgic evocations. As exemplars of contemporary protest performance, these artists demonstrate that restorative nostalgia is more than an allegiance to preserving a history that never really existed, but rather a desire to embed oneself within a historical lineage of black social and political resistance. Restorative nostalgia is more than an abstracted affect that serves as the domain of the political right. Black restorative nostalgia serves as the site and source of an activist aesthetic that actuates new subject formations and enables new articulations of political belonging.

3
(Nostalgic) REGENERATION

Absent Archives and Historical Pleasures in Contemporary Black Visual Culture

And this is the domain of the strange, the Marvelous, and the fantastic, a domain scorned by people of certain inclinations. Here is the freed image, dazzling and beautiful, with a beauty that could not be more unexpected and overwhelming.
—Suzanne Césaire, "The Domain of the Marvelous"

Black life—which lies, after all, at the center of black literary and cultural production—is in this moment bounded by vulnerability, by death's ubiquitous proximity, as well as by resilience, everyday wonder, and deliberate joy.
—Candice M. Jenkins, "Black Refusal, Black Magic: Reading African American Literature Now"

Kerry James Marshall's painting *Vignette* (2003) features two opaquely black figures—a man and a woman, afroed and dreadlocked—running through a lush field amid a covey of butterflies and birds (figure 2). Everything in this image suggests joy: the bright blue sky, the smiles, the liberating nakedness of bodies, the lush vegetation, and the animals, like the people, in flight and with abandon. I was so moved by this image of unabated black bliss that I decided to show it to the students in my Introduction to African American Literature class, mostly as a counterpoint to our more somber discussions of slavery and the nation's failed Reconstruction. For me, Marshall's images portrayed a blackness that was agential, blithe, and unbothered. Yet when I asked my students about what

2. Kerry James Marshall, *Vignette*. 2003. © Kerry James Marshall. Courtesy of the artist and Jack Shainman Gallery, New York.

they saw, the responses were all about slavery, specifically that the man and woman in the image were running away from their plantation or they had run away and found peace "up North." I pressed them about why they had imagined the couple in the painting as slaves or runaways, given the absence of any markers that would suggest such a reading. They offered nothing but the blackness of the figures and the nakedness of their bodies as evidence of their bondage. The mere fact of blackness was enough to intimate that this scene was implicated in a larger narrative of subjugation. Such an interpretation is a classic example of projection.[1] Perhaps it was because our class was in the thick of reading slave narratives that their first interpretations recalled the antebellum era. But projections, especially collective ones like this, are the social data we accrue over time. Marshall's *Vignette* is but one example of how visual art seeks to retrain its audience by giving us what we believe to be familiar or "stock" images and revising those images, thus producing an unanticipated affect. In other words, the "slaves" that we may expect to see on the canvas might instead be read as the not-yet-shamed, Africanized versions of Adam and Eve frolicking about a Garden of Eden.

I begin with this anecdote because it underscores two key concerns of this chapter. The first is to point to the supremacy of oppression narratives as the structuring logic of black lives, black experiences, and black pasts; the second is to reimagine black origins in nostalgic terms, a larger endeavor among contemporary black visual artists. Michel-Rolph Trouillot offers a provocative thesis that is readily taken for granted in most conceptualizations of black history, which is that "the past is constantly evoked as the starting point for an ongoing traumatism and as a necessary explanation to current inequalities suffered by blacks."[2] Trouillot refers to persistent narratives of historical subjugation as providing an uncomplicated through line from African American history to the present. I consider works like Marshall's *Vignette* in the context of nostalgia because the concept, at its core, connotes the desire for an idyllic past that possibly never existed. To examine nostalgia in this light, it is necessary to move from a narrow conception of the term as an embodied experience to one that operates within a broader cultural register. While nostalgia is often interpreted as an embellishment of the past, nostalgic memory can also be produced through the past's effacement. In writing about contemporary African American playwrights, visual artists, and writers, Harry J. Elam Jr. asserts that "these artists see history not as static fact, but as malleable perceptions open to interpretation, as a place to envision the past as it ought to have been in order to understand the present and to achieve the future they desire."[3] The work of the imaginary can generate two distinctive modes of nostalgic memory: one that derives meaning and affect through amplification, and one that does so through negation.

While the literary texts I discuss in the first chapter take a nostalgic look at the Civil War era to question, challenge, and cocreate (black) nationalist narratives, this chapter examines the work of contemporary African American visual artists who materialize nostalgic pasts that unmoor, through imaginative invention, the traumatic roots of the black historical past. Literary texts and visual art perform different kinds of aesthetic work. Yet images, much like literary texts, are equally invested in the process of worldmaking—that is, of presenting audiences with the possibility of a past, present, and future that may only vaguely resemble our own. While many contemporary novels of slavery engage the "historical period of chattel slavery in order to provide new models of liberation by problematizing the concept of freedom,"[4] these artists are less interested in recalling slavery's traumatic afterlife or troubling the notion of freedom in the years since emancipation. Instead, these artists turn to re-creation in the form of regeneration to approach the inevitable and irreparable voids of black history. The term *regeneration* connotes, among other things, the (re)formation of something new after a loss or injury.

Here, I introduce the concept of *regenerative nostalgia* as a constructive counterpoint to a traumatic narrativizing of the black historical past, one that centers healing and revitalization rather than the repetition of pain. A rich body of scholarship has traced the legacy of slavery to modern-day feelings of depression and psychic instability.[5] In her reading of Saidiya Hartman's *Lose Your Mother*, Ann Cvetkovich interprets Hartman's memoir as an attempt to seek "reparation for the past in the affective dynamics of cultural memory rather than in legal reform or state recognition." As Cvetkovich argues, Hartman's project is one that refuses to "find solace in an African past before slavery" and thus "provides a model of emotional reparation in which feelings of loss and alienation persist."[6] Similarly, the artists I examine contend with the everyday persistence of cultural trauma through the inventive renegotiation of black historical memory. Their aesthetic projects address those "feelings of loss and alienation" through the solicitation of black pasts that decenter a traumatic origin story. The nostalgic concepts of retribution and restoration that I invoke in the previous chapters of this book center the project of historical recompense and rectification. Aligned with these ambitions, nostalgic regeneration attends to the psychic and emotional damage produced by the traumas of history through the creation of alternative pasts and the production of blithesome affective sentiments.

I use the term *regenerative* to describe this artistic praxis because it inheres a medical and a spiritual connotation. Regenerative medicine works toward repairing illnesses and injuries previously thought incurable; it thrives on the premise that the body has everything it needs to heal itself and uses what is already present to establish a course of treatment. The body is thus re-formed in its original state or, in some cases, better than it once was. The term *regenerate* also means to be "spiritually reborn," to "invest with a new and higher spiritual nature."[7] In my conception, then, regenerative nostalgia is firmly grounded in its origin as illness, maintaining a therapeutic imperative with a focus on spiritual or psychic renewal and revivification; it acknowledges that an injury, trauma, or loss has taken place but deploys the creative processes of memory to narrate new black historical pasts and our relation to them. The primary function of regenerative nostalgia is to assemble sanguine "memories" to enable wellness and healing as a response to the psychic, spiritual, emotional pain brought on by cultural and ancestral loss or trauma.[8]

For the artists I discuss, nostalgia is not necessarily tied to a time or place but to an idea of the past as a space of black historical possibility. These visual artists return to the past not to retell or reframe familiar historical tragedies, but to (re)form new histories that translate into new ways of being in the present. I examine the visual art of April Banks, Krista Franklin, and Rhonda Wheatley because they each, in disparate and equally compelling ways, deploy nostalgia as a sanative to reframe the inevitable voids of black historical memory and fabulate black pasts that hinge on the absence of cultural suffering while using their works as a source of remediation.

It is not entirely surprising—in the cultural moment that produced enough contemporary novels of slavery to constitute an entire subfield of literary study—that there would simultaneously emerge a series of black visual works that endeavor to imagine the black historical past in the absence of slavery and racial terror. While contemporary African American literature has been preoccupied with reconceiving the antebellum era, visual art has been equally immersed in revising the historical moment of US chattel slavery. Huey Copeland's important *Bound to Appear* (2013) is illustrative of this thematic fascination in African diasporic visual culture. Copeland emphasizes the intricate dialogue between black literature and black diasporic visual art in re-representing the slave era, arguing that the cultural productions in his study "resonate with Morrison's invocation of slavery in *Beloved*" by "engaging resistive African diasporic traditions and summon[ing] up the ghosts of the past."[9] While Copeland's project centers on black artists who also refuse the traumatic framing of black experience, his analysis of visual artists like Glenn Ligon and Lorna Simpson focuses on how they "reframed the siting, subject, and appearance of blackness through recourse to the material coordinates of slavery."[10] In that vein, this chapter asks: What do we make of African American visual representations of the historical past that are "unbounded" and provide no "coordinates" to the site of slavery? In light of the rich corpus of contemporary visual narratives of slavery, how have artists diverged from such narratives to create alternative black pasts? How do these aesthetic elisions of slavery read as nostalgic endeavors? This chapter is motivated by such questions and is concerned with how these visual works decenter the memory of slavery with remedial imaginings of alternative black historical pasts.

I begin this discussion by examining the photographic images of April Banks, which rely on the historical voids of African American history and the inherently fictive nature of nostalgic memory to produce diverse black histories dating as far back and away as seventeenth-century Iran. Banks's "peregrinations with time travel through historical archives and memories" effect a nostalgic impulse to embed her own black familial ancestry within a multiplicity of potentially desirable historical pasts, a process she calls "re-fabling."[11] Banks makes use of the fissures within existing historical scripts to craft new black memories, while the collages of Krista Franklin produce nostalgic affects by marshalling the excesses of history to form an "archive of feelings."[12] Contrary to Cvetkovich's "archive of feelings" as a chronicle of everyday trauma, Franklin's collages produce a different kind of catalog, one in which traumatic pasts are refigured as "something that can potentially become beautiful."[13] Franklin's *Afrimerica Archive* (circa 2013) acts as a site of assembly and recovery, of abandoned black pasts and of joy. Regenerative nostalgia in Franklin's oeuvre manifests through the processes of assemblage in terms of both content (the aggregation of traumatic histories and sublime memories as a point of aesthetic and psychic reconciliation) and form (her chosen medium of collage). This chapter concludes with an analysis of Rhonda Wheatley's exhibition *A Modern Day Shaman's Hybrid Devices, Power Objects, and Cure Books* (2017). Wheatley extends Banks's and Franklin's imperative to reconceive the past in a way that translates into "good feelings" in the present. However, Wheatley's project is distinguishable by its acute focus on the psychic power of the individual (black) subject to reclaim happiness through conscious reorientation to the past by harnessing the healing properties of her devices and objects. The contemporary black body becomes part of the aesthetic project to effect nostalgic memories from potentially traumatic pasts. This endeavor is less about erasing or effacing trauma than about using our individual agency to process healing. As Christina Sharpe has aptly stated, "I am interested in ways of seeing and imagining responses to the terror visited on Black life and the ways we inhabit it, are inhabited by it, and refuse it."[14] Part of this "refusal" is imagining (and, possibly, inhabiting) alternative spaces of historical belonging. Banks, Franklin, and Wheatley engage in nostalgic practices that produce a complementary frame for living "in an ongoing present of subjection and resistance"[15] by troubling the black origin narrative and the linearity it assumes.[16]

Because these artists do not engage the history of black bondage as a starting point for African American experience, it would be easy to argue that their works are inclined less toward nostalgic remembrance than toward historical erasure. Refiguring the African American origin narrative opens up the space to consider the way that trauma and pleasure operate as simultaneous and layered ontologies of blackness. As Michelle Wright explains, "When deployed as the de facto 'origin' of established Black populations in the West, [slavery] effectively (re)creates the illusion of all Blacks in the West as always already disempowered."[17] These artists are part of a larger critical conversation that attends to resituating black-ness along alternative historical trajectories. What we have then is the expression of the (re)generative capacities of nostalgic memory, which do not reflect longing for a time now passed but rather reclaim lost time as a form of solace, healing, and even joy. The visual works I explore in this chapter are indebted to and resonant with black feminism as an emancipatory praxis that maintains, at its core, an ethic of care. Before it became Instagram chic, the notion of radical self-care was (and is) a foundational politic of Audre Lorde, Sylvia Wynter, bell hooks, Patricia Hill Collins, Jennifer Nash, and Joan Morgan, along with a wealth of other black woman scholar-activists who enact pleasure and self-love as a revolutionary enterprise. To wit, regenerative nostalgia in the works of Banks, Franklin, and Wheatley contributes to this black feminist endeavor by resituating blackness and pastness in the service of creating an eclectic archive of black joy.

April Banks: The Re-Fabled Self

In an attempt to trace her ancestral origins and as a starting point for a potential new artistic project, April Banks underwent scientific DNA testing. For African Americans, genealogical projects have been part of a centuries-long effort to claim an ancestral home that predates the trans-atlantic slave trade. The ability to mark a moment that is not tethered to one's slave ancestry has figured prominently in the African American con-sciousness as a form of racial affirmation and cultural pride. However, such efforts to recover the African country—or, more specifically, the "tribe" to which one's ancestors belonged—have been frustrated, given both the commodified status of Africans upon their arrival to the New World and the lack of archival records that would make such ancestral knowledge possible. Now, for the low, low price of ninety-nine dollars, companies like AncestryDNA and 23andMe promise to "uncover your ethnic mix" by analyzing your DNA through more than "700,000 genetic markers,"[18] making the prospect of knowing one's past viable. A small sample of saliva sent to a third-party testing lab can now offer "millions" of African Ameri-cans knowledge about their ancestry, an endeavor once thought entirely impossible. However, as Alondra Nelson explains, "Genetic ancestry test-ing is about more than unearthing of facts. . . . They hold, and we hold also, more intangible aspirations for DNA."[19] When Banks took the test in 2011, she learned that her genetic markers linked back not to Africa but to the Middle East, specifically along the Caspian Sea, in an area that is now Kurdish. What she found was that she was "made up of all these ancestors that go in multiple directions." In a personal interview, Banks claims to have been surprised by this revelation while also admitting that it did not bear much meaning on her present identification as a black woman. ("What does that really mean for my identity now?")[20] While the expectation is that this past will begin to fill the gaps of a stolen familial legacy—especially for African Americans, for whom the past is largely lost and unknowable—the reality is that such knowledge often begs more questions than answers.

Admittedly, I know this sensation firsthand. I received an AncestryDNA analysis kit as a birthday gift and learned that my "ethnicity estimate" is 82 percent African (mostly from the Ivory Coast and Ghana), 15 percent English (UK), and 3 percent Irish. I found the markers unremarkable. Not one to believe in the myth of racial purity, I had assumed that there would be some configuration of African and European. What did startle me was that none of the markers indicated any connection to a Native American heritage. In the words of Zora Neale Hurston, "I am colored but I offer nothing in the way of extenuating circumstances except the fact that I am the only Negro in the United States whose grandfather on the mother's side was not an Indian chief."[21] As Hurston mocks, like many African Americans, my family proudly incorporated a Choctaw lineage within our ancestral lore. My maternal grandfather (apparently) was nicknamed "Red" because of his light complexion and because his grandmother was Choctaw, or so we thought. As further evidence, our family has widely circulated among ourselves a sepia image of my maternal great-great-grandmother Catherine Lowe, a short woman with a slight smile, light skin, and coarse gray hair (figure 3). As I look at her image now, I can project onto it any number of ethnic origins, but I also wonder whether my own family did not simply invent its own lineage and assign her an ethnic status that she did not possess.

Genealogical projects are but one way in which African Americans have attempted to fill the historical gaps produced by slavery. The 2011 exhibit *re-FABLE*, which featured Banks as well as fellow artist Amanda Williams, imaginatively reconstructed the past, not to recover it but to exploit its chasms. Banks's artistic endeavors suggest that the inevitable voids in our ancestral legacies are as much a part of our memory as are those moments we can immediately recall. Williams notes, "As the artifacts of each generation become less legible, they are simultaneously more cherished. We embellish and fabricate the details that have become elusive. We re-fable the missing pieces."[22] The notion of "re-fabling" suggests that any and all

3. The author's maternal great-great-grandmother,
ca. 1915. Author's personal collection.

histories are inherently fictitious. The repetition of "fabling" is then part
and parcel of the historical process. *Fable* operates as both a noun and
a verb, referring to the fact and the act of storytelling—in this case, filling in the gaps of what cannot be mined via "facts" and "artifacts." One
merely continues to reproduce extant fictions in the process of making
history. In broaching the concept of "re-fabling," Banks offers imaginative possibilities for black histories and black futures that treat the gaps
of memory not quite as an absence but more as a specter that haunts. The
act of "re-fabling" takes on a regenerative character in that it aggregates
sentimental affect with each successive iteration. Regenerative nostalgia
is evident in the process of "re-fabling" if, as Williams suggests, objects
accrue currency through attrition. This mode of regenerative nostalgia

is exemplified in Banks's piece *Possession Is Nine Tenths* (figure 4), which tells the story of her family's "missing" Stradivarius violin.

According to familial lore, someone in Banks's family once owned a Stradivarius violin. From generation to generation, the through line of this narrative has been that the never-seen violin was simply misplaced. In revisiting this narrative, Banks questioned whether this violin ever existed.[23] In Banks's project, a succession of plastered violins, the mythological dimension of the "missing" violin becomes a metaphor for the uncertainty that belies any family history. As Banks explains, "Stories about its speculated worth and possible demise have morphed over time and by storyteller. Its absence becomes stronger than its presence."[24] The materiality of the violin matters less than the reproduction of the narrative surrounding it; the stories, rather than the object, become the family heirloom. Reasoning that history is as much about ephemera as it is about tangible artifact, Banks created twenty plaster encasements that reflect the absence, rather than the presence, of the object.

The idea that "possession is nine-tenths" of the law reinforces the notion that memories have multiple owners, each of whom can make legitimate claims on the past. As Banks's work suggests, the actual existence of the Stradivarius violin is less important to her family's history than what its

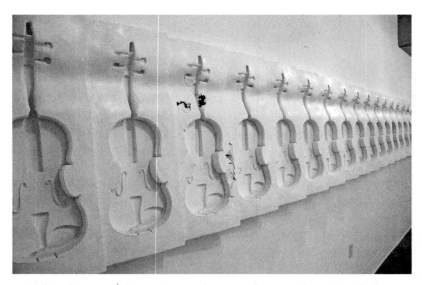

4. April Banks, *Possession Is Nine Tenths*. 2011. Plaster sculpture installation, 18′4″ × 28″.

absence signifies; the violin acquires meaning through the generational act of storytelling. I view this process of acquisition as exemplary of regenerative nostalgia because it recontextualizes the experience of loss and creates a renewed narrative of the past that works to cohere generations of this family through making meaning of an absence. The act of re-fabling raises the question: what kind of narrative about the family does this object, real or imagined, enable? Given that Banks is African American and her family has roots in the South, there is also the more obvious question: how would this family have managed to own a Stradivarius? What I am suggesting here is that perhaps the violin maintains such centrality in this family history because it suggests something about how this family wishes to perceive its past—specifically, in nostalgic terms.

Handcrafted by Italian luthier Antonio Stradivari, Stradivarius violins are regarded as the paragon of string instruments. Stradivari's best violins were made between 1700 and 1725, though he made more than a thousand violins during his lifetime, of which approximately 550 exist today. Stradivarius violins gained their reputation due to what many claim to be their unique quality of sound, which has not been reproduced even with the advantages of twenty-first-century sound technologies.[25] Given the instruments' rarity and reputation, the owner of a Stradivarius violin would reasonably be assumed to occupy a particularly privileged or even elite status. Perhaps it is this association that forms the basis of Banks's family narrative: the idea that somewhere in the recesses of this history lies a much more complex narrative of race, class, power, and geography than any archive or history book would allow. The story of the "missing" violin demonstrates more than the power of the imagination to foster a sense of historical continuity; it also exceeds what we may deem to be historically possible for a southern black family in the nineteenth century. The regenerative capacities of nostalgia are evident in the narrative of the "missing" violin, which highlights a familial desire to sustain and sentimentalize not only the object itself but a particular vision of familial history signified by that object's esteemed value. *Possession Is Nine Tenths* is the fabrication of a lost past, signified by a violin that may (or may not) have gone missing, originally the property of an unknown possessor. The accretion of absences, in this case, produces a surplus of half-rememberings and misrememberings that radiate a multiplicity of potential familial histories. The multigenerational act of attempting to resolve the mystery of the prized Stradivarius evokes a frustrated attempt at *consignation*, the desire to "articulate the unity of an ideal configuration."[26] The narrative assemblage—or what Jacques Derrida would describe as the *archival desire*—that circulates around the violin functions as a form of regeneration to reconcile the loss of this missing piece of the familial past. In contrast to the physicality of the archive to which Derrida refers, the archival processes in this instance are meant to consign not actual documents but rather ephemera.

Banks extends this archival play in her digital photography project *Make. Believe.* (2011), which was also featured in *re-FABLE*. In the process of scrolling through historical archives and her family photographs, Banks melds the two sources to re-create her own family history. Enmeshing old family photographs within random historical scenes, Banks plays with the possibility that any imagining of the historical past can be as "real" as an "actual" past, since both are equally unknown. As Banks explains, she creates "an imagined family history, filling in what science, oral histories and archival documents cannot."[27] The project of creating these imagined spaces or inserting herself and her family into them highlights the gaps and mysteries that constitute most family histories but take on special relevance for African American familial narratives. The idea of "finding your roots" emerges as a troubling and frustrating enterprise for black subjects whose ancestors were marked as chattel or property within the account books of their "owners." Even a casual viewer of Henry Louis Gates Jr.'s television show *Finding Your Roots* (2012–) can recognize a familiar pattern: African American celebrity guests routinely express shock that the only reliable way to access their family's past is through the more stable archive of the family that once owned their forebears. Entangled within the narrative of the black family, and black history more broadly, is the inextricable bind to that peculiar institution. As such, the slave past often functions as the locus of the black experience in the United States. In one episode, Sean Combs beams with pride after being told that his great-great-grandfather—a man by the name of Robert Allsup—was never enslaved. The episode carries a celebratory ethos made possible by the fact that someone in Combs's family had managed to escape the horrors of chattel slavery and, more markedly, the common narrative of black subjugation in the nineteenth century.[28]

Make. Believe. begins with the question "what if?" to explore narrative alternatives to blackness in the absence of slavery's origin story. By taking historical images—like that of a long-ago proposal (figure 5)—and embedding old family photographs, Banks effectively reshapes two histories: her family's and that of the original image. *Make. Believe.* tugs at the historical threads intimated by that DNA test to explore the possibilities of alternative histories that interrupt/disrupt an immediate through line to a singular black traumatic past. Banks's endeavor is a compelling riff on Carrie Lambert-Beatty's concept of *parafiction*, in which "real and/or imaginary personages and stories intersect with the world as it is being lived." A "crucial ingredient" of parafiction is plausibility, which allows us to "make a new reality sensible."[29] Banks's project evokes a parafictional praxis by recontextualizing her own familial narrative in unlikely historical contexts, motivated by a broader imperative to make black subjects "at home" across a multiplicity of historical times and spaces. However, Banks's photographs sharply depart from parafictional projects that portray imaginative representations as "fact," leading to what Lambert-Beatty calls a "deception" or even a "hoax."[30] Banks's family images are not so seamlessly integrated within those found in historical archives as to dupe the viewer. To borrow from Jacques Rancière, the redistribution of the sensible is apparent here through the image's comedic and anachronistic effect, as opposed to an attempt to evince a presumed reality or historical authenticity.

The slightly confused/shocked/concerned expression of Banks's brother infuses a sense of humor into the otherwise stoic scene of the historical

5. April Banks, historical photograph, blended with photograph of the artist's brother. 2011. From the series *Make. Believe.*

proposal (figure 5). Despite Banks's careful melding of her brother into this historical scene, his presence does not offer a clear, alternative narrative; it is evident that he is both out of place and out of time. His puzzled gaze more closely resembles that of an unwitting subject who has been thrust back into the annals of history, evoking a sense of time travel rather than historical continuity. Banks's image resonates with the results of her mitochondrial DNA test, which traced her ancestry to the Middle East rather than Africa as she expected. The "shock" of the DNA results is amplified and mirrored in the above image and has influenced Banks's aesthetic choices, encouraging her to forge interstices between West African, African American, and Middle Eastern cultures, defying the Middle Passage epistemology on which so much of African American subjectivity relies. Michelle Wright argues that blackness is best understood within the context of "epiphenomenal spacetime," which would allow for an understanding of blackness as it is produced through intersections with "other bodies, other times, and other histories."[31] *Make. Believe.* enacts these intersections, creating for the viewer a spectrum of blackness that is produced in and through a series of randomized historicities.

The multitude of ancestries unearthed in Banks's DNA test is acutely represented in a photograph in which Banks situates herself alongside Liz Taylor during Taylor's famous visit to Tehran in 1976 (figure 6). Unlike the previous image, Banks's inclusion within this scene seems historically possible. Why wouldn't this stylish black woman be a part of that entourage? By immersing herself within the more contemporary history of the 1970s, she extrapolates the possible ethnic and racial intersections of her DNA results and her present lived experience.

Banks's image also competes with Taylor's; Taylor is no longer the focal point of the scene but part of a fabulous ensemble, of which Banks is now also a part. Banks takes the information about her Middle Eastern "origins" and explores what could have been. Interestingly, Banks does not position herself as an Iranian woman, which would suggest a connectedness with her "roots," but as a black woman—the subject position with which she identifies.

And it's pretty funny.

Part of the humor here is that the other people in this story would have likely viewed her as an interloper who did not belong in their world—at least not standing beside them as a peer. Yet she has created, despite them, an alternative reality where they are comfortably smiling and accept her presence as natural. If we read the image as humorous, the joke is on the

6. April Banks, historical photograph, blended with photograph of the artist. 2011. From the series *Make. Believe.*

figures in the original photograph. Banks's insertion into the picture creates a "photobomb"; however, her presence enriches rather than spoils the image. While the historical possibility of a black woman keeping company with Liz Taylor on a private jet in the 1970s reads as unlikely, Banks's egalitarian positioning of herself next to Taylor and her entourage offer an air of plausibility, unlike the Middle Eastern proposal scene with Banks's brother.

The formation of new narrative pasts in *Make. Believe.*, like in *Possession Is Nine Tenths*, does more than fill the gaps of black ancestral pasts. It exceeds those realities by inserting black subjects within spatial temporalities that register at the level of truth but are also historical impossibilities. In this respect, both pasts—that of Banks's own family and that in the original photo—are made anew. Banks's work reimagines the historical photographic object as a projective space in which to swell the voids of unknowable pasts and, in doing so, produce sites of contact, knowledge, and affect that transcend the boundaries of space, time, and circumstance. Banks's transmogrified photographs remap the coordinates of possible black pasts by rerouting the Middle Passage journey across a spectrum of alternative narratives that enable historical points of intimacy and plausibility.

Krista Franklin's *Afrimerica Archive*

If we consider Banks's project to be a semi-parafictional enterprise that reframes and explodes extant familial and historical archives, then we should consider Krista Franklin's collages as contributions to a largely absent archive of black (ancestral) joy. Her collages are a nostalgic sojourn through the black historical past, mining objects, events, persons, and personas that (re)create new narratives of pleasurable black histories. Franklin admits that "black ritual, the metaphysical and the black nostalgic are core concerns in [her] art practice."[32] D. Scot Miller's observation that afro-surrealists "take up the obsessions of the ancients and kindle the dis-ease, clearing the murk of the collective unconsciousness as it manifests in these dreams called culture" is broadly reflected in Franklin's aesthetic practice.[33] The act of "kindling the dis-ease" functions as a defining trope of Franklin's collages, which account for the layered histories of black trauma while also creating spaces in which black subjectivity exceeds that condition as a mode of healing and regeneration; to "kindle the dis-ease" is to actively and intentionally manifest healing or "ease."

Franklin's collages and cyanotypes express what Miller identifies as the afro-surrealist praxis of using "excess as the only legitimate means of subversion, and hybridization as a form of disobedience."[34] The archive Franklin produces might also be considered an "archive of feelings" that highlights sublime moments of black memory through processes of layering and assemblage to extract moments of the Marvelous from the history and afterlife of the black traumatic.[35] Unlike Cvetkovich's archive of feelings, which contextualizes the "everyday" nature of trauma and the "idiosyncrasies of emotional life" that constitute traumatic experience,[36] Franklin's archive is one of black pleasure, play, and bliss—a subjective status that reads, for many, as peculiar and dissonant.[37] Cvetkovich admits that her interest in the archive was partly inspired by Cheryl Dunye's film *The Watermelon Woman* (1996), a fictionalized endeavor to recover the lost history of a black queer actress, Fae Richards. In the movie, a black filmmaker ("Cheryl") searches for a black lesbian ancestor, piecing together the story of an actress from the 1930s and 1940s who is often listed in the credits of the films in which she appears as simply "The Watermelon Woman." Cheryl's desire to make Richards's history visible is frustrated through the absence of the histories of black women, particularly black lesbians, in both traditional and alternative archives. At one point, the film proffers its own solution to the elision of black (queer) bodies from history, suggesting, "Sometimes you have to create your own history." The aesthetic desire to "create your own history" is one that has marked much of the recent (post-1990) work in African American literary and visual cultural productions. Dunye's project speaks to the need to create histories where there are none, to fill in the voids of history with imagination and affect when no institutional archive is available. Cvetkovich explains that she was motivated by

> the epistemological and political challenges of the absent archive. What happens if the histories you want to know have left no records? What about, for example, the history of black lesbians that led Dunye to invent Fae Richards, or the minor queer figures in the shadows of Hollywood cinema or in famous times and places like 1920s Paris? What archives and historical methods are necessary to figure out who those lesbians were and what they were doing in their intimate lives? There are many roads that led me to the archive as a relevant category for feelings.[38]

African American histories are largely constituted by (arti)facts of traumatic experience: from slave narratives to neo-slave narratives, from black-heritage tours to blues music. This is not to say that archives of slavery and black trauma are not important or necessary; indeed, they are crucial. Yet I read Franklin's *Afrimerica Archive* as a complement to existing, dominant historical narratives of black trauma. Franklin's collages enact the desires expressed in Miller's manifesto to "reject the quiet servitude that characterizes existing roles for African Americans, Asian Americans, Latinos, women and queer folk."[39] For Miller, "Only through the mixing, melding, and cross-conversion of these supposed classifications can there be hope for liberation."[40] In the *Afrimerica Archive*, "mixing, melding, and cross-conversion" happen at the level of subject matter and artistic medium. Franklin's collages emit an emancipatory affect/effect; they are playful, wistful mirages that advertise the quotidian merriment of black life.

Franklin's compositions incorporate fragments of commonplace items, recycled and resurrected from the mundane and transformed into felicitous objects enacting the processes of regenerative nostalgia. Collage has been considered an intensely feminist praxis because "women have always collected things and saved and recycled them because leftovers yielded nourishment in new forms."[41] The African American expression of this medium is found, perhaps most famously, in the work of Romare Bearden, who drew on the antiestablishment impulses of collage to destabilize viewers and bring the complexities and contradictions of black life to light. His project was, in his words, "to reveal through pictorial complexities the richness of a life I know."[42] The intersectionality of blackness and womanhood situates Franklin's collages within a rich lineage of womanists, to borrow from Alice Walker, who deployed collage as a "strategy for collecting their heritages and connecting them to their own lives and to current political and cultural concerns."[43]

Franklin's collage work is an archival practice that extends the fruitful projects of black feminists who have created new paradigms of black happiness and black love, particularly in the form of well-being and self-care, which have been distinct features of black feminist discourse for decades.[44] Scholar Rosi Braidotti considers happiness to be "a political issue" that should stand at the center of the feminist movement rather than be left to the devices of "pharmaceutical companies, the managers of diversity and human capital experts." Indeed, "well-being, self-confidence and a sense of empowerment" are both "fundamental ethical concerns" and "fundamental human rights."[45] I posit that regenerative nostalgia works in the *Afrimerica Archive* to recast black historical nostalgia as an affirming affect.

By way of example, Franklin's 2006 *Wanderlust Wonderland* (figure 7) offers a mirthful image of "black boy joy" in the pose of a young black boy surrounded by contrasting images of urban landscapes, tropical flowers, and excerpts from Lewis Carroll's *Alice's Adventures in Wonderland* and the 1940s children's tale "The Little Red Hen."[46] The composite picture reflects Franklin's archival and aesthetic imperative to consider black subjectivity within narratives of freedom, fantasy, and enfranchisement. This is not to suggest that these themes are altogether absent in African American visual and literary texts. Rather, I am suggesting that Franklin's expressions of freedom in the form of "carefree-ness," bliss, and even euphoria are so absent as to be inconsistent with black experience and, by extension, black feelings. The literary snippets from children's stories underscore the fantastical nature of the image but also serve as Franklin's nod to the intersection of the visual and the textual. Indeed, in her artist statement, Franklin admits that she "appropriate[s] image and text as a political gesture that chisels away at the narratives historically inscribed on women and people of color, and forges imaginative spaces for radical possibilities and visions."[47] The inclusion of both stories evokes the innocence of childhood, a life stage that is often denied to black children: a recent psychological study confirmed that "black children are more likely to be seen as similar to adults prematurely."[48] Franklin's luminescent and floral framing of the image's black boy serves, then, as a reclamation of the happiness that all children deserve. The pose, the shoulder "pop," and the direct gaze into

7. Krista Franklin, *Wanderlust Wonderland.* 2006. Collage on canvas.

the camera's lens point to this black boy's sense of self-assuredness and self-possession.

The subtle yet centrally positioned inclusion of the word *drapetomania* in *Wanderlust Wonderland* captures the emancipatory ethic of the collage and of the *Afrimerica Archive* more broadly. Coined by physician Dr. Samuel Cartwright in the 1850s, *drapetomania* refers to the impulses of the enslaved to run away from their plantations and masters. An 1855 edition of the *Buffalo Medical Journal* published an excerpt from Dr. Cartwright's original essay. In this piece, Dr. Cartwright extended the ancient Greek definition of drapetomania, "the fact of absconding," to account for the runaway slave, given that this particular manifestation of drapetomania was "a disease not heretofore classed among the long list of maladies that man is subject to."[49] Referring to drapetomania (as it pertained to the

American slave) as "a disease of the mind," Cartwright proposed a "cure" that was aligned with the "Creator's will in regard to the negro; it declares him to be the submissive knee-bender." With an explication that was part theological, part biological, and part pseudo-psychological, Cartwright asserted:

> In the anatomical conformation of his knees, we see "*genu flexit*" written in the physical structure of his knees, being more flexed or bent, than any other kind of man. If the white man attempts to oppose the Deity's will by trying to make the negro anything else than "*the submissive knee bender*," (which the Almighty declared he should be,) by trying to raise him with a level to himself, or by putting him on an equality with the negro; or if he abuses the power which God has given him over his fellow man, by being cruel to him or punishing him in anger . . . the negro will run away.[50]

Oddly, the "illness" by which the slave was afflicted was not entirely biological but rather a consequence of the master's inability to exercise proper control over his slaves. Franklin's invocation of drapetomania sharply contrasts both the title and the sentiment of *Wanderlust Wonderland*. The concept of drapetomania recurs throughout Franklin's oeuvre as an "illness" that the black subject willfully accepts. In a play on the conventions of the slave narrative, for example, Franklin created a sculpted image of a book entitled *A Natural History of My Drapetomania, fragments from a girl who refused to be contained. WRITTEN BY HERSELF* (2010). Drapetomania, much like nostalgia, was once thought to be a medical illness, but it is reconfigured in these instances as a mark of healthy resistance to manifest forms of black containment—slavery, surveillance, policing, and marginalization. Reframing drapetomania as wanderlust, Franklin effectively defies the destabilizing regimes of race and the culture of the plantation by rethinking the relationship between blackness, spatiality, and mobility.

Wanderlust, or the eagerness to wander or travel, resituates the black body as a free agent; in this contemporary context, the desire to run away is depathologized, functioning instead as a rejection of the "quiet servitude" that informs Cartwright's characterization of the black body as anatomically and theologically created for the purpose of subjugation. Franklin's *Afrimerica Archive* fills a critical void, given the absolute dearth of cultural narratives in which black bodies are seen as explorers, adventurers, tourists, trekkers, flaneurs, wanderers. The text in the upper-right corner of *Wanderlust Wonderland* recounts the rise of Timbuktu, a city founded by nomads in the twelfth century that eventually became a major trading hub. The nod to nomadism aligns with the collage's general theme of wandering. Taken to its theoretical extension, the idea of nomadism has a specific currency in feminist discourse as a "critical consciousness that resists settling into socially coded modes of thought and behavior."[51] Wanderlust, though an undertheorized dimension of black mobility, becomes an essential mode of affective resistance to dominant and totalizing representations of black bodies in stasis or in various stages of escape. The floral framing of *Wanderlust Wonderland* further evokes a sense of tranquility, adventure, leisure, and pleasure. The striking vividness in the piece is a hallmark of Franklin's collage work, which evokes an unregulated and unbounded spirit: black happiness exists in and of itself, for itself.

The memories—or, rather, histories—that *Afrimerica Archive* appears committed to preserving and collecting are those of positive black affect, memories that function as complements to the extant archive of black trauma. Franklin is concerned not with a nostalgia for the black historical past as we know it, but with the way that future generations will interpret it. As exemplified in the 2009 collage *Lush Life* (figure 8), Franklin's collage work contrives an archive that animates the felicity of black experience and that offers surreal journeys through black pasts and presents, spatialities and temporalities, all punctuated by hyperpigmented colors. The "lushness" of the image reflects both the rich fecundity of the natural life represented—the leaves, the grass, the trees—and the joviality of the figures at the center. The verdant scene evokes a hyper-"aliveness" exemplified by saturated colors. The moment represented here is one of excess. The glimmers of gold that lace the collage animate the luxuriance that lushness effects; the gold leaf hovers and falls over the central figures like stardust, transforming a simple moment of lounging into an enchanted landscape. Despite the image's vividness, which nods to the contemporary, even the futuristic, the scenes within the piece call forth a pastness—the afroed couple, the turntable, the half-nude figure situated in Franklin's semi-Technicolor forest. More than harking to a generalized black past, the image evinces a nostalgic sensibility. It is a romantic return to an analog, unprocessed past—natural hair and natural landscapes. In a vein reminiscent of Marshall's *Vignette*, the romance of blackness is front and center, as is the predominance of leisure. More than a depiction of simple joys and pleasures, *Lush Life* reflects a historical (and even present-day) dissonance between blackness and happiness—or, to state it more broadly, between blackness and being. Leisure is a luxury, a luxury of time, that is often perceived as antithetical to blackness, in which time is "stolen"

8. Krista Franklin, *Lush Life*. 2009. Mixed media on watercolor paper.

rather than "left over."[52] Regenerative nostalgia, in *Lush Life*, emerges as a site of affective reclamation—of laughter, of leisure, of joy.

Franklin, also an esteemed poet, uses her poetry—specifically the 2015 poem "Manifesto, or Ars Poetica #2"[53]—to articulate the manifold resources from which she draws. The range is extensive; "Hottentot&Huey

Newton," "black dahlias," "Afro-Sheen," and "deep brown apple butter" are among a wealth of objects, persons, sounds, and sentiments that Franklin cites as her muses. "Manifesto" documents an eclectic archive of black cultural artifacts that, collectively, culminate in one of the poem's final lines: "I'm on a quest for the Marvelous." Taking up the dictums of the late theorist, intellectual, and matriarch of the afro-surrealist aesthetic Suzanne Césaire, who once wrote that "surrealism is living, intensely, magnificently,"[54] Franklin extends the contemporary afro-surrealist endeavor to "strive for rococo: the beautiful, the sensuous, and the whimsical."[55] Césaire's 1943 essay "Surrealism and Us" offers surrealist thought as an analytic through which to consider the possibilities of black life outside of the frame of subjugation. Césaire believed that surrealism held the potential to "finally transcend the sordid antinomies of the present: whites-Blacks, Europeans-Africans, civilized-savages."[56] Though far less known than her husband, Aimé Césaire, famed poet and leader of the Negritude movement, Suzanne Césaire found inspiration in surrealism—a new way of being, of thinking, of finding freedom for black subjects mired in the dregs of European colonialism. Indeed, scholars like Brent Hayes Edwards have argued that "Césairean Negritude contributed to the shaping of the surrealist movement, rather than simply adopting it as a preformed system."[57]

Franklin's "quest for the Marvelous" makes explicit her aesthetic intertextuality with Suzanne Césaire, but it also bridges the earlier afro-surrealist project to a more contemporary political and aesthetic imperative: the fantastic. The "search for the black fantastic," described by Richard Iton as the "minor key sensibilities generated from the experiences of the underground, the vagabond, and those constituencies marked as deviant," resonates deeply with Césaire's, and later Franklin's, "quest." For Iton, the "*black* in black fantastic" refers to "a generic category of underdeveloped possibilities and the particular 'always there' interpretations of these agnostic, postracial, post-colonial visions and practices generated by subaltern populations."[58] Franklin's revered "hot combs," "back alleys," "gold grills," and "beads at the ends of braids"—all named in "Manifesto"—are signifiers for a colloquial blackness that constitute her nostalgic project of affective archiving. The collection of these artifacts aligns with Franklin's worldmaking process of collage; in "Manifesto" she playfully points to the power to create new worlds deemed historically (im)possible, if only for her own amusement ("Under my knife, El-Hajj Malik El-Shabazz laughs with Muhammed Ali. . . . Under my knife, Marilyn Monroe enjoys an evening out with Ella Fitzgerald"). In this light, Franklin's aesthetic archive is informed by black nostalgic impulses that manifest a constellation of unapologetic blackness and unconditional love.

Rhonda Wheatley: For Self-Use Only

While Franklin's collages revisit "old ways" with "new eyes," Rhonda Wheatley's art installations enable her audience/participants to (re)construct a compassionate relationship to the past to alleviate trauma and manifest healing. Wheatley's objects, devices, and elixirs encourage a return to the past to compensate for any number of losses, traumas, and injuries, so that their "users" can resituate their present selves in the context of a renewed relationship to that past with the promise of forming a more holistic and healthful self. Such a process requires interpreting the past nonjudgmentally and sympathetically, with an eye toward repairing a fractured and damaged present self. For example, Wheatley's *African Diasporic Ancestral Memory Transmutation Device* (2016) claims to possess the power to "quell effects of trauma passed down genetically from ancestors" and to "inhibit passing to descendants traumas caused by 20th and 21st Century anti-black racism and brutality." The device, importantly, only "operates at individual soul's discretion."[59] A common theme in Wheatley's project is the insistence that healing is not projected onto others but that individuals bear responsibility for enabling curative processes to begin.

The devices Wheatley constructs are largely vintage and found objects that contain their own histories and past users. Common to her works are analog devices like rotary phones, record players, and TV antennas that possess their own nostalgic value for predigital times yet take on new meaning as they are transformed into life-altering apparatuses for users in the now. Perhaps on its own, the individual object might read as little more than a dated contraption—a throwback to another time, a slice of nostalgia that jogs a recessed memory, real or imagined. But collectively, these items take on new meaning; their assemblage exceeds their individual banality to produce more than a romantic remembrance of the past, of "simpler times," but an agentic relation to the past in which one holds the power to resituate oneself within it. The transformation of these objects from their original intended use becomes a metaphor for the possibility of individual power and promise for those that interact with these creations, which Wheatley terms "power objects" and "hybrid devices." While the works of Banks and Franklin capture expressions of nostalgia, Wheatley's interactive objects facilitate its making. There is an intentionality with Wheatley's devices, objects, and books that resonates with the processes by which nostalgia is often experienced. While it is certainly possible to be taken back to a moment in time by spontaneously glancing at an image, for example, nostalgia can also be summoned expressly for the purpose of producing "good feelings."

In spring 2017, I took the honors students in my Contemporary Novels of Slavery course to view Rhonda Wheatley's exhibit *A Modern Day Shaman's Hybrid Devices, Power Objects, and Cure Books* at the Hyde Park Art Center (HPAC) in Chicago. Wheatley was kind enough to meet us at the HPAC, where she patiently and comprehensively answered my students' questions about the sculptures and collages on display. We ended our tour with Wheatley giving a few student volunteers a tarot reading. Many wanted to know about the fate of their love lives and their next steps in life, fairly predictable questions from college students quickly approaching graduation. Like her hybrid devices and power objects, Wheatley's readings encouraged my students to be cognizant of their own agency; while a person cannot escape their past, they do have the power to reframe their relationship to it. Her art, in all its manifestations, focuses on the choices one makes that can (or cannot) contribute to one's own happiness and well-being. Wheatley noted that the power objects, hybrid devices, serums, elixirs, and potions that constituted her exhibit were for "self-use only," and many of the items on display were explicit in this directive. Some students wanted to purchase the "Elixir for Un-Learning Race-, Gender-, and Sexuality-Based Hatred" and spread it into the world. However, the directions for use explain that it is made specifically to "target the roots of one's learned prejudicial hatred and hostility." Thus, one has to decide to use the elixir to change one's own behavior. This notion is at the core of Wheatley's exhibit: she provides the tools, but the "user" provides the impetus to shift his or her behaviors, thought processes, and circumstances by "targeting" their "roots."

It is perhaps most useful to consider Wheatley's project within the broader discourse of what is known as the "healing arts," much of which emerges in feminist studies. The notion of returning to the past to heal present-day trauma is at the core of the work of many writers, scholars, and activists: Audre Lorde, Aurora Levins Morales, and bell hooks, among many others. Levins Morales's historical memoir *Remedios: Stories of Earth and Iron from the History of Puertorriqueñas* (1998) creates what she calls a "curative history" that weaves together an alternative history of the world, upending conventional and dominant historical narratives that privilege white, Western, male power and authority. Interspersed within her wide-ranging histories of figures like Juana de Asbaje, Ida B.

Wells, and Gracia Nasi are recollections of Levins Morales's own history of trauma and recovery, highlighting the healing power of memory. Writer and healer Cassie Premo Steele offers that "healing from memory means remembering the split aspects of our existence, reclaiming the goodness of our bodies and our spirits, and re-storing to us the ability to use creativity as power."[60] What Wheatley's exhibit shares with these works is the use of memory to creatively engage with these objects and, in doing so, fill in the blanks of a past that may not be otherwise be fully knowable or available.

In the absence of access to the truth of the past, users must imagine their own pasts and create the narratives in which to situate themselves as part of the healing process. For example, Wheatley's 2017 exhibit included a device called the *Post-Traumatic Soul Restoration and Brain Rewiring Device* (figure 9)—constructed from a vintage record player, vintage movie cameras, a television antenna, and moss, among other elements—that "traces a user's negative repeating patterns and life cycles back to the traumas from which they originate."[61] This is the work that the machine performs. However, the "restoration" and "rewiring" cannot take place unless the "user is willing to release the pain." As Wheatley explained to my class, she believes that recovery is a choice that cannot and should not be foisted on others. Her rationale is that some people are attached to their pain and use it as a point of identification. She recalled a story in which she offered to perform energy work for a woman who experienced constant pain in her hip. The woman flatly refused, claiming that her hip injury could not be cured and that she was prepared to deal with the pain for the rest of her life. Thus, in order for the soul to be restored and the brain to be rewired, the user has to be ready to release her attachment to the pain of the past. Lastly, the device is designed to "uproot the ingrained effects of trauma (addiction, self-sabotage, codependency, etc.) freeing the consciousness to begin unraveling those negative, repeating patterns as it assists in healing the soul and rewiring the brain." *Post-Traumatic Soul Restoration and Brain Rewiring Device* most poignantly identifies Wheatley's aesthetic endeavor to promote psychic and emotional healing vis-à-vis a mediated relationship with one's real or imagined past. In an African American historical context, locating or "tracing" the origin of one's trauma would necessitate an imagined return to the past in order to facilitate the process of restoration. Wheatley's objects and devices work to stimulate the imagination, a necessary step in the course of healing. Wheatley's medium encourages active engagement with these objects, and the HPAC exhibit explicitly referred to visitors as *users*, not *viewers*.[62] If a person is in need of healing (and aren't we all?), they are drawn to the

9. Rhonda Wheatley, *Post-Traumatic Soul Restoration and Brain Rewiring Device*. 2017. Portable turntable, movie cameras, snakeskin, plastic spider plants, and earphones.

objects, which are compelling from a tactile perspective but also spark curiosity: do these objects really "work"?

In viewing the devices and objects that constituted the exhibit, I was reminded of a podcast I had recently heard about a phone booth in Japan that allows its "users" to commune with the dead.[63] In 2010, grieving the death of a beloved cousin, a man named Itaru Sasaki living in the town of Otsuchi purchased an old phone booth and placed it in his backyard. He added an old rotary phone and set it on a small shelf in the booth. Sasaki designed this space to communicate with his deceased family and process his grief. The following year, in March 2011, the town of Otsuchi was devastated by an earthquake and tsunami that left more than twelve hundred people dead and four hundred missing, of a total population of approximately sixteen thousand. Sasaki began inviting others to use the booth to "speak" with their lost loved ones, and it has since attracted hundreds of visitors who use the booth not only to commune with the dead but to work through their feelings of the tragedy that devastated the entire community.[64] Like Wheatley's power objects and hybrid devices, Sasaki's Wind Phone, as it is affectionately called, points to the enhanced materiality of these objects—or "things." According to scholar Bill Brown, "You could imagine things . . . as what is excessive in objects, as what exceeds their mere materialization as objects or their mere utilization as objects—their force as a sensuous presence or as a metaphysical presence, the magic by which objects become values, fetishes, idols, and totems."[65] Like Sasaki's unconnected rotary phone, Wheatley's vintage cameras and TV antennas no longer possess any value in accord with their original function. The found objects that constitute Wheatley's devices are transformed from their original usage in order to effect a transformation in the subject. Wheatley's endeavor, importantly, differs from the surrealist practice meant to reveal "the object as a form of commodification and as a subjective act of creation."[66] The repurposing of these objects into things, specifically things that "users" employ to help them reconcile the past, makes clear Wheatley's (and even Sasaki's) nostalgic imperative—to heal the "user" by facilitating a sympathetic return to the past using objects (now things) as a vehicle for the journey.

Similar to Sasaki's Wind Phone, one of the objects featured in Wheatley's 2017 exhibit was a repurposed phone, albeit one with no buttons or mechanism for the user to dial out. Instead, the user can only employ the phone once they have reached an advanced stage of psychic awareness and are ready to be guided toward the next step. The object that was once a "vintage Ukrainian telephone" is now a *Guidance Counselor* (figure 10)—a "one-way communication device" that "calls out from spiritual realms to users who are on the brink of profound transformation in their three-dimensional lives on earth." By answering the call, users can restore some of the memories of "their eternal selves, i.e., who they are as limitless energies outside time and beyond all other earth-based lifetimes." The instructions that accompany the device note that the call "triggers the dauntlessness necessary to complete the transformation and next stage of their purpose and mission in this lifetime."[67] Resonant in all of Wheatley's works is an opening for users to recover their pasts and progress toward an elevated space of awareness and well-being. The possibility to transcend one's current circumstances is readily available, should one choose to use it.

The *Guidance Counselor* taps into a part of the self that has been lost, and the device thus serves as a mediator between one's past self and one's

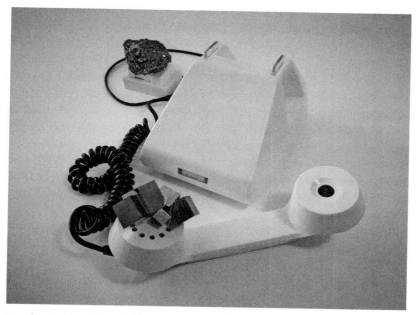

10. Rhonda Wheatley, *Guidance Counselor*. 2017. Vintage Ukrainian telephone, pyrite clusters.

present identity. While thing theory and object studies offer an attractive way to consider the critical value of Wheatley's devices and objects, I read her project less as an attempt to animate objects and more as an investment in animating the memories of the users who manipulate them. The focus is not on the objects themselves but on what the user can achieve through conscious engagement with them.

Such is the case with the *Life Review Device* (figure 11), which is meant to spark a "life reboot" for users battling "depression and despair." In the spirit of nostalgic return, users can "re-experience their entire lives in a full/extra-sensory consciousness download, infused with the hope and purpose with which they entered this lifetime." By "releasing blame and grudges, forgiving one's self and others," users can get "back on mission," which ostensibly leads to the living out of purposeful lives.[68] A thread running through Wheatley's project is its subtle acknowledgment of past trauma and loss, yet in each object there exists an emphasis on agency, choice, and transformation. Given that we all (apparently) enter this world with a distinct "hope and purpose," the objects help us remember ourselves as "limitless energies," each with a role to play on this earth. I refer to the

11. Rhonda Wheatley, *Life Review Device*. 2017. Three vintage clock radios, vintage TV antenna, and quartz crystal cluster.

mediated recall in Wheatley's exhibits as nostalgic because it is inspired by a desire to return to and approach the past with a sense of compassion and longing—a longing, specifically, for a return to the self that one never knew existed within a time and space that cannot readily be accessed.

Black historical nostalgia that offers little to no regard for the inevitable circumstance of traumatic experience can easily—and, arguably, rightfully—be deemed an act of self-deception at best and, at worst, politically dangerous. Each of the artists I discuss imagines the concept of regeneration as a progressive "healing" that privileges the psychic health of the contemporary (black) subject with regard to a renewed conception of the past. Regenerative nostalgia is about recovery, both as a curative for the self and as a reclamation of affective black histories. If the previous chapters situated black historical nostalgia as a matter of revision and redress, the work of Banks, Franklin, and Wheatley imagines it as a function of recovery and (re)creation. The preceding chapters demonstrate that the public history of black trauma is complicated, multilayered, and incomplete; this chapter shows that the same is true for the public history of black happiness, health, and romantic sentiment. As the previous chapter made clear, black aesthetic practices serve a political imperative to reclaim nostalgia as a fecund site of resistance to narratives of white dominance over black feelings, black psyches, and black sound. The making anew of black historical pasts with an eye toward wistfulness, sentimentality, and a touch of the sublime emerges as a much-needed dimension to explore the full range of black affect. To be cognizant of and even to honor black joy is not to disregard or dismiss black pain; rather, it is to affirm that the romance of the past is available to black folks too.

4

(Nostalgic) RECLAMATION

Recipes for Radicalism and the Politics of Soul (Food)

My childhood in the Nation of Islam (NOI) is marked by three lingering memories: addressing my parents and their friends with the greetings "Assalamu alaikum" and "Wa alaikum assalaam," not being allowed to wear shorts in the sweltering heat of Chicago summers, and believing that pork was the devil. Being restricted to pants and long skirts all summer was an annoyance, but it was nothing compared to the public shame associated with not eating pork. Because "pigs eat shit" they have been taboo as a source of human sustenance in multiple cultures.[1] But this was the 1970s: there were no gluten-free menus, no waitstaff asking whether there were "any allergies the kitchen should consider," no vegetarian main courses. Children in the NOI who had to partake in the school lunch program either ate the sausage pizza, peeled off the layer of pork-laden industrial cheese, or went hungry. The school's hot dogs were pork, and even if the meat of the hamburger was "safe," I had to consider whether lard was an ingredient in the bun. At sleepovers, I tried to avoid the bacon that accompanied the morning's requisite pancakes and eggs, and I feared having to explain to the parents of friends why my pile of crispy pig remained uneaten. On multiple occasions, I was accused of "wasting food." My earliest recollections of food are accompanied by fear, shame, and guilt—especially during those weak moments in which I carefully stripped pepperoni from my pizza but consumed the remnants of pork that lingered behind. Even though I no longer identify as Muslim and have accepted bacon into my diet, I still cannot bring myself to try ham or pork chops. My father's insistence that "pigs are poison" still resonates sharply.

My aversion to pork was undoubtedly associated with upsetting my father and disappointing my mother. But it was also linked to disrupting and disobeying the larger cultural and religious community to which I belonged. My father insisted that "eating swine" was racial treachery: pork was something that the "white man" enjoyed, profited from, and forced into the diets of black people (according to the Honorable Elijah Muhammad).[2] Refusing it was an act of defiance. Jennifer Jensen Wallach points out that according to the NOI, "healthy black bodies belonged to the nation . . . and the failure to obey dietary rules could be seen as a form of community betrayal."[3] The absence of pork from our family diet was, in many ways, as significant as my parents' decision to change our last name from "Patton" to "Abdul-Ahad." Pork was the medium through which my father expressed his vitriol for "the West." If his black nationalist utopia seemed impossible in the United States, then he would at least attempt to realize it in his own household. The foods we consume constitute who we are, in the most base and biological sense. Our family's culinary choices reflected a commitment to black nationalist ideals and a resistance to white supremacy. What I learned from my father at a very early age is that food is political: it is not only a reflection of one's identity but an assertion of it. While nostalgia, in general, often originates from feelings of depression and ambivalence, food nostalgia operates in a converse fashion, carrying with it a range of good feelings.

In this chapter, I explore more fully how the positive emotions associated with food nostalgia are entangled with broader political and racial nostalgic desires, and how contemporary black chefs, in particular, navigate this shifting terrain. Generally, we think of nostalgia as mired in a sense of longing for a past to which one cannot return. However, since food offers an opportunity to re-create the past in sensory terms, it complicates the notion of nostalgia as mere loss that can never be recaptured.[4] For example, culinary historian Michael Twitty has embarked on an ambitious project to uncover his African roots through food. Guided by a fear of forgetting where he came from and alarmed by his "own apathy and amnesia," Twitty began a project he calls the "Southern Discomfort Tour." He set out to "travel the South looking for sites of cultural and culinary memory while researching [his] family history and seeing the food culture of the region as it stood in the early twenty-first century."[5] I see Twitty's work as a response to and a revival of the 1960s and 1970s complex and mutually constitutive relation between black radical consciousness and food consumption and restriction.

This chapter looks at the contemporary culinary practices of two chefs, Bryant Terry and Marcus Samuelsson, and their nostalgic retreats to moments within the black historical past, specifically precolonial Africa, the Harlem Renaissance, and the Black Power movement. These retreats translate into what I refer to as a *nostalgic reclamation*. References to the black historical past in recent artistic and cultural contexts are indicative of the symbolic hold that these moments have on the contemporary black consciousness. Margo Natalie Crawford expertly defines this relation as "black post-blackness," a "nonlinear, back-and-forth, black radical tradition of continuity *and* rupture."[6] The murkiness of the multiple black nostalgias from which Terry and Samuelsson draw their inspiration points to how nostalgia often operates in the sphere of black cultural memory. As I noted in the introduction, Jessie Fauset's essay "Nostalgia" identifies the lack of an identifiable homeland as creating a free-floating and ever-present malaise for African Americans. Yet contemporary black cultural producers like Terry and Samuelsson grapple with this lack of specificity vis-à-vis the imaginative accretion of black historical moments without an allegiance to a particular site of memory—or of home, for that matter. As Kyla Wazana Tompkins has keenly assessed,

> It is not simply the "what" of what one eats that matters. It is the "where" of where we eat and where food comes from; the "when" of historically specific economic conditions and political pressures; the "how" of how food is made; and the "who" of who makes and who gets to eat it. Finally, and most important, it is the many "whys" of eating—the differing imperatives of hunger, necessity, pleasure, nostalgia, and protest—that most determine its meaning.[7]

The amalgamation of eras within the black historical past from which Terry and Samuelsson cull reflects a complexity of nostalgic desires: Terry's black nationalist culinary aesthetic echoes that of Elijah Muhammad, whose own dietary framework is inspired by nostalgia for precolonial Africa ("The so-called American Negro is a Divine member lost from the Divine circle").[8] Similarly, Samuelsson—who was adopted by Swedish parents at two years of age and taken from Ethiopia after losing his mother to tuberculosis—expresses nostalgia for his lost homeland and his mother. In his memoir, *Yes, Chef*, this nostalgia is enmeshed with his emerging identification as African American. That identification is reflected in his romantic attachment to the Harlem Renaissance and his incorporation within post-black artistic circles, specifically his friendship with Thelma Golden, director and chief curator of the Studio Museum of Harlem. Both Terry and Bryant also perform significant "ruptures" from these moments in black history that reflect shifts in contemporary political and racial sensibilities. As Crawford explains, their work "shows how blackness remains that elusive 'flash of the spirit' that moves through the Black Arts Movement to twenty-first-century black aesthetics."[9] I argue that it is this "flash" that animates the nostalgic culinary practices of Terry and Samuelsson. Many chefs reflect on the black culinary past to craft new forms of African American cuisine;[10] I have chosen to discuss Terry and Samuelsson because of the explicit and pervasive deployments of nostalgia in their written works, specifically their cookbooks and memoirs. The predominance of nostalgia and the imperative of self- and cultural continuity in their work position Terry and Samuelsson as exemplars of the way that black nostalgia functions in the complicated space of food studies.

Inherently, nostalgia indicates a break with the past; the concept itself relies on the irrecoverable nature of a moment or a place that no longer exists. For this reason, nostalgia is generally read as an especially unproductive form of recollection. But, as we have seen so far, efforts to reconceive this term in a more progressive and positive light have been significant, especially within the past two decades. Nostalgia represents a point of departure, a picking up of the mantle of history to continue an interrupted project; the "break" signifies a gap, which suggests the possibility of connection. Nostalgia, in these chefs' culinary practices, is more than a romantic nod to the black past: it extends the dietary programs of their culinary forebears. Reconnecting black people to their culinary roots offers obvious health benefits, but it also revives a sense of racial and cultural pride and self-awareness. In this way, Terry and Samuelsson extend the conceptual link between contemporary black consciousness and food practices. In the previous chapters of this book, I have deployed the concepts of retribution, restoration, and regeneration as the varied means by which nostalgia operates as an emotional and psychological counter to the historical, generational, and psychic trauma produced by US chattel slavery. This chapter's focus on reclamation centers the phenomenological experience of food production and consumption that black people employ as a matter of recovering a culinary history and heritage that is intimately tied to an emancipatory politic of black radicalism.

I begin this chapter with an analysis of the cultural work of Elijah Muhammad's dietary guide *How to Eat to Live* (1967–72) and the self-titled *Dick Gregory's Natural Diet for Folks Who Eat: Cookin' with Mother*

Nature (1973). I start with these works because they offer a clear lineage and point of continuity from which to consider how food, aesthetics, and black radical politics operate in Terry's oeuvre. Though I reference other black cookbooks and recipes from this era to point to the broader cultural phenomenon of racial identification through the creation and consumption of particular foods, Muhammad's and Gregory's texts move beyond the "how-to" cookbook paradigm to offer extended meditations on the relationship between black diet and black politics. In different ways, they make explicit how the foods we consume reflect a broader political sensibility: in this case, African American cultural and political agency. They argue that food and diet are integral to the projects of black self-awareness, black pride, and black nationalism, and their respective programs function as acts of resistance to white hegemony over black bodies. As Wallach explains, "Culinary black nationalists did not conceive of food decisions as a series of trivial personal consumer choices but rather as an arena for communal activism."[11] Muhammad, in particular, was concerned with the incorporation of whiteness—meaning "white" values, culture, and spirituality—into the black body. He associated whiteness largely with American institutionalism (such as Christianity or the prison-industrial complex), and thus eating foods like "swine," which were part of the diet of "Nordics," meant that black people were ingesting a set of cultural, social, and political values that were not their own. These black culinary enterprises of the 1960s and 1970s sought to mark African American foodstuffs as distinct from the (white) American diet.

I then turn to Bryant Terry's cookbook *Afro-Vegan: Farm-Fresh African, Caribbean, and Southern Flavors Remixed* (2014), in which Terry takes up the imperatives of Muhammad and Gregory and reconceives them to reflect and address contemporary issues of racial disparities, injustice, and identification. Terry's work reflects a post-black sensibility that simultaneously honors and critiques, continues and ruptures, the dicta of the Black Power movement. Significantly, he establishes continuity between the contemporary present and the Black Power movement by drawing directly on historical moments in the narratives that inspire his recipes. However, he fashions a culinary perspective that complicates the black nationalist precepts of Muhammad's *How to Eat to Live* as well as the integrationist ethos of *Dick Gregory's Natural Diet*.

I complete the chapter by turning to Marcus Samuelsson's post-black culinary endeavors, in which the nostalgic turn to black culinary pasts is decidedly less straightforward than in Terry's reclamation of the Black Power moment. Samuelsson's praxis is informed by the loss of his mother and his homeland, Ethiopia; his migration from Sweden to the United States; and his inclusion within a contemporary post-black artistic scene of cultural arbiters. While the two chefs' ventures are inspired by different markers within the black historical culinary landscape, they converge at the site of endeavoring to make visible America's Africanist origins, which have been universalized (whitened) and thereby erased. In unearthing the Africanness of the American culinary landscape, Samuelsson and Terry advance a dietary politic that is indelibly linked to the articulation of a post–civil rights identity and recast US culinary culture within a contemporary afro-diasporic framework.

How to Eat to Live (Black)

My father had not invented this relation between pork avoidance and black nationalist ideals. He was merely echoing the insights provided by the Honorable Elijah Muhammad in his dietary guidebook *How to Eat to Live* (1967–72). Under the mentorship of Master Fard Muhammad, Elijah Muhammad developed a series of guidelines that NOI members were advised to follow. In many respects, Elijah Muhammad's dictates were ahead of his time and would fit squarely within the food-conscious culture of the present moment. In "Right Way to Eat," the introductory chapter of *How to Eat to Live*, Book 1, Muhammad condemns the "Christian people" for killing animals when they are in a state of "fright and excitement," thus "murder[ing] the animals they eat."[12] At the time this book was published, in 1967, the average consumer was unable to choose among a range of meat products that had lived "cage-free" lives and were "humanely" put to rest. Muhammad also advises against buying processed foods, eating soybeans, and consuming catfish, which he calls "the pig of the water."[13] For women, taking birth control is an act Muhammad describes as a "bold offer of death."[14] Despite the NOI's reputation for its rampant anti-Semitism,[15] Muhammad continuously praises Orthodox Jews for "still trying to obey that which they were ordered to do by Allah," making them the "only people, the Holy Qur-an teaches, whose food we can eat."[16] He advises, "If you would like to find good food, such as lamb, beef or even chicken—if you are a Muslim—buy it from the strictly Orthodox Jew."[17]

A number of scholars have studied the culinary program of the NOI.[18] Most read Muhammad's dietary guidelines as merely part of a larger program of indoctrination for NOI members, but various interpretations exist concerning the Nation's dictums on food and health. At one end of this spectrum, scholars like Edward E. Curtis IV read Muhammad's *How to*

Eat to Live as part and parcel of the Nation's curriculum of "ritual purity" by which "black men and women could save their bodies from emasculation, violation, and contamination."[19] Curtis's study of the "Islamization" of the black body persuasively argues that "members of the NOI adopted many turn-of-the-century black middle-class 'uplift' themes like thrift, sexual propriety, industriousness, and temperance by recasting them in an Islamic mold."[20] He further argues that although the NOI's theological and political program emphasized black self-sufficiency, Muhammad "was not first and foremost a black nationalist."[21] In prioritizing Muhammad's rank as prophet first and black nationalist second, Curtis draws on Wilson Jeremiah Moses's definition of black nationalism, which states that "the essential feature of classical black nationalism is its goal of creating a black nation-state or empire with absolute control over a specific geographic territory, and sufficient economic and military power to defend it."[22] Curtis asserts that the "religious, political, and economic activities" of the NOI were byproducts of and in response to the "prophetic commandments" of Elijah Muhammad.[23]

While Curtis's study offers a view of the NOI and its ritual practices as indicative of broader political and theological concerns, Kate Holbrook argues that the NOI's dietary program was "deeply influenced by mainstream American values, rather than religious mandates."[24] Holbrook acknowledges that the NOI's food restrictions were part of a larger process of "racial rehabilitation," but she insists that while there were "clearly strong racial themes in Muhammad's culinary directions . . . he did not tell his followers to eat small navy beans in search of a new, postslave, post-American identity." Instead, Holbrook argues, "[Muhammad] taught them to eat small navy beans because they were healthy."[25] She points to the NOI's famous bean pies as a revision of "familiar American staples like sweet potato pie," which reflect the Nation's "endorsement of broader American ideals."[26] Though Curtis and Holbrook construct two different arguments around the NOI's dietary program and its relationship to the NOI's larger mission—whether spiritual or political or both—the scholars converge by de-emphasizing the political, specifically black nationalist imperatives of Elijah Muhammad and the NOI. I agree with Curtis and Holbrook that one of the imperatives behind the Nation's food proscriptions was health and that these dietary restrictions were part of a larger program of purification and ritualization. However, the relationship that I draw between the NOI's culinary and ideological concerns resides in a broader understanding of black nationalism as a praxis that maintains a number of dimensions: social, economic, psychological, and physiological.

Here, I am draw on James Taylor's nuanced "transhistorical" treatment of black nationalism "from its religious foundations in early-nineteenth-century protest fulcrums to the hip-hop generations' attempts to activate it to articulate the social and political circumstances that confronted them in the late twentieth century."[27] In fact, I would argue that there is no material object more nationalistic in nature than food. A consideration of black nationalism as not only a socioeconomic practice but also a gastronomic one allows us to extend the parameters of black nationalist ideals to encompass the multivalent ways that such ideologies simultaneously function as material, social, and biological praxis.

When I was a child, the logic behind not eating pork in our household was that it was meat that was consumed and enjoyed by white people. As my father explained, and as was noted by Elijah Muhammad, for "them" pork was a perfectly acceptable meal option. It was part of their ancestral heritage, and they were merely following a centuries-long tradition in their consumption of pig. In Book 2 of *How to Eat to Live*, Muhammad writes, "When they were in the hillsides and caves of Europe, they ate the foods other wild beasts ate. That is why you see white people eating all kinds of food today."[28] Much of Muhammad's rhetoric concerning the dietary habits of white Americans resulted from the idea that they, white Americans, forced black people to partake in a dietary regimen that was "unnatural." Muhammad repeatedly refers to slavery and his own time in prison as circumstances in which black folks were made to submit to the forces of white hegemony by eating foods that were not part of their ancestral diet. Slavery is the most explicit example of the inability of black people to maintain possession of their own bodies, as exemplified by the capitalist exchange of black bodies on the slave market, the pervasive sexual violation of black women and men, and the phenomenon of runaway slaves being charged for theft (of themselves). Muhammad merely extends this logic to include the foods that black people were made and then conditioned to consume. For instance, Muhammad advises against eating "peas, collard greens, turnip greens, sweet potatoes and white potatoes" because they are "cheaply raised foods" and "slave masters used them to feed the slaves, and still advise the consumption of them."[29] He says nothing about the nutritional makeup of these foods or their (perceived) lack of health benefits. These foods are, put simply, harmful by association. Based only on the fact that they constitute part of a diet that is indelibly linked to a slave past, Muhammad warns against their consumption. For Muhammad, it is through food that the "white race" has sought and "tried throughout their civilization, to change the very natural religion of the black man."[30]

Muhammad constructs food as a primary source of oppression during slavery and assimilation in the decades that followed. Muhammad explains that a "doom is set for the whole race of them, and you will share their doom with them if you continue to eat and drink intoxicating drinks just because you see them doing such things."[31] Notwithstanding the prophetic ruin that will befall the white race, Muhammad cautions against assimilating what he considers "white" practices (dietary and otherwise). "Swine" was deemed the most offensive betrayal, not only of a NOI member's religion but of their race: "White America will do its utmost to test you if you say you do not love the swine. This proves, beyond a shadow of a doubt, that the white race is an enemy to the law of Allah (God) and wishes to make everyone of us disobey the law of Allah (God)."[32] So while it is clear that Muhammad understood himself as a prophet and the NOI as a religious entity, this platform was inextricably linked to a larger sense of cultural and racial self-determination that characterizes black nationalism.

The bean pie, for which the NOI is perhaps most recognized, emblematizes the ways that black nationalist thought was at the heart of the NOI's culinary practices. Although Muhammad offers no specific health detriments associated with sweet potatoes, he claims that they too are "unfit" for human consumption. In their place, *How to Eat to Live*, Book 1, praises the navy bean not only as a magnificent source of "protein, fats and starches" but as a food that can prolong one's life to possibly "240 years."[33] Mike Sula describes the evolution of the bean pie, made with "a filling of strained and mashed beans, butter, raw sugar, evaporated milk, eggs, cinnamon, and other baking spices,"[34] which could reasonably be mistaken for a sweet potato or pumpkin pie. According to Lance Shabazz, a historian of the NOI, the recipe for bean pie was given to Elijah Muhammad and his wife, Clara, in the 1930s by the Honorable Fard Muhammad, whom Elijah identified as a teacher, a mentor, and a prophet taking the form of Allah. Sula notes that the prohibition of sweet potatoes "might have been a tough sell for African-Americans new to the Nation,"[35] and while there is no clear evidence that the navy bean pie was developed as a substitute for the sweet potato pie—a gem of the southern diet—this may have made the transition for those new members easier to digest (pun intended). According to Sula, "bean pie wasn't the only Nation of Islam dish made with the miraculous navy bean—there was bean soup and bean bread—but it was certainly the most iconic, not just in Chicago but in any other city with a Nation of Islam presence."[36]

There are several reasons why the bean pie became the culinary face of the NOI: (1) it was delicious; (2) it tasted like sweet potato pie, which made it an appealing and healthful alternative for Muslims and non-Muslims alike; and (3) it was sold on the street by members of the Nation, making the pies, the people, and, by extension, Islam, accessible to a broad public. I would like to linger on this last point for a moment because it is an important one, especially in understanding why the bean pie signifies a larger black nationalist culinary aesthetic. Catching the stoplight at Seventy-Ninth and Stony Island in Chicago was more of an opportunity than an inconvenience. In the 1980s and into the early 1990s, there was always a flutter of activity. Male members of the Nation hustled throughout the intersection maneuvering between the stalled cars, smartly dressed in their requisite suits and bow ties, selling copies of the *Final Call* (the NOI newspaper) and bean pies. Sometimes we would purchase the *Final Call*, but we would always purchase the bean pies. Although Shabazz finds the time when "brothers [were] stopping cars at the light trying to sell a pie" an "embarrassing" moment of the Nation's history, the image of these men approaching vehicles to sell these products served as a potent and distinct counternarrative not only to pervasive negative images of black men but also to perceptions of members of the Nation as "odd" or "foreign." Their style of dress, their manner of speech—particularly their references to customers as "my brother" or "my sister"—and the bean pies they sold collectively fashioned a less militant and more genial and even familiar/familial vision of the NOI and black nationalism. The life cycle of the bean pie illustrates an alignment with black nationalist thought from production to consumption: the pies were created with ingredients that adhered to the Muslim diet, they were made by NOI members in their own bakeries and sold in black communities, and the revenue from these sales went back to the Nation. While the practice of selling pies on the street may not have been "professional," as Shabazz notes, it was effective in demystifying the Nation by making a black nationalist politic visible and accessible to the urban masses. Elijah Muhammad's dietary program, at the center of any serious discussion of the intersection of black radicalism and culinary consumption, was part of a larger and less acknowledged discourse of food as a significant aspect of black nationalist thought. Recipes, cookbooks, and dietary guides from the 1960s and 1970s reveal an investment in the shoring up of a distinct African American subjectivity through food choices and dietary guidelines. Similar to Muhammad's *How to Eat to Live*, a number of publications from the Black Power era articulate a connection between black pride and dietary choice.[37] For example, and contrary to Muhammad, Amiri Baraka, "used soul food to show connections within the African diaspora, whether it was ingredients such as black-eyed peas, collard greens, and okra, or cooking methods such as deep-fat frying."[38] Despite the differing ideologies concerning food consumption and black political culture, there existed an overwhelming interest in carving out and articulating a space of black politics using food as evidence of such.

Laretta Henderson notes that establishing a relationship between food choices and cultural pride was essential for black children during the Black Power era to maintain a sense of racial integrity in an ever-changing, integrated cultural landscape. She takes up this issue in the context of print culture through an analysis of the important, though short-lived, publication *Ebony Jr!* Arguing that "during the 1960s, middle-class blacks used their reported consumption of soul food to distance themselves from the values of the white middle class, to define themselves ethnically, and to align themselves with lower-class blacks," Henderson notes that this logic was extended in the discourse of soul food in *Ebony* magazine's print publication for children.[39] Even though Henderson admits that most middle-class black folks were not eating soul food as part of their daily diet, black print culture posited the preparation and consumption of soul food as part and parcel of a demonstrated racial allegiance: "soul food as a symbol of blackness would have been understood by the child reader."[40] A number of definitions, sometimes competing, exist as to precisely what qualifies as soul food—ranging from foods that date back to slavery to any food that is prepared by a black person—but Henderson establishes the ways in which the culinary choices made by black folks have reflected a broader political and racial politic, even in its insistence on authenticity.

In their introduction to *The Integrated Cookbook or the Soul of Good Cooking* (1971), Mary Jackson and Lelia Wishart make clear that the recipes in their book are not to be confused with "so-called Southern cooking," which they describe as "a thin, white man's parody."[41] While the "unique dishes" Jackson and Wishart offer are "the means by which Blacks have been able to survive and develop over hundreds of years of oppression," their *Integrated Cookbook* is "meant for everyone."[42] The cookbook appears especially geared toward "young Blacks who have been away too long from mother's cooking [and] may revive the old flavors of their ancestors and take pride in their origin," though white people are also invited to experience the "tantalizing savor" of their soul food recipes.[43] Jackson and Wishart also make the compelling claim that "Southern food may be found in many cookbooks and restaurants, but soul food always stays close to its origin in the Black slave's kitchen. It is, of course, purely American, perhaps the most American cooking there is."[44] The insistence on the fundamental Americanness of soul food offers a nuanced perspective of the authors' deployment of the term *integrated*. Their recipes are not a fusion of Africanist and "American" foods; rather, the authors claim that their "authentic" soul food creations are inherently American, and they imagine that "soul food will lead to a deeper, better understanding for us all."[45] Not only, then, does soul food carry with it an originary history of American cuisine, but its consumption is interpreted as a potential path toward reconciling America's racial ills.

Fasting for the Nation

Similar to Jackson and Wishart, famed comedian and activist Dick Gregory attempted to link principles of nonviolence to a reformed and natural diet. Gregory began his career as a comedian in the early 1960s. While Gregory was popular among black audiences, he was catapulted into mainstream celebrity after Hugh Hefner offered him a job at the Chicago Playboy Club. Gregory leveraged his fame to support the civil rights movement, and he eventually became a close ally of Dr. Martin Luther King Jr. In 1967, he ran an unsuccessful Chicago mayoral campaign against Richard J. Daley. The following year he ran for president as a write-in candidate as part of the Peace and Freedom Party in response to the announcement of segregationist George Wallace's candidacy for the office. In the early 1970s, Gregory extended his political ideologies to dietary culture, emphasizing healthy eating as a radical form of self-care and as an ethical practice.

While Gregory's dietary program differs from Muhammad's in significant ways, it shares a similar perspective on the relationship between racial pride and dietary health. For Gregory, a "clean diet"—one that includes both vegetarianism and fasting—is inherently linked to the idea of racial "cleansing" and purification. The idea that a pure body is tied to a pure mind and a pure conscious belies Gregory's politics of integration, which does not preclude his resistance to American institutionalism or white authority. In fact, Gregory advocates fasting as a form of alternative health and as a mode of political resistance. In his book *Dick Gregory's Natural Diet for Folks Who Eat: Cookin' with Mother Nature*, Gregory identifies his journey with the civil rights movement as instructive to his own diet:

> The philosophy of nonviolence which I learned from Dr. Martin Luther King, Jr., during my involvement in the civil rights movement was first responsible for my change in diet. . . . Under the leadership of Dr. King, I became totally committed to nonviolence, and I was convinced that nonviolence meant opposition to killing in any form. I felt the commandment

"Though shall not kill" applied to human beings not only in their dealings with each other—war, lynching, assassination, murder and the like—but in their practice of killing animals for food or sport. . . . Violence causes the same pain, the same spilling of blood, the same stench of death, the same arrogant, cruel and brutal taking of life.[46]

Gregory credits Dr. Alvenia Fulton, whom he refers to as a "teacher in the 'ancient tradition,'" for helping him establish a healthful way of living.[47] Fulton—whose natural health food store, Fultonia, was an institution in the Englewood neighborhood on Chicago's South Side—introduced Gregory to the benefits of fasting. It was at the Fultonia Health Food Center that Gregory broke his first fast, on January 9, 1968. As a brief aside, given this project's investment in twenty-first-century nostalgic iterations of the black radical past, I would be remiss not to mention the revival of Alvenia Fulton's health project that has emerged in concert with a series of redevelopment projects in the Englewood community. The organization Fultonia, named after Fulton's landmark store, is now a collective of health advocates and urban cyclists who are committed to reestablishing Fulton's legacy through a series of meatless communal dinners and collective "Friday fasts" as well as health programs, particularly urban cycling.[48]

Fulton introduced Gregory to fasting, which he had done previously only in the form of hunger strikes to protest the Vietnam War, yet Gregory's dietary politics were part and parcel of a broader resistance to American institutionalism: for Gregory, healthy living and black political consciousness were inextricable. His defiance was explicit in the naming of his oldest child, Gregory: "His birth certificate does not read 'Gregory Gregory,' but rather simply 'Gregory.' In the American system, whose computers, bureaucracy and institutional requirements *demand* two names to function, my son Gregory is a symbol of independence of the built-in entanglements which predetermine the destiny of the 'two-namers' in a controlled society." Similarly, he named his first daughter "Miss" so that people would be forced to address her as "Miss Gregory." He chose this name because "racial hangups in the United States made it difficult for some white folks to call a black woman 'Miss' and a black man 'Mister.'"[49]

In the pages of his book, Gregory applauds the Black Power–era ideology that encouraged African Americans to appreciate their natural beauty and, in particular, to stop processing their hair (hence the popularity of the afro). However, he is critical of the fact that Black Power politics start and stop at the socioeconomic level and fail to account for the physiological.

He credits the arbiters of the Black Power movement for "telling black folks to take pride in their blackness and be as Black and as Beautiful as Mother Nature intended them to be," yet he is disappointed that "most black folks decided to go 'natural' in every phase of their life except diet."[50] Arguing that soul food "seems to have survived the period of Reconstruction in a way political power for black folks did not," Gregory urges African Americans to extend their politics to dietary concerns.[51] There are many moments in Gregory's narrative in which he seems baffled by what he perceives as black people's resistance to changing their eating habits. By invoking humor, science, and anecdotal experience, Gregory advocates a healthy diet not simply for the maintenance of one's own body but interprets acts like growing an afro and engaging in social protest as dimensions of black radicalism. But he also makes the case that nothing is more radical than (literally) internalizing those politics. He goes so far as to implicate black people in working against their own best interests by not adhering to a healthful diet: "One of the tragedies is that the very folks in the black community who are most sophisticated in terms of the political realities in this country are nonetheless advocates of 'soul food.' They will lay down a heavy rap on genocide in America with regard to black folks, then walk into a soul food restaurant and help the genocide along."[52] Despite the parity between Gregory's dietary proscriptions and that of the NOI, he makes little reference to Muhammad's *How to Eat to Live*. A reasonable assumption for this absence would be the disparate nature of their politics as it relates to food. While Muhammad deployed the rhetoric of black nationalism in setting forth his dietary guidelines for members of the NOI, Gregory's path takes a decidedly integrationist bent.

Though Gregory was clearly at odds with American imperialism, at home and abroad, he saw the promise and possibility of the United States. In the same way that Gregory advanced a natural diet for black Americans as a full commitment to the health of the individual body and the health of the race, he extended the metaphor of purification to include the national body, which he claimed was in desperate need of cleansing:

> Just as individual Americans need to realize the beauty and marvel of their own bodies and clean out their systems, the national body must realize that its own system needs cleaning. America needs to go on a long purifying fast to realize it has one of the most beautiful systems the world has ever known—the United States Constitution—if Americans would only treat that system with respect and allow it to work as it was intended. And that

realization and practice will only come when individual Americans start treating their own bodies with respect, cleaning both body and mind, and tuning in to the Universal Wisdom of Mother Nature.[53]

The notion that food is often a way to establish and assert a political consciousness is not new. Wallach notes that "although Gregory's strict fruitarianism inspired few wholesale converts, his commitment to maintaining the physical health of the black community was widespread in nationalist circles in the late 1960s and early 1970s."[54] What I hope to have made clear thus far is the centrality of food to the emergence of a black radical consciousness. Gregory's admonition that nutrition and diet remained the least realized aspects of black revolutionary thought is also reflected in the larger cultural and scholarly discourse around the Black Power movement. He signaled in his book a hope (and a call) for the US nation to engage in what might today be called mindful living. His vision reflects an integrationist ideal, which many would consider the antithesis of a black radical agenda. Yet, Gregory remains explicit in referencing the particularized racial, social, economic, and dietary experiences and needs of black folks.

Muhammad and Gregory highlight the connection between black resistance to white hegemony and the consumption (and rejection) of particular foods. Though their dietary programs are distinct, Muhammad and Gregory both offer a clear foundation from which to interpret the contemporary resurgence of black radicalism within the culinary arts. Contemporary black chefs are similarly attempting to create a food revolution in the United States—one that acknowledges and celebrates the Africanist origins of the "American" diet. Through their aesthetic creations, these chefs draw upon yet complicate the dietary dictums of the black culinary past to reflect new forms of black radicalism in the present.

The "Original Green People"

While chefs Bryant Terry and Marcus Samuelsson come from distinct geographic and cultural backgrounds, they share the ambition, in Bryant's words, to "move Afro-diasporic food from the margins closer to the center of our collective culinary consciousness," or as Samuelsson succinctly notes, "to capture African cool."[55] In a 2014 interview, Terry conveyed his project of taking "[black people] back to the root and really reminding us that people of African descent—African people—are the original green people, the original farm-to-table and garden-to-table people."[56] If eating, as Elspeth Probyn notes, is yet another act of identity formation, then cooking or creating dishes for others to consume reads as an act of agency or, perhaps more precisely, of articulation. In *Carnal Appetites*, Probyn extends Stuart Hall's conception of *articulation* to discuss how the act of eating "conjoins us in a network of the edible and inedible, the human and non-human, the animate and the inanimate." Significantly, she asserts that we are "'articulated' subjects, the products of the integration of past practices and structures," but "also always 'articulating' subjects: through our enactment of practices we reforge new meanings, new identities for ourselves."[57] Probyn's analysis denotes the point I want to make here concerning how Bryant's and Samuelsson's culinary projects reflect alternative formulations of black subjectivity. Their respective remixes of African culinary traditions recall a shared ancestral past as well as to a more recent African American history in which the politics of food have been intimately and inextricably connected to the formation and articulation of a distinct twenty-first-century black identity.

It is not too often that cookbook readers are invited to peruse a copy of Jamaica Kincaid's *A Small Place* (1988) while preparing a recipe for corn broth, or to pick up George Jackson's *Soledad Brother* (1970) while making millet and sweet potato porridge, but such is the case with chef Bryant Terry's 2014 *Afro-Vegan: Farm-Fresh African, Caribbean, and Southern Flavors Remixed*. In addition to suggested readings, his cookbook also provides a sound track with each recipe, a little something-something to give the home cook a sense of inspiration and history. Admittedly, when I first embarked on this study, I wondered, "What the hell does 'Putting Up Resistance' (a song by Beres Hammond) have to do with All-Green Spring Slaw?" Some connections were a bit more self-explanatory; "Butter" by A Tribe Called Quest is paired with Maple-Plantain Spread. But some of the more esoteric accompaniments do not so much dictate a clear relation as tempt the senses. If a sommelier is someone who has a keen sense of the synergy that exists between wine and food, then Terry's literary and sonic complements are meant to produce a similar dynamic response. Though Terry does not tie his approach to food within a black nationalist framework, he offers a persuasive argument that links modern-day veganism to a project of racial and ancestral reclamation. Specifically, Terry delineates a connection to an African past via the Black Panthers' revival of that past. Further, his inclusion of music, films, and books demonstrates the extent to which he constructs his culinary practices within a broader contemporary black aesthetic context, one that is interwoven with other artistic practices that feed into and animate his own culinary projects. The term *remix* in Terry's book title proves useful in considering his appropriation of black radical history to produce a more neoteric inflection of post-black identity. With respect to sound recording, the *Oxford English Dictionary* offers the following definition of *remix*: "a reinterpretation or reworking, often quite radical, of an existing music recording, typically produced by altering the rhythm and instrumentation."[58] The concept of nostalgia figures prominently here in that Terry's remix emerges as a wistful reminiscing toward multiple and diverse black pasts, which he then deploys as a point of departure for his own culinary creations.

Terry is perhaps best known for his accessible and ethnically centered approach to a vegan diet. Not only does Terry credit veganism with providing the best possible means through which to heal African American communities—which suffer disproportionately from health diseases that are attributable to poor dietary habits, including hypertension and heart disease—but he also affirms that a plant-based diet allows black people to reconnect to their African heritage. However, the nostalgia to which I refer is not for an "authentic" African self but for a more recent black historical moment, the Black Power era. Terry made this connection himself in a 2014 interview when discussing his time as a graduate student in history at New York University, where he researched "the activism of the Black Panthers in the late 60s and 70s in the San Francisco Bay area that looked at the intersection of poverty, malnutrition, and institutional racism." The organization—most readily known for its black leather jackets, rifles, and berets—made access to food (albeit not specifically vegan food) part of its famous ten-point platform: "We want land, bread, housing, education, clothing, justice and peace." To encourage these ends, the Panthers established the Free Breakfast Program for children in 1969. Lauded as one of the most successful outcomes of the Black Panther Party, the breakfast program became a keen example of the Black Panthers' politics of the everyday. During the course of his research, Terry "discovered that a number of the Panthers had become vegans" and that "some of the sites in the Bay area serving breakfast were serving vegan foods."[59] Bryant makes an important linkage between black nationalist ideals and a natural diet.

In a 1969 essay titled "On Meeting the Needs of the People," Black Panther Eldridge Cleaver drew the distinct connection between good nutritional health and social justice: "Black children who go to school hungry each morning have been organized into their poverty. This is liberation in practice."[60] Nik Heynen has read the Panthers' breakfast program as an "emancipatory political agenda based in direct action."[61] The Free Breakfast Program was a symbolic and material practice of black nationalism that functioned as a model of communal self-sufficiency, sharply countering forces of structural racism. Similarly, Terry's activist work has included exposing children to the world of organic farming, farmer's markets, and community gardens, and getting them off the "industrial treadmill of eating chips, candy, sodas, fast food." Terry, having been inspired by the Free Breakfast Program, sought to expose children to "a visceral, practical way to help them think more about the politics and ideas of food."[62]

In addition, Terry's imperatives resonate with Elijah Muhammad's, though perhaps not as vehemently, in that he links a vegan diet to a larger notion of black subjectivity. He notes in his book that "as Afro-diasporic people have strayed from our traditional foods and adopted a Western diet, our health has suffered,"[63] and he uses nostalgic references both to resist the "whitening" of what is considered to be the healthy American diet and to enact a mode of cultural and ethnic reparation. One key notion that distinguishes Terry's philosophy from his black culinary forebears is that Terry advocates a natural diet to "reclaim our ancestral knowledge and embrace our culinary roots."[64] Whereas Muhammad and Gregory discuss the benefits of a plant-based diet in contrast to soul food, Terry understands veganism as the original soul food. He maintains an activist approach to food, concentrating primarily on issues of food justice, specifically "the basic human right to fresh, safe, affordable, and culturally appropriate food in all communities."[65] However, Terry's emphasis on food justice is tied to an understanding of what it means to be black in the twenty-first century. Terry uses his "remixed" African diasporic recipes as the canvas on which his formulation of a twenty-first-century black subjectivity is captured. Food, for Terry, is part and parcel of a larger political and aesthetic endeavor that conveys the insistence and complexity of blackness in the contemporary moment.

In American popular culture, concepts like organic, farm-to-table, vegan, and sustainable have become largely synonymous with a particular type of hipster whiteness. Andrea Freeman notes that "many African Americans and Latina/os view the healthy food movement, including vegan, vegetarian, raw food, and macrobiotic diets, as well as farmers' markets, as driven by and intended for white people."[66] This relationship is further buttressed by the "conscious capitalism" of Whole Foods, which, despite its efforts to open stores in food deserts and poor communities, is indelibly associated with a kind of bourgeois existence that is barely attainable by the middle class.[67] As Rachel Slocum notes, "While the ideals of healthy food, people and land are not intrinsically white, the objectives, tendencies, strategies, the emphases and absences and the things overlooked in community food make them so."[68] Terry argues that alternative food practices like farmers' markets, food co-ops, veganism, and sustainability are an inherent part of black cultural heritage, and that they have been usurped from black people and then made economically inaccessible to an entire class of black folks. In an ironic twist, two popular vegan cookbooks—*Thug Kitchen: Eat Like You Give A F*ck* (2014) and *Cookin' Crunk: Eatin' Vegan in the Dirty South* (2012)—were at the center of a blogosphere debate regarding the authors' appropriation of black culture to make vegan eating seem "cool" (the authors of both cookbooks are white). Notably, Terry emerged as one of the most vocal critics of the cookbooks' authors. In a scathing piece for CNN, Terry wrote, "Whether or not the hipsters and health nuts charmed by Thug Kitchen realize this, vegetarian, vegan and plant-strong culture in the black experience predates pernicious thug stereotypes."[69] Thus, the privileged representation of veganism emerges in two predominant forms in mainstream American culture: as a symbol of bourgeois whiteness or as a form of cultural theft. Even in the wake of Black Lives Matter protests following the May 2020 murder of George Floyd, the authors of *Thug Kitchen* voiced their support of the movement yet remained both tone deaf and ahistorical. In a statement posted to their website, the authors admitted that the name of their brand "has been twisted, particularly by our president, who has used the word 'thug' in a weaponized and racist way." In the meantime, the authors promised to "reflect on how we can best move forward to have our brand name better reflect our values."[70] As Terry observes:

> There is a notable failure to (1) acknowledge that the modern world is indebted to ancient Africans for basic farming techniques and agricultural production methods; (2) appreciate the agricultural expertise (rice production), cooking techniques (roasting, deep-frying, steaming in leaves), and ingredients (black-eyed peas, okra, sesame, watermelon); and (3) recognize the centrality of African-diasporic people in helping define the tastes, ingredients, and classic dishes of the original modern global fusion cuisine—Southern food. You see, it is not enough to celebrate the food of the African diaspora without appreciating the *people* who gave birth to this rich culinary tradition.[71]

Terry's emphasis on *people* in the above passage points to the easy assimilation of foodstuffs normally associated with African and African

American culture, while vitriolic racism against black people endures. Further, Terry places black people at the very center of what is generally considered to be either white or racially neutral ways of cooking and eating. Essentially, he identifies the consciously convenient erasure of black people from the broader conversations surrounding African American foodways.

Writing about Food Network, Lisa Guerrero argues that this behemoth of food programming's "overarching predominance of a white upper-middle- and middle-class perspective . . . belies the network's implied belief that food is universal."[72] Guerrero adds that while "the network presents food as a language that everyone speaks and understands; . . . it is clear that the network is only interested in hearing a particular group of people, white middle-class *Americans*, speak it."[73] The popularity of the blog-turned-cookbook *Thug Kitchen* brings to bear one of many problematics with the way that veganism is represented by the mainstream. Critics of *Thug Kitchen* have referred to the authors' appropriation of black markers of identification as the "latest iteration of nouveau blackface."[74] In the case of *Thug Kitchen* and *Cookin' Crunk*, elements of black culture are deemed acceptable and even hip, but black people . . . not so much. This is only one example that underscores the significance of Terry's efforts with *Afro-Vegan*, in particular, to re-place African diasporic food and culture at the center of dialogues within national food media and to create a space of visible representation.

Freeman points to a catch-22 in the way that black folks have slipped through the cracks of the nation's broad culinary enterprises: "while food justice advocates have largely failed to embrace issues of race, class and other sites of oppression, social justice groups . . . rarely consider food oppression issues to be paramount." She argues that food oppression has the same deleterious effects as mass incarceration on black communities. Both issues are "forms of social control that successfully reduce the strength and numbers of besieged communities while placing the blame for this diminution squarely on the harmed individuals."[75] Through imprisonment, food-related illness, or death, both mass incarceration and food oppression "lead to the physical removal of black and brown bodies from public spaces, rendering them invisible to the mainstream."[76] The consequence of these factors is that black folks' contributions to American culture, particularly in a culinary sense, have gone virtually unrecognized. Even soul food, which had largely been the domain of the African American culinary experience, has slowly morphed into

"Southern cooking," represented by the likes of Paula Deen and Paul Prudhomme.[77]

The connection between the past and the present emerges as a fundamental impetus of *Afro-Vegan*. Terry wants to make black people aware of their own culinary heritage. He asserts, "people of African descent should honor, cultivate, and consume food from the African diaspora."[78] Thus, nostalgic impulses in his cookbooks are deliberate and strategic. Terry not only looks to an African historical past to devise new culinary creations, he also looks to the black radical past of the Black Power era by contextualizing these creations within a larger political tradition of black resistance to white hegemony—in this case, in the culinary world.

Afro-Culinary Interdisciplinarity

Terry made his Black Power–era influences explicit in a 2014 conversation with Julianne Hing for *ColorLines*, in which he shared the six books that inspired *Afro-Vegan*. Among them were *The Autobiography of Malcolm X* (1965), Toni Morrison's *The Bluest Eye* (1970), and Robin D. G. Kelley's *Race Rebels* (1994). While these texts do not speak explicitly to a culinary praxis, they do offer a sense of the political import of Terry's gastronomic project. For example, he credits Kelley's text with helping him "understand the political nature of seemingly apolitical acts like growing one's own food, cooking meals from scratch at home, and building community around the table," which Terry refers to as "crucial acts of rebellion and resistance." Terry rereads *The Autobiography of Malcolm X* "every few years," and he credits *The Bluest Eye* with giving him a clearer sense of the "impact of white supremacy on black minds, bodies and spirits."[79] Terry's brand of black consciousness is not only reminiscent of the culinary projects of Elijah Muhammad and Dick Gregory, but also formed by the same kind of political sensibilities that inspired these earlier figures. That Bryant looks to and engages Malcolm X, in particular, demonstrates the way in which a racial nostalgia is infused in his "remixed" culinary practices. Even Terry admits that his ideas around food and politics were originally conceived as an academic project but that he realized that writing a tome on the subject "would not be as effective as writing actual recipes that gave people something practical and immediate to do."[80]

Terry's decision to write a cookbook rather than a "heavy intellectual book" characterizes his efforts to make tangible and accessible the relationship between food and emancipatory politics. Given his admitted points of influence, he brings to the culinary table a politics of food that resounds deeply with the motives and imperatives of the Black Power movement, and he strategically incorporates this radical past in his twenty-first-century conceptualizations of food politics.

I would like to examine what Terry "does" and what he encourages readers of *Afro-Vegan* to do in the process of exploring his recipes. I realized quite quickly that I would have to follow the recipes, listen to the music, and read the text in order to get the full range of experience that Terry's book offers. So, I picked one: Fresh Corn Grits with Swiss Chard and Roasted Cherry Tomatoes. Terry's recommendations to accompany this recipe are the song "Solace" (1909) by Scott Joplin and the book *The New Jim Crow: Mass Incarceration in the Age of Colorblindness* (2010) by Michelle Alexander. The inspiration for this recipe, Terry explains, is Juneteenth, "the oldest known celebration commemorating the ending of slavery in the United States." Specifically, the dish is meant to be served at a "Juneteenth sweet and savory brunch."[81] Bryant's acknowledgment and remembrance of Juneteenth emerges here as a moment of afro-nostalgia. While the origins of Juneteenth may not have been in resistance to white authority, present-day iterations of this celebration use the holiday to continue the conversation about slavery and reparations.[82] Within this frame, Terry's evocation of Juneteenth is an example of the way that "the past is remade in the image of the present or a desired future."[83]

The juxtaposition of freedom from slavery and Alexander's argument in *The New Jim Crow* that African Americans have become imbricated in a modern-day form of slavery—the prison-industrial complex—begs for a consideration of the continuity between the black historical past and the present, as well as the many ways in which structural and institutional forms of black subjugation evolve over time. While Terry implores readers to celebrate Juneteenth, he simultaneously acknowledges and encourages those enjoying their fare of corn grits and chard to consider what black freedom means now. Joplin's "Solace," made famous globally as the sound track to the 1973 film *The Sting*, nails the nostalgic impulses summoned by Juneteenth yet channels the grim reality that Alexander's work reveals. Joshua Rifkin, a pianist and Joplin scholar, describes Joplin's "Heliotrope Bouquet" as "balanced flawlessly in an emotional fault line between forlorn melancholy and aching wistfulness, this piece wears smiles you only see once they have already begun to fade."[84] "Solace," arguably, creates a similar ambivalence. The composition strains to exude a joy that it never quite reaches. The corn grits recipe (which is delectable, I may add) almost becomes an afterthought in this mélange of sound and sorrow, though I would imagine that Terry's readers, especially those of African descent, cannot help but associate grits with a comforting childhood memory. Terry's recipe, along with his reading and listening recommendations, produces an intellectual and sensory experience of the continuity of black negotiations with freedom, agency, and citizenship.

Terry's project is, in many respects, a throwback. His relationship and indebtedness to the Black Power past is clear and straightforward. His work is indelibly characteristic of the post-soul generation, which draws on predecessors from the civil rights and Black Power past to understand and articulate the meaning of blackness in the contemporary moment. Terry's not-so-subtle afro-centricity is reminiscent of the Black Power rhetoric and resistance to white hegemony and Western aesthetics. His fundamental argument is that black culture *is* American culture, despite the centuries of historical erasure and amnesia that effectively detached African Americans from their own rich, gastronomic legacy. While Malcolm X and the Black Panthers have notably influenced Terry's food justice projects, he also clearly aligns himself with post-soul intellectuals who are equally invested in remapping the terrain of black culture and politics for the twenty-first century. Alexander's *The New Jim Crow* is but one example of Terry's engagement with other black public intellectuals; *Afro-Vegan* also features Mark Anthony Neal's *Looking for Leroy* (2013), Imani Perry's *More Beautiful and More Terrible* (2011), and Tera Hunter's *To 'Joy My Freedom* (1997), among other recommended readings. His intertextuality with the post-soul intelligentsia undergirds a conscientious attempt to link food practices to radical new ways of expressing black subjectivity in the twenty-first century.

The New Harlem Renaissance

Terry's indebtedness to the Black Power past in the formulation of his own post-black culinary aesthetic resonates throughout his opus. Chef Marcus Samuelsson's racial nostalgia, in contrast to Terry's, is decidedly more circuitous. The November 2008 issue of *Food and Wine* featured an article titled "The New Harlem Renaissance," highlighting the easy friendship and culinary collaboration between Samuelsson, owner of the Red Rooster restaurant, and Thelma Golden, director of the Studio Museum of Harlem. The article in *Food and Wine* details Golden and Samuelsson's plans for an elaborate dinner party to celebrate the publication of his cookbook *The Soul of a New Cuisine* (2006), which pays homage to the African food cultures that Samuelsson believes have gone virtually ignored

in Western culinary spheres. Among the invited guests were famed artist
Kara Walker, jazz pianist Jason Moran, and choreographer Bill T. Jones, the
last two of whom were "touring with new works and in the past six months
[had] been in more than 45 cities, from Rio de Janeiro to Melbourne."[85]

This august group was assembled at a gathering cohosted by Golden,
who is, perhaps, most well known in academic circles for her coinage
of the term *post-black*, in reference to the 2001 *Freestyle* exhibition at
the Studio Museum of Harlem. Golden, along with artist Glenn Ligon,
defined post-black artists as "adamant about not being labeled 'black' artists, though their work was steeped, in fact, deeply interested in redefining
complex notions of blackness."[86] Indeed, many artists featured in the exhibition—including Ligon, Rico Gatson, Rashid Johnson, and Susan Smith-
Pinelo, among others—have been less (if at all) invested in representing
the celebratory notes of blackness and more intent on signifyin' tropes
of blackness through various forms of satire and play.[87] After Golden's
iconic exhibition, the expression post-black quickly morphed from merely
describing a singular artistic event to characterizing the experiences of
an entire generation of black people who came of age in the post–civil
rights era. This generation is marked by the critical distance from its civil
rights forebears (who are most often and most directly their parents),
at the same time that its members have benefited both materially and
socially from the activist struggles that exemplified the civil rights and
Black Power eras. However, what truly distinguishes this generation is its
desire to live outside what had previously been the rather tight strictures
of racial allegiances and expectations.[88] In fact, the most common strain
in post-black works is the expression of a desire to exist as an individual
composed of many distinct attributes. Blackness, in this case, operates
within a vast sea of subjectivity.

The shared sensibilities of the artists in attendance at Golden and Samuelsson's dinner party reflect a post-black/post-soul aesthetic in which the
concept of blackness has been negotiated and renegotiated both as a site of
subjectivity and as an aesthetic object. But the intention of this fellowship
was not to provide a discourse about visual or musical art but to familiar-
ize guests with Samuelsson's take on contemporary African cuisine. To set
the mood, Samuelsson played a CD entitled *Afrikya* that includes "Cape
Verdean, Arabic, Afro-Cuban and Bahian sounds." Similar to Samuelsson's
cookbook, "the CD mirrors the cultural exchanges between Africa and
the rest of the world—Europe, Latin America, the Middle East, Asia."[89]
The menu that Samuelsson prepared—"crunchy okra in a roasted sweet

potato salad tossed with wilted spinach and tangy capers" and "quince *sambal* served with lamb"—is much less a straightforward presentation of traditional African fare and more so a diasporic riff that echoes his own complex travels.[90] For Samuelsson, who was born in Ethiopia and adopted by Swedish parents at the age of two, the project of remixing African cuisine is both personal and professional, driven by his desire to reclaim the African "home" he lost as a child and by an urge to "chase flavors," a phrase Samuelsson frequently invokes to describe his never-ending quest to create a fundamentally "new" cuisine.

Afro-nostalgia operates in funky ways in this dinner party scene: the unconventional African fare, the remixed diasporic mood music, and the event's moniker, "the New Harlem Renaissance," are all indicative of a complex engagement with different forms and figurations of blackness. Samuelsson's distinct imperative to revise and elevate African cuisine reveals the extent to which his culinary style evokes a narrative of post-blackness that hinges on nostalgic allusions to a multiplicity of flavors and homelands. His aesthetic and culinary mission is to productively distort history and tradition. Using Samuelsson's memoir, *Yes, Chef* (2012), as a framework, I examine the nostalgic impulses of post-blackness vis-à-vis food culture, specifically the ways in which taste, space, and subjectivity materialize as a function of both real and imagined histories, homes, and flavors. The nostalgia evinced in Samuelsson's memoir is not the oft-derided futile sentiment that disables the subject from progressive movement or action. In fact, Samuelsson's memoir provides good evidence to defy such critiques; nostalgia is front and center in *Yes, Chef*, but not as a commemoration of what was; rather, it is a portal to contemporary modes of being that are in process and in flux. Nostalgic invocations of food become the medium through which, in this case, racial and ethnic identities are forged, reimagined, and remixed to convey a post-blackness that speaks to the future of the racial imaginary and the unleashing of static and seemingly fixed structures of blackness. While Terry's culinary aesthetic provides a rather seamless through line with Black Power–era food practices, Samuelsson brings to this conversation a diasporic sensibility that forges a nostalgic nexus between a series of homelands, both real and imagined. The "new" Black Power positionality from which Terry draws is an attempt to "return"—if only culturally and culinarily—to an African homeland he has never known. Samuelsson's food mission is also guided by a similar desire, but his return functions less as a site of the imagination and more as a recollection of lost remembrances from a traumatic past.

Chasing Flavors

In Samuelsson's case, the act of "chasing flavors" emerges as a pursuit of a space with which to identify and reconcile, though not collapse, the collectivity of cultural, ethnic, and racial experiences by which he has been constituted. Through the manipulation of food and flavor, the chef, as both a historian and an architect of taste, self-fashions a culinary style. With Samuelsson, such self-fashioning is enabled through a nostalgic reclamation of the past. His role as a chef grants him agency with respect to how that past is internalized, psychically and physiologically. What we have in *Yes, Chef* is a delicate push and pull between past and present. Samuelsson's imperative to engage a range of personal, ethnic, and cultural histories in his food designs is propelled by the seemingly contradictory desire to fashion an entirely new breadth of tastes, moving our culinary sensibilities forward. In this way, Samuelsson's project as a chef exemplifies the inherent value and potentiality of nostalgia, not only in terms of the acts of creation manifested through food preparation but also in terms of the series of identifications that emerge in the process. In Samuelsson's case, his shifting set of geographies and corresponding identifications collude to produce an afro-nostalgic sensibility that departs from what Michelle Wright has conceptualized as a "Middle Passage epistemology" that draws a linear narrative of "our cultural practices and expressions, our politics and social sensibilities, to the historical experience of slavery in the Americas and the struggle to achieve full human suffrage in the West."[91] Samuelsson's diasporic blackness challenges this epistemic logic in ways that enable us to consider afro-nostalgia's malleability and simultaneity as a site of racial and ethnic recovery and production, and it animates the diasporic nature of African American foodways. In his oeuvre, post-black culinary praxis is not simply a recuperative project to locate what was, but an intersection of space-times that, as Michelle Wright points out, "produce diverse but coherent narratives" of blackness.[92]

Like Terry, Samuelsson endeavors to shift culinary paradigms to reflect the perspective of the Global South. As one of the few prominent black celebrity chefs, Samuelsson seeks to acclimate Western palates to cuisines that are more reflective of the world they inhabit, specifically by reintroducing Americans to their African origins through the production of a "new African" cuisine. Without question, French-style cooking techniques serve as the gold standard in the culinary world. But as Zilkia

Janer notes, such superiority was only made possible by the "subordination of indigenous and many other culinary knowledges."[93] For Janer, the "belief that knowledge of French technique enables cooks to prepare any world cuisine is based on the assumption that other cuisines lack their own techniques or that such techniques are expendable. Academics, cooks and diners alike seem resistant to revise the myth of the superiority of French cuisine in spite of the influence of postcolonial and postmodern analyses and their critique of Eurocentric metanarratives."[94] Samuelsson's desire to expose the American palate to a new African cuisine was inspired by a trip back to his homeland, Ethiopia, at the age of twenty-eight. About this visit, he notes that "on the plane from New York to Addis, I was so aware that for the first time in my adult life, I was traveling not as a chef, chasing flavors—but as an orphan, chasing history."[95] Despite the fact that Samuelsson makes a distinction between his journey as a chef and the journey to locate his past, the two remain interrelated. His story describes how cuisine, like his own subjectivity, (im)migrates. His goal has since been to "communicate the sense of a vibrant, sophisticated Africa."[96]

Fittingly, Terry offers a shout-out to *Yes, Chef* as a complement to his recipe for Berbere-Spiced Black-Eyed Pea Sliders. Berbere is a key ingredient in Ethiopian cuisine and consists of a blend of spices including cardamom, fenugreek, cumin, allspice, and chilies, and it is a key point of nostalgia for Samuelsson. The memoir opens with Samuelsson's imagining of the mother whose face he cannot remember. Drawing on his sister's memories of their mother's sacrifice—walking miles to a hospital so they could all be treated for tuberculosis, navigating the crowded space so her children could see a doctor, and then finally succumbing to the disease herself—Samuelsson wistfully attempts to access his sister's memories and re-locate himself in a past of which he has no memory. It is also fitting that Samuelsson begins his memoir with this absence as this void guides one of his foremost objectives as a chef: to reconnect with his homeland and (symbolically) his biological mother, through food. In the opening pages of the narrative, Samuelsson writes, "I have never seen a picture of my mother, but I know how she cooked. For me, my mother is *berbere*, an Ethiopian spice mixture."[97] His identification of berbere with his deceased mother structures his feelings of loss as well as the culinary process he undertakes in an attempt to recapture them both. Further, he notes, "I have taught myself the recipes of my mother's people because those foods are for me, as a chef, the easiest connection to the mysteries of who my mother was. Her identity remains stubbornly shrouded in the past, so I feed myself and the people I love the food that she made. But I cannot see her face."[98]

In an interesting riff on Jean Anthelme Brillat-Savarin's maxim, "Tell me what you eat and I'll tell you what you are," Samuelsson attempts to reconstruct the past and re-produce the self through the creation and consumption of food. This endeavor is a way to fill the void of his maternal loss and a sincere approach to reclaim some aspect of his shrouded past. Given that his mother died while he was young, he has no actual memory of the foods that she made. The nostalgic impulses of this scene operate entirely at the level of the imaginary. Ethiopian food becomes a synecdochic medium that enables the fantastical reconstruction of his maternal memory. Samuelsson describes time and again his desire to see his mother, either through gazing at his own image in the mirror or by using berbere. Inextricably tied to the search for his mother of whom no photograph exists is Samuelsson's own project of piecing together his history. The memoir begins with the recognition of his own fractured subjectivity that he can only try to reconcile through the invocation of his own imagination and the smell and taste of an indigenous spice mixture. In his discussion of the term *wei* or "flavor" in Chinese literary criticism, Eugene Eoyang briefly introduces the concept of *hui-wei*, which refers to "a recollection of previously encountered flavor."[99] For Samuelsson, berbere is this flavor, but *hui-wei* as described in the above scene has nothing to do with revisiting what he once knew; it is a matter of creating memories of a never-experienced past.

As Samuelsson acknowledges in *Yes, Chef*, his goal was never to create a cuisine that was "authentic" to a geographic locale, but rather to create something that was indicative of his own sense of authenticity, specifically his multiethnic, multicultural subjectivity.[100] However, given that his Ethiopian past is partially constructed in an imagined nostalgic fantasy, this authenticity is largely of his own making. The external pressure of authenticity—to make something or someone conform to a popular or accepted version of the "real"—is absent in this case though Samuelsson maintains the agency as a chef to construct what is real on his own terms. As Inga Bryden notes, "nostalgia makes way for adaptation and an acknowledgement that food is provisional, always on the move, and that recipes are not perfect."[101] In Samuelsson's case, nostalgia makes adaptation possible. With no concrete remembrance to romanticize, nostalgia emerges as a catapulting force that allows Samuelsson to produce innovative recipes in an attempt to both recapture a lost past and fashion himself anew. Samuelsson's emphasis on "chasing" is imperative here as it signifies a consistent refusal of stasis in terms of both food and race. The act of "chasing flavors" is inextricably tied to Samuelsson's own sense of ethnic and racial mobility.

Eoyang notes, "for the Chinese critic, the distinctiveness of a work lies in that quality called flavor . . . the mark of true savor lies in the authenticity with which the writer expresses his feelings."[102] "Flavor" and "savor" are terms that resonate for Samuelsson in similar ways. In Samuelsson's case, the fragmented multiculturalism by which he is constituted align with the processes he undergoes in order to construct a "new" cuisine. His culinary creations reflect not only technical skill but, more importantly, his interiority. Particularly useful is Eoyang's idea that "savor" or "flavor" both "establishes [the] original character" of a work and "makes it new."[103] The simultaneity of the past and present as the "flavor"-defining element of the poem, for example, is an expression of the possibilities inherent in nostalgia and delineates a constructive relationship between these terms. Nostalgia is not simply a concept that suggests a longed-for past; it is a gateway to future experience. An attempt to locate that quality we can't quite put our finger on, the subtle indetermination of "some particular ingredient," forms the core of Samuelsson's journey as a chef and also speaks to how important nostalgia is to the formation of his identity.

While Samuelsson documents his experiences of racism—growing up as an African child in Gothenburg, Sweden, and coming of age in a predominately white culinary industry—those moments are presented to the reader as mere inconveniences rather than as identity-forming experiences. In a direct address to his audience, Samuelsson notes, "it's important that you know that growing up black in Sweden is different than growing up black in America. I have no big race wounds."[104] In a 2012 interview, Samuelsson admitted, "I'm an American chef. I'm American. I live here. I love being here. But, of course, it is different. A black man's journey is different."[105] Though he identifies as black, his blackness is unlike that of black Americans; yet his experience as a "black man" in America is also distinct from the "journey" of (white) Americans. His reference to the race wounds suffered by many black Americans identifies racism as both a traumatic experience and a traumatic memory, something with which he cannot readily identify, although his memoir is peppered with accounts of the racism he has experienced through his life. For example, Samuelsson recalls that a "little Sambo had long been used to advertise *negerboll* cookies in Sweden and [he] felt a sense of dread anytime [he] saw a boy open a package of them at lunch because [he] knew that the wrapper would soon be coming [his] way."[106] And yet, Samuelsson characterizes such racist acts as random incidents rather than formative experiences. Since Samuelsson did not grow up in the United States or in any territory indelibly marked by the specter of slavery, he appears relatively unscathed from the racial trauma that African Americans bear.

While Samuelsson's European blackness allows him to escape black American race wounds, his decision to make New York his home was due to the perceived lack of possibilities available to raced and ethnic subjects in Europe. He notes, "My decision [to move to New York] was made when I saw that there was a black Other—there was David Dinkins, mayor of New York. There was a black middle class, upper middle class. I didn't see that in Europe anywhere. In Europe I couldn't be anything but a black cook working for somebody. Which was fine, but my inspiration was to own, to be the chef."[107] In New York, Samuelsson was able to use as a model multiple instances of black achievement and success in order to craft his own narrative of possibility. The expansiveness of blackness as it played out in an American context enabled him to realize the various ways in which his distinct "flavor" of African Americanness did not have to be subverted to a more revered and respected (French) European culinary tradition. By maintaining his own flavor, or *wei*, he was free to create dishes that were expressive of his own cultural and culinary aesthetic.

At first glance, it might seem curious that Samuelsson, a global chef and a global citizen, has chosen to call the 3.8 square miles that constitute Harlem "home." However, he notes, "I spent so much of my life on the outside that I began to doubt that I would ever truly be in with any one people, any one place, any one tribe. But Harlem is big enough, diverse enough, scrappy enough, old enough, and new enough to encompass all that I am and all that I hope to be. After all that traveling, I am, at last, home."[108] The notion of home is, of course, fraught within the context of immigrant or diasporic subjects. While it is tempting to read Samuelsson's journey as a chef and as a black subject within the framework of immigrant and diasporic experience, his journey lacks the explicit sense of dislocation or nebulousness that often structures such narratives. Instead, Samuelsson appears entirely at ease with his ability to claim a psychic and geographic space of his own, even if this space is, in part, constructed through a largely imagined nostalgic sensibility. In fact, his movements have enabled him to choose a home as yet another site of self-conscious identification. The space in which he chooses to identify becomes as central to his subjectivity as the cultural, racial, ethnic, and culinary identifications he incorporates over the course of his life. Samuelsson's Harlem restaurant, Red Rooster, serves as the cultural and social space through which Samuelsson merges his global experiences with his localized identity. In a 2011 *New York Times* review of Red Rooster, Sam Sifton observed,

> There were four elderly black women in hats at Red Rooster Harlem the other night, across the aisle from a group of white men who had come north to 125th Street by subway. Also present were a mixed-race family sharing apple pie, a stroller beside them; an Asian same-sex couple, drinking wine; and mixed-gender black couples eating Swedish meatballs. Above them all was a Philip Maysles painting depicting the artist Norman Rockwell staring into a mirror and painting a portrait of himself—as Ruby Bridges, the African American girl who integrated an all-white elementary school in New Orleans in 1960.[109]

The image Sifton paints in this moment further exemplifies the nostalgic riffs Samuelsson engages to collapse the present and the past. Maysles's painting, *Self-Portrait of Norman Rockwell as Ruby Bridges* (2008), evokes Rockwell's *The Problem We All Live With* (1964), which speaks to the collective tragedy of segregation and its attendant violence and, as Maysles's painting represents, the complicity of everyday citizens in that everyday tragedy. By collapsing the figures of Ruby Bridges and Norman Rockwell, Maysles's work reinforces the idea that racism remains a "problem we all live with," even on a psychic level. Inspired by the question, "to what degree have we been able to transcend those same racial issues today?"[110] Maysles's painting suggests that race and racism are still very much operative in the day-to-day lives of America's raced and ethnic citizens. And yet, the "problem" in *Self-Portrait of Norman Rockwell as Ruby Bridges* appears to be the failure of a liberal whiteness to contend with its (unconscious) complicity and reproduction. Specifically critiquing white studio artists, Maysles sets out to "articulate the way in which White masculinity is both affirmed and challenged through contradictory feelings towards its perceived Black other."[111] Maysles's painting is less an interpretation of the larger problem of racism that Ruby Bridges's image signifies than a meditation on the racial unconscious. Through this act of resignification, Maysles engages in his own memory project by challenging a normative and seemingly objective view of historical representation. The image also subverts romantic remembrances of the civil rights movement as a time now passed. While little black girls may no longer need to be escorted to school by the National Guard, the racial problems of today remain pernicious. Rockwell's painting externalizes "the problem we all live with," while Maysles's painting considers the extent to which the white artist is also part of that problem. In his 1953 essay "Stranger in the Village," James Baldwin wrote that "at the root of the American Negro problem is the necessity of the American white man to find a way of living with the Negro in order to be able to live with himself."[112] It is this dilemma that Maysles evokes at the level of the aesthetic through his representation of Rockwell, and that he provokes on a broader scale concerning the conditions under which racial transcendence would be possible (or even desirable).

The scene that Sifton observed at Red Rooster seems to offer a positive response to this question of racial transcendence: the presence of the "four elderly black women in hats," the "mixed-race family sharing apple pie," and the "Asian same-sex couple," all sharing together in this space, speaks to the degrees of racial and social progress that have been made since 1960 when Bridges entered William Frantz Elementary School. The scene exemplified by Maysles's painting is a deft reminder that our present condition is only made possible by that dark and turbulent past, and that the trauma of racism and segregation remains ever present in our contemporary lives, yet Sifton's description of Red Rooster is a vision of a post-racial fantasy.

Samuelsson's project almost paradigmatically invokes a post-soul/post-black artistic endeavor through the strategic deployment of black historical memory to create a new black aesthetic: "When I think about my purpose as a black chef, the mission seems clear: to document, to preserve, to present, to capture, to inspire, and to aspire. I'm documenting Harlem's history at the Rooster, preserving the fine history of African American cuisine while presenting it through my own unique Swedish-Ethiopian lens. I want to capture the imagination of New York's dining communities, inspire a new generation of chefs and I aspire, always, to make food that makes a difference."[113] Samuelsson's reference to himself as black evinces a diasporic consciousness that envelopes the identifications by which he is constituted—African American and Swedish Ethiopian. The desire to "chase flavors" through the process of accession and experimentation is analogous to the way that Samuelsson has, in many respects, self-constructed a transnational black subjectivity through a combination of accretion and mobility. Of course, Samuelsson (as self-described archivist of African American, specifically Harlem, culinary history) begs the question: what happens to black culinary nostalgia when it is embraced and evoked through a Swedish-Ethiopian lens? What Samuelsson's adoption of African American culinary nostalgia establishes most clearly is that nostalgia operates well outside the parameters of individual consciousness; we would do well to consider nostalgia as a social, cultural, historical (and even, political) production that has less to do with experience and more to do with feeling.

Nostalgia is, above all, a product of the imaginary, and it is generally invented to foster a sense of both self-continuity and community. Thus, in addition to Samuelsson's racial and ethnic identifications, his positionality as a refugee, an adoptee, and an immigrant speaks to a level of dislocation that could well facilitate the appropriation of any number of potential homelands. In a 2016 interview, Samuelsson acknowledged, "Being black, I had some ties to Harlem, and I felt connected to Harlem through the African-American history, but I didn't know it."[114] How does one feel connected to something that they do not know? The phrasing is peculiar in that Samuelsson identifies a connectedness to Harlem—whether through friendships, racial kinship, or perhaps a broadly black diasporic "tie"—but he admits to feeling "connected" to a place, a history, a people that he knew little about. Samuelsson's project to not only "document" but "aspire" in his engagement with African American food histories points to the ways that the "mission" he undertakes is a matter of both historical and affective reclamation.

Samuelsson's Red Rooster is more than just a restaurant. It is a site that enmeshes the sensibilities of the "old" Harlem Renaissance with the post-black imperatives of the "new."

> Just as Thelma transformed the Studio Museum into an institution that preserves the legacy of African American artists while promoting new voices in art from around the world, I dreamed of creating a similar space for food. I wanted Red Rooster to guard the history of black cooks in America while starting new conversations in food. During the long, doubt-filled, crazy-making months between my exit from Aquavit and the opening of Rooster, I had little more than a logo to show for my dream. But in my head, I used that time to immerse myself in the history of Harlem.[115]

Samuelsson's approach demonstrates the role that nostalgic history plays in shaping his post-black culinary praxis. His emphasis on "guard[ing] the history of black cooks in America" underscores the importance of preserving the past while at the same time "starting new conversations in food." This dynamism between preservation and generation also establishes nostalgia's creative possibilities. Further, by acknowledging Golden's influence on his approach to food as art and history, Samuelsson positions his work as part of a larger cultural and racial post-black aesthetic.

A New Harlem, a Dangerous Nostalgia

One can argue that Samuelsson's project of nostalgic restoration has come at a price. The release of *Yes, Chef* shortly after the opening of Red Rooster has been interpreted negatively as the neighborhood grapples with the perils of gentrification. Chef Eddie Huang publicly denounced Red Rooster in a 2012 article in the *Observer*, referring to *Yes, Chef* and Red Rooster as "an embarrassing exercise in condescension" rather than an act of "homage." Huang points to the expensive menu items and the thirty-day advance reservation policy as examples of why Red Rooster may be in Harlem but not of it. Referring to the memoir's persistent themes of dislocation and home, Huang writes that "in [Samuelsson's] quest for a home and a business success, he's doing a gross injustice to a neighborhood, a culture and a history that has already seen its share of struggles."[116] Samuelsson has since responded to critics who believe that his culinary venture in Harlem is yet another act of gentrification. His primary defense appears to be that Red Rooster "creates jobs," but Samuelsson is, admittedly, wrestling with the restaurant's positioning within a changing Harlem. In reference to gentrification, Samuelsson writes that "it bubbles in our stomach. . . . The worry is who Harlem's going to end up being."[117] In this book's introduction, I identified black conservative nostalgia as animating community restoration projects in urban areas, particularly Bronzeville in Chicago and Harlem in New York. These projects exemplify the dangerous manifestations of nostalgia that get deployed in the name of progress and renewal. Samuelsson's emphasis on creating jobs points to a difficult negotiation between Harlem's historic preservation and the creation of economic opportunities for its residents. But questions still remain: For whom does nostalgia "feel good" in circumstances such as this? Do the nostalgic imperatives of the "new" Harlem Renaissance require sacrificing the contemporary lived experience of Harlem in the now?

In his *New York Times* review of the restaurant, Sifton wrote that "the racial and ethnic variety in the vast bar and loft-like dining room are virtually unrivaled. The restaurant may not be the best to open in New York City this year (though the food is good). But it will surely be counted as among the most important. It is the rarest of cultural enterprises, one that supports not just the idea or promise of diversity, but diversity itself." He added that "it is a restaurant for a modern Harlem, a gentrifying one, a business at ease with well-heeled patrons of whatever skin tone, that has more in common with the integrated Savoy Ballroom of the 1940s than the whites-only Cotton Club or, for that matter, the tourist-trapped Sylvia's soul food restaurant down the block. There may be fried chicken on the menu (and oxtails, too). But there are some greatest hits from Aquavit as well, and a 2005 Brunello that costs $229."[118] In Sifton's review, gentrification is presented as a natural, inevitable, and (largely) positive force that facilitates "authentic" diversity and access to vintage wine. Within Sifton's assessment of the kind of community that Red Rooster makes possible is the assumption that such diversity is always desired or deemed desirable. His is a vision of the fantasy of post-racialism that marked Barack Obama's 2008 campaign (a fantasy swiftly eroded by Obama's presidency) and much of the cultural criticism in the mid- to late 1990s. The kind of racial and ethnic diversity that Sifton describes may be beautiful to see, especially if we are blind to the social violence that makes such visible diversity possible. Projects like Red Rooster enable the revival of Harlem as a lively cultural and aesthetic center, but at what cost?

Much has been written about gentrification projects that masquerade as historical and cultural restoration designed to return blighted communities to their "heyday."[119] At heart, these are nostalgic endeavors that privilege the economic benefits of the return to a presumably more glorious past over the immediate needs of the residents of these communities. It is difficult to distinguish Samuelsson's revamping of Red Rooster from other black restoration projects in which residents of these communities are not the ideal or, in many cases, desired consumers of new developments. The fact of gentrification both problematizes Samuelsson's nostalgic refashioning of Red Rooster and captures the complexities of nostalgic forms of remembrance; in this case, the ways that social and political realities intersect/interfere with the individual and intimate manifestations of nostalgia (loss of mother, loss of homeland, the sensory act of eating, etc.). These contradictions are not easily resolved, though the example of Samuelsson's re-conception of Red Rooster highlights the way that nostalgic sentiment—an intensely personal feeling—can operate in the social and political sphere with potentially dangerous and debilitating consequences.

Samuelsson takes up the subject of gentrification more explicitly in *The Red Rooster Cookbook: The Story of Food and Hustle in Harlem* (2016), published four years after *Yes, Chef*. In the book's preface, Samuelsson offers a poetic assessment of Harlem's shifting topography and the inevitability of gentrification in Harlem. But rather than read it as enhancing the diversity of Harlem, Samuelsson paints a neighborhood in transition and interprets Harlem's metamorphosis as a mix of pleasure and pain. He writes,

> Right now in Harlem authorship is on the move. This is ours, we tell each other. We have made it, chopped it, cooked it, played it. This is our story. . . . Right now and since forever, the world keeps telling us there's only room for one: Serena and that's it. Toni and that's it. I wonder if they can hear Harlem across the divide. *Come one, come all.* That's how we wrestle with urban renewal, black removal. The church ladies know this, and so do the hustlers. Right now in Harlem, we don't shy away from the ugly; we don't bow our heads to what's beautiful. We just keep asking, how does all this new shit fit with the old?[120]

This preface reveals the ways that the Red Rooster has become part of the broader conversation concerning gentrification in Harlem. The question "how does all this new shit fit with the old?" is a persistent one that evokes the urban dilemma in Harlem and extends to Chicago, Oakland, and New Orleans. This question also complicates Samuelsson's culinary project because it simultaneously erects and erases black nostalgic memories within this community. The racialized nostalgia that leads Samuelsson to create his restaurant disrupts and interrupts the nostalgic memories of those ("the church ladies," "the hustlers") who were there long before Samuelsson imagined Harlem as home.

But even "the old" cannot defend itself against time. Sifton's mention of the "tourist-trapped Sylvia's" offers yet another example of how nostalgia functions as a process of memorializing, and how this process reproduces models of black authenticity. Soul food or southern cuisine is most associated with black folks in the United States, and this is what made Sylvia's Restaurant of Harlem so notable when it opened in 1962. The 1960s are defined by the civil rights movement and Black Power, as well as their attendant (global) programs of protest, politics, and black liberation. The 1960s may also be defined as that moment when the concretization of blackness reached its apex. The sociopolitical imperative to construct visible symbols of black unity and empowerment consciously created the conditions of black authenticity. Sylvia's Restaurant functioned, then and now, as a space of black cultural authenticity. Sifton's reference to Sylvia's as tourist trapped indicates the extent to which the restaurant has ceased to exist as a hangout for Harlemites. In a touching memoriam to Sylvia Woods, who passed away in July 2012, the *New York Times* compiled the recollections of her family and famous New Yorkers who were also her customers. Half jokingly, David Paterson (former governor of New York) recalled, "One day I went in there, and it was all white and Japanese. I said to Sylvia: 'Hey, when are we going to have some affirmative action? When are you going to let some black people in here?'"[121]

Like most tourist destinations, Sylvia's is reminiscent of an older era, and it culminates any tour in Harlem: after snapping photos of the Apollo Theater and the Savoy Ballroom from the comforts of an air-conditioned bus, what better way to satiate one's appetite than scarfing down a plate of collard greens and fried chicken at a Harlem institution? Certainly, the reason that Sylvia's is tourist trapped is because it stands as a monument of black southern cuisine and of blackness more generally, its dishes consumable historical objects. To Paterson's point, Sylvia's serves as such an authentic marker of blackness that black folks no longer maintain a dominant presence there. It has become a place, for many, where blackness is no longer lived, but objectified. This is not meant to critique traditional soul food but rather to point to the difficulties of escaping the forces of memory and memorialization that often attend both public and intimate forms of nostalgia. Without constructing a reductive (and unnecessary) binary between Sylvia's Restaurant and Red Rooster, I want to make the point here that Samuelsson's imperative to "chase flavors" can also be read as an attempt to avoid the pitfalls of "monumentalizing" blackness. The kind of consistent motion that the term *chase* connotes is as much a culinary dictum as it is a strategic refusal to be pinned down and objectified as historical object. In considering how processes of monumentalizing versus chasing emerge in afro-nostalgic practices, I would suggest that contrary to the comforting fixed memories a place like Sylvia's contrives, the act of "chasing flavors" points to a multiplicity of origins or "homes" from which to fashion (or, perhaps more accurately, reflect) a contemporary black subjectivity, one that is not defined by or restricted to a Middle Passage epistemology but that "[radiates] outward from the individual and [achieves] meaning through the continual updating of intersecting interpellations in the 'now.'"[122] If we consider "chasing" to be the process of "continual updating," then Samuelsson's Afro-European engagement with a specifically African American nostalgic history only further elucidates the ways that both memory and blackness function as intersecting and ever-evolving sites of subjectivity.

Toward a Post-Black Culinary Praxis

The through line of Samuelsson's text is the notion of "chasing flavors," a phrase that he uses to describe his global culinary quest to locate new foods and spices and then combine them in unexpected ways to create a signature dish. "Flavor" emerges as something more local, culture specific, and distinctive, especially when contrasted with "taste," which is used to express an often-indescribable sensation we experience when food touches our tongues. Allen Weiss describes taste as the "sense by which we distinguish flavors; the discriminative activity according to which an individual likes or dislikes certain sensations; the sublimation of such value judgments as they pertain to art, and ultimately to all experience; and, by extension and ellipsis, taste implies good taste and style, established by means of an intuitive faculty of judgment."[123] In this sense, the origin of one's taste can be biological or psychological (or both), yet it is highly individual and, as Weiss notes, largely "intuitive." Undoubtedly, taste is indelibly tied to history and to memory, assuming that it is, like most aspects of our subjective being, constituted by and through a series of identifications and disidentifications over time. Weiss continues to observe that

> selectiveness of memory creates both identities and differences, so that culinary idiosyncrasy is in the vanguard of invention, and any adequate answer to the question of taste must entail a discourse of inclusion, not exclusion; of openness, experimentation and risk, not reticence, denial and reaction. Thus a recipe is not a canon, code or regulation, and the typicality or "authenticity" of a dish is but a range of possibilities, an indeterminate ideal, a pole of transformations. Taste is the mark of a personal singularity that draws its sense from collective tradition, and its possibilities from continual creativity. This is not to discount tradition, but merely to historicize it, in the context of a hedonism that is a moveable feast.[124]

Weiss's assessment of a recipe as "a range of possibilities, an indeterminate ideal" speaks directly to the relationship I posit in this chapter between Samuelsson, food, nostalgia, and post-blackness. The ever-shifting nature of taste evinces similar processes of memory and subjectivity that form the core of Samuelsson's culinary praxis but also challenge our conception of culinary nostalgia as individuated and experiential. If nostalgia is indeed "prospective" rather than merely retrospective, then Samuelsson's incorporation of African American tastes reads as part and parcel of the project of challenging conventional nostalgia's provinciality and immobility.

Samuelsson's formulations of nostalgic memory and post-black identity couched within his mission to "chase flavors" make his memoir less the quintessential ethnic/immigrant bildungsroman—in which the subject reconciles the self through various trials and errors—and more a celebration of the various fragmentations that constitute the self. Weiss's rendering of taste as "a sign of individual style, a mode of constituting the self, a mark of social position, an aesthetic gesture" speaks to the way that Samuelsson ultimately constructs his brand of blackness as an aesthetic gesture that is intimately connected to his role as a (post-black) chef.[125] Flavor, as opposed to taste, is defined by the *Oxford English Dictionary* as "an olfactory *suggestion* of the presence of some particular ingredient."[126] This sentiment is echoed in Eoyang's discussion of flavor, when he explains that the "student of Chinese literary criticism will notice how frequently one encounters the word *wei*, meaning 'flavor' or 'savor,' in discussions of literature. For the Western-trained critic, this reliance on such an elusive quality is an inevitable source of frustration. *Wei* cannot be abstractly described or defined." In a literary context, "flavor, then, is the soul of writing; while sounds and images convey some of the thought, only flavor can convey its essence."[127] Taste, therefore, acts as the body, while flavor is the soul.

Through the nostalgic reclamations of Samuelsson and Terry, we see that nostalgia functions as a product of memory and as a quality that makes possible continual creative imaginings of a present and a future. Food is, arguably, the most visceral way in which we access memories, making it a central point for a study of the way in which nostalgia informs our day-to-day lives socially, psychically, and (in the case of this chapter) gastronomically. The culinarily informed genealogies I have attempted to construct in examining the oeuvre of Samuelsson and Terry exemplify the way in which a post-black/post-soul aesthetic makes use of the black historical past to conceive of new articulations of blackness in the now. Nostalgia emerges in these works not as a form of longing or as recuperation of a "lost" past but rather as a point of departure in which the past functions as a form of embodiment and affect.

Even though I still avoid ribs and ham, I admit to having developed a more adventuresome and omnivorous diet as an adult. While I cannot bring myself to try the infamous Wood Oven Roasted Pig Face at Chicago's Girl and the Goat, I find it hard to resist a crispy sprinkling of lardoons on my salad or a good pork belly ramen. Undoubtedly, my culinary tastes reflect a different sense of spatial mobility and socioeconomic status than that of my parents. It is not lost on me how the foods I consume and the places where I purchase and consume them reflect a politics of class, gender, and race. I break my children's hearts each time I refuse their requests to go to fast food restaurants and insist that they try my homemade grit cakes with collards and roasted tomatoes. I recognize this as an attempt to globalize their young palates but also to introduce them to the food of their ancestors, as well as a past and a politics that become hazier with each successive generation. I am aware that the simple act of eating yams will not magically transport me or my children to the memory of an African (or even southern) homeland, but the act of purchasing sweet potatoes from black farmers at the Healthy Food Hub and jamming out to Erykah Badu's "Back in the Day" while preparing sweet potato granola provides its own nostalgic possibilities for the future.

Postscript

A Future for Black Nostalgia

> There's just a lot of videos of terrible things happening to black people. I mean, it's literally, like, almost a genre. And there's got to be a parallel narrative, you know what I mean? There's got to be a parallel narrative.
> —Neil Drumming, "Afrofuturism"

When I was a teenager, one of my favorite movies was *Coming to America* (1988). The film starred Eddie Murphy in the role of Akeem Joffer, a young African prince who comes to the United States (Queens, New York) in order to find love and, hopefully, his future princess. While *Coming to America* garnered lukewarm reviews from critics,[1] it was well received among African Americans and has since become a black pop culture classic. *Coming to America* struck a chord with late 1980s black audiences, who identified with the film's brand of humor, which was particularly resonant with black culture at that moment: excessive Jheri curl "juice" jokes, classic barbershop scenes, and the lackluster but utterly comical soul band Randy Watson and Sexual Chocolate. *Coming to America* also featured Eddie Murphy's comedic acting genius (he plays over a dozen roles in the film). Akeem Joffer hails from the fictional country of Zamunda, which is more of an African American fantasy of Africa and Africans than a representation of any particular place on the continent or the people who inhabit it. The Joffers are Zamunda's aristocracy, and even the livery of their "subjects" is luxuriant. Four years after *Coming to America*, Michael

Jackson released the music video "Remember the Time" (1992), which featured supermodel Iman and Eddie Murphy as an Egyptian queen and king. The video was described by one critic as a "gorgeous ancient Egypt extravaganza."[2] At the center of both Murphy's film and Jackson's video (which, at nine minutes in length, can be considered a short film) lies a grandiose reflection of afro-nostalgic desire.

Foregoing, for a moment, the problematics of Murphy's and Jackson's imaginings of Africa, which are but facsimiles of Western power and privilege with a veneer of Africanness (mainly symbolized by feathered headdresses and animal-skin sashes), I want to look at the imperative of such portrayals, which drives both my curiosity and my reading of these representations as nostalgic. In the project of presenting a counternarrative to the well-worn stereotype of Africans and Africa as perpetually impoverished, famine ridden, and in need of the West for salvation (both materially and spiritually), Murphy's and Jackson's works expose a larger black popular cultural desire to install a new memory of Africa within the black American historical imagination. If we follow the narrative of Jackson's video, the "time" we are meant to "remember" is one in which black people were not tragically and traumatically severed from their homelands to labor as slaves along the diaspora. On its face, Jackson's song is merely a plea from a former lover to recall the good times they once shared in the hopes of rekindling a romance. But beneath the surface, "Remember the Time" is plea for a romantic African American history. As Elizabeth Amisu notes, "Jackson highlights not just blackness in 'Remember the Time,' but far more important, black affirmation."[3] Notably the story lines of both *Coming to America* and "Remember the Time" elide the problematics of whiteness and white supremacy in manifesting a vision of Africa (and, in the case of *Coming to America*, a black Americanness) that is in and of itself; or rather, a blackness that is not created in tension with white dominance and white subjectivity. The desire to exist in and of oneself, outside the confines of a pervasive white supremacist logic that dominates everything from historical memory to the circadian rhythms of black life, is at the core of afro-nostalgia.

This aesthetic manifestation of black nostalgic memory is unlike a postracial utopia or a black nationalist promised land; it is neither regressive nor fearful of the future, as critics of nostalgia often contend. The desire to create a different past is not new for any culture at any point in time, but the active confrontation with historical trauma is one that has certainly resonated among African Americans for centuries. As David Blight has noted, "From sermons, and from the 'race histories' and theological works

written by blacks at the turn of the century, a spiritually reassuring form
of memory emerges that helped many people cope with the desperation
of Jim Crow. Many blacks found not only a link to a glorious, if unreal-
izable, African background but also a historical theodicy that provided
them the spirit to redeem Africa, if only symbolically."[4] The desire to reform memory was thus developed as a coping mechanism to address not
only historical trauma but the ongoing injuries of Jim Crow. The African
American impulse to craft a new history can easily be read as a kind of
revivalism through the persistent and cyclical reanimation of the past. But
I understand these efforts as nostalgic rather than revivalist because the
former is constituted by a deep sense of longing and affect, whereas the
latter is largely concerned with reanimating the fervor of a past moment.
Blight points to black theologians who were keen to "provide not only
a usable past, but a sense of ultimate 'racial triumph' for black folk in
America. . . . In such interpretations, old collective memories could be
discarded and new ones imagined."[5] The project of nostalgia can be read
as yet another form of historical revisionism, and—in some ways—it is
exactly that. Yet a key distinction I would make between revisionist history
and nostalgia is the role that feeling and emotion plays in the construction of each. Nostalgia is emotionally driven and emotionally charged;
it works at the level of the conscious and unconscious, and it creates the
psychic conditions for the production of revisionist histories. The creation
of a usable, more redemptive past can be construed as an act of historical
erasure, a willingness to simply forget and start anew. Yet such obscuring
is also a rejection of incessant narratives of oppression and subjugation
that offer few to no redeeming features of black life or black people. The
consequence is that black history and, by extension, black folks are ren-
dered static, fixed, and "outside" of history.

One of this book's primary goals has been to consider nostalgia as a
relevant and meaningful concept in constructing new narratives of black
life that resist, complicate, and complement its dominant traumatic framing. Nostalgia is often evoked as an expression of one's discontent with
the present, and the recollection of a more glorious past—whether real
or imagined—is seen as a respite from the ills of the current moment.
The "past," for many African-descended people, does not bring with it
sentiments of good feelings. I find that expressions of afro-nostalgia often
show up as desires for precolonial African pasts, which are really about
the desire for freedom in the contemporary moment. In Paul Louise-Julie's
comic *The Pack* (2015–16), for example, the project of black worldmaking
is explicit. In an interview, Louise-Julie discussed traveling to Africa to

begin constructing "Black fantasy completely unrelated to racism or social commentary." *The Pack* is motivated by Louise-Julie's desire to "create a mythology for the black diaspora based on the tales of our ancestors," and thus "redefine how we see ourselves—how the world sees us. If Tolkien could do it, so could I."[6] Throughout this book, I have explored manifestations of black worldmaking in the absence of white domination, and the multivalent ways that black subjects imagine historical freedom and historical pleasure.

Michelle Commander maps the many ways that "writers, tourists, urban planners, and activists imagined Africa to which African descendants might return, belong, and feel free."[7] It is this idea of "feeling free" that interests me, and, specifically, the role that afro-nostalgia plays in invoking and imagining spatiotemporal "memories" in which black bodies are unshackled, literally and figuratively. For African-descended people throughout the diaspora, one's history has always been inextricable from a broader narrative of human bondage, and thus the invention of Africa as a relief from the psychic burden of slavery has been a feature of black mythologies since the eighteenth century. Commander articulates contemporary reimaginings of Africa as a "complicated, transnational spectrum of longing . . . that is perpetually in flux, reinforcing the impossibility of literal returns despite the perpetuity of yearning as well as the hybridity of Afro-Atlantic identities."[8] Though nostalgia is not referenced explicitly in Commander's examination of these cultural productions, her reading of Afro-Atlantic speculation is couched in the language of longing, yearning and homeland, which signals a multitude of nostalgic processes at work even if not precisely named.

In a 2017 interview, Nnedi Okorafor, the author of the 2010 novel and soon-to-be HBO series *Who Fears Death*, troubles the label of afro-futurism because it is too tightly bound to an African American perspective of Africa: "My relationship to the label Afrofuturism is complicated because, Afrofuturism is a word, a label that, over the years was typically assigned to African-American visions of the future. . . . The roots are African-American and I feel very strongly, that the roots of Afrofuturism—if we're talking about narratives of whatever kind be it visual art, music, whatever—it should be rooted in the continent first. Because that's where we came from, and then we left. Some of us left, and some of us stayed, and some of us go back."[9] Okorafor is right. To consider afro-futurism as an African American enterprise is both limiting and reductive. She has since declared that she writes "Africanfuturism," which is distinct from afro-futurism in that "Africanfuturism is specifically and more directly rooted in African culture, history, mythology and point-of-view as it then branches into the Black Diaspora, and it does not privilege or center the West."[10] The distinction is important because it highlights the ways that afro-futurism is less about "African-American visions of the future" and more about African American historical desires. In the absence of an "actual" or "authentic" originary history in which to return, such "visions of the future" are intimately bound to the fiction of what has been.

In the process of writing this book, I encountered a rather obscure term, *Heimat*, which means "to conjure something which has never been or rather: something that has always been but only imagined and still not realized."[11] The term has no English equivalent. Entrenched in the concept of *Heimat* is a vision of freedom that is intimately bound to recapturing the past and locating oneself along a historical trajectory that shores up who we are in the now. It is through the processes of nostalgic recall that the subject invokes a way of being in the world as an agent, or what Nietzsche would call a "free spirit."[12] Hegel's construction of "an intermingling of past, spirit, and present in *Heimatlichkeit* does lead to a freedom at once mental and spatial, in which a 'free and beautiful' contact with history is possible."[13]

Heimat is largely understood as a form of longing that produces "a selectively idealized memory of the past."[14] Yet, this idealized memory proves necessary for imagining the self as truly emancipated. As Allen Wood puts it, Hegel's concept of freedom is a "model of human agency," in which "modern individuals cannot be truly free until they create a social order in which this is possible. Surely the most wretched unfreedom would be to lose the ability even to conceive of what it would be like to have the freedom we lack, and so dismiss even the aspiration to freedom as something wicked and dangerous."[15] While Hegel could have never imagined such a relationship between black people and historical memory (or black people as having a historical memory or even a history, for that matter), *Heimat* proves fruitful in considering blackness in a social order absent white supremacy, where black freedom and Being exist in and of (and for) themselves. At face value, the concept of *Heimat* appears problematically regressive; *Heimat* is but a longing to return to the pastoral to resolve anxiety about the pace and pressures of modernity. It is not surprising that *Heimat* was oft conjured by German Nazis as a *völkisch* nationalism. But what can a concept like *Heimat* mean for black subjects and their imagining of African homelands?

To bring this book to a close I focus on a particular fantastical representation of the African past, the 2016 comic *Black Panther: A Nation under Our Feet.* The mythical African spaces in *Black Panther* represent an African American utopian ideal, which is an imagining of blackness outside of and beyond its relation to whiteness. What I find in *Black Panther* is the self-conscious referencing of the function of memory as instrumental to the formation of emancipated black subjectivities.

Marvel Comics' release of the Black Panther comic in July 1966 predated, by three months, the founding of the Black Panther Party in Oakland, California. While there exists some debate about whether the comic's creators, Stan Lee and Jack Kirby, were aware of the burgeoning Black Panther Party, one could reasonably argue that they were attuned to the prolific independence of African nations from their former European colonizers and an emergent Black Power movement in the United States.[16] The early iterations of *Black Panther* portrayed Wakanda, the African kingdom over which the Black Panther (T'Challa) rules, as a "composite of colonial imagery," as Martin Lund notes: "Lee and Kirby's Wakanda reproduces notions about Africans as peoples without history, whose opportunity for progress and a future—their way out of their 'savage' past—comes from engaging in international trade, ignoring the fact of centuries of intra-continental trade and of European complicity in keeping Africa underdeveloped. . . . Africans can begin making history only after whites arrive."[17] In 2016, Marvel tapped acclaimed writer Ta-Nehisi Coates to write its next series. In this version, Coates made certain to retain the premise of the original comic but extend and revise the broader narrative to include "black diaspora mythology."[18] Given that "Wakanda, as originally imagined by Lee, Kirby, and later Don McGregor, was a collection of characterless and problematic locations, with names like Piranha Cove, Primitive Peaks, and Serpent Valley that traded on Western stereotypes and ignorance,"[19] Coates sought not only to portray an African society that had its own rich history but to make Wakandans' knowledge of that history the key to its future. Coates's version emphasizes the import of historical and collective memory as a basis for imagining an emancipated blackness.

In the opening pages of *Black Panther: A Nation under Our Feet*, Book 1, readers learn the following about the comic's protagonist, his homeland of Wakanda, and the predicament in which he currently finds himself:

Black Panther is the ancestral ceremonial title of T'CHALLA, the king of Wakanda. T'Challa splits his time between protecting his kingdom, with the aid of his elite female royal guard, the DORA MILAJE, and helping protect the entire world, as a member of super-hero teams such as the Avengers and the Ultimates. The African nation WAKANDA is the most technologically advanced society on the globe. It sits upon a large deposit of an extremely rare natural resource called Vibranium. Wakanda long boasted of having never been conquered. But recent events . . . have humbled the kingdom. T'Challa recently spent some time away from the throne. His sister SHURI had been ruling as both queen and Black Panther in his absence, but she died defending Wakanda against Thanos' army.[20]

What readers later learn is that T'Challa has preserved Shuri's corpse with the ambition of finding a way to resuscitate her body. In the interim, Shuri's spirit travels to the Djalia, the "plane of Wakandan memory." The Djalia is a liminal space that collapses the past, present, and future. While there, Shuri is mentored by a griot, a "caretaker of all our histories,"[21] who leads her through a journey of her ancestral past. When Shuri became Queen of Wakanda, she earned the title of Black Panther, and after her journey in the Djalia is complete, she shares a spiritual connection with the Panther God (Bast) and gains superpowers of transformation.

The narrative's section on the Djalia opens with the griot introducing Shuri to a lush green space with verdant trees and purple rivers. When Shuri asks, "Where are we?" the griot responds with a single word: "Home." The griot explains to Shuri, "You are in Djalia—The plane of ancient memory. All of it is here, all of the triumph and tragedy of your people. And I am a caretaker of all our histories, now lost to the acolytes of machine and the prophets of this metal age. . . . Here we will arm you not with the spear, but with the drum, for it is the drum that carries the greatest power of all . . . the power of memory, daughter, the power of our song."[22] The Djalia is the brainchild of Coates, who explains that previous issues had defined Wakanda as technologically advanced but given no attention to its history. For Shuri, the return to the Djalia is a return to a homeland that she never knew existed. Shuri's residence in Djalia empowers her on multiple planes (psychological, spiritual, physical), and the narrative is fairly explicit in linking the acquisition of historical knowledge to the power one holds. It is here that I want to draw a connection between history, historical memory, and nostalgia because the text uses these interrelated concepts to project an image of emancipated blackness. Armed with "the drum," Shuri gains access to ancestral knowledge, which the text equates with power and agency. While the text does not cede T'Challa's power to the returned Shuri, when she leaves the Djalia in Book 2 she is charged by the griot to "go off to teach those who have forgotten your name—the Aja-Adanna, Keeper of Wakandan lore. The bearer of what was . . . what is

. . . and again shall be."[23] In Book 3, with this newfound knowledge, Shuri fully embodies her new form as sage and advisor to T'Challa. Notably, Shuri's quest centers on instantiating a form of collective memory that will inspire Wakandans to reestablish their country's eminence.

Nostalgic sentiment plays an important part in the moral, social, and historical agency that emerges as part of the Djalia. Shuri's voyage to the Djalia can easily be read as the age-old sentiment that in order to know oneself (and one's future), one must know the past. It is there that she learns the story of Ife, a descendant of the Nri people, who were capable of growing wings and taking flight; the tale of Oronde, the "village boy" who was consistently defeated in his race against the cheetah until he remembered that he was more than a mere village boy and thus became "Oronde who mastered the flame"; and, lastly, the story of Sologon, the Queen-Mother, who leads her tribe into battle, where they learn that "spirits of iron, make skins of stone." With each narrative, Shuri's acquired knowledge translates into the acquisition of a new "power"—the ability to fly, the gift of speed, and the capacity to turn skin to stone. Shuri's process of cobbling together fragmented narratives, retrieving historical artifacts, and journeying to ancestral homelands mirrors the methods by which African Americans work to create an unknowable past, the threads of which are held together by the imagination. This process creates its own brand of power, specifically the manifestation of a "parallel narrative" in which the nostalgic past is more than an impotent retreat but a repository of black memory that inspires a resistant, critical subjectivity.

The homeland Coates creates not only builds a history for Wakanda but reflects a broader African American yearning for home. It is not that Wakanda was missing a history; the missing historical memory that Coates implants is for that of displaced Africans throughout the diaspora. If Wakanda represents the enmeshing of an African past and future, what does Coates's Wakanda (or that of Ryan Coogler, writer-director of the 2018 film *Black Panther*) tell us about the historical desires and utopian fantasies of African Americans now? Coates's and Coogler's versions of Wakanda appear to express layered nostalgic desires: for a precolonial Africa, for black nationalist aspirations in the United States and African independence from Europe in Africa in the 1960s, and, according to Salamishah Tillet, for the Obama era.[24] This most recent expression of nostalgia emerges in light of an ever-hostile political climate in which blackness is fervently under attack and erasure. Ironically (or not), the spark that has inspired racial backlash in the late 2010s is yet another brand of nostalgia—one for an imagined white homeland within the United

States. We can trace this fantasy back to Thomas Jefferson, who, in his *Notes on the State of Virginia*, expressed a plan for the enslaved persons inhabiting this nation to be "colonized to such place as the circumstances of the time should render most proper."[25] In other words, send them away, anywhere but here. The desire to render black Americans invisible, in our time, is set against a narrative like *Black Panther* that amplifies our visibility. Such a narrative also capitalizes on our own fantasies of black nationalism, in which our existence is not subject to the forces of white hegemony; Wakanda stands in for our own unknowable histories and is, thus, readily available and accessible to us all.

Alongside recollections of trauma, contemporary black aesthetic projects have been highly invested in romancing the past to produce diverse representations of black history and black identity. Ultimately these projects have been motivated by a cultural want to be read as something other than "victim"; as Suzan-Lori Parks has written, "We have for so long been an 'oppressed' people, but are black people only blue?"[26] I do not position nostalgia as at odds with important and necessary studies and stories of the ways that the transatlantic slave trade and its afterlife maintain a pernicious presence in the social, psychic, and biological existences of modern-day black people. Yet, I read afro-nostalgia as an opening to consider other important and understudied sentiments produced by and through the afterlife of slavery, particularly those emotions, feelings, and memories from which black folks are considered "immune." Afro-nostalgia figures in black lives as a desire to experience the past as a site of romantic reclamation and to build from it a future worth being nostalgic for.

Notes

Introduction

1. Z. Smith, "Novelist Zadie Smith."
2. Levin, "The Case against Vandalizing Monuments."
3. Blight, *Race and Reunion.*
4. Levin, "Why I Changed My Mind."
5. Silva, "Nostalgia and the Good Life," 126.
6. Jefferson, *Notes on the State of Virginia,* 139, 140.
7. Jefferson, 138 (emphasis added).
8. B. Williams, *The Pursuit of Happiness,* 15.
9. Atias and Davies, "Nostalgia and the Shapes of History," 184.
10. Baldwin, Biernat, and Landau, "Remembering the Real Me," 128, 144.
11. Routledge et al., "Nostalgia as a Resource."
12. Here I am inspired by numerous scholars thinking through the ways that affect is operative across a range of bodies, spaces, and temporalities, particularly those sites that are generally overlooked as fruitful or legitimate sites of critical inquiry. Key among those are Sara Ahmed, *The Cultural Politics of Emotion;* Lauren Berlant, *Cruel Optimism;* Alexis Pauline Gumbs, *Spill;* Jennifer Nash, "Practicing Love"; Kathleen Stewart, *Ordinary Affects;* and Rebecca Wanzo, *The Suffering Will Not Be Televised.*
13. Fauset, "Nostalgia," 157.
14. Edwards, *The Practice of Diaspora,* 143.
15. Bonnett, *Left in the Past,* 10.
16. R. Williams, *Marxism and Literature,* 122.
17. Cvetkovich, "Affect," 15.

18. This idea forms the central concerns in José Muñoz's *Cruising Utopia* and Tavia Nyong'o's *Afro-Fabulations*, for example.

19. Levy-Hussen, *How to Read African American Literature*, 2–3.

20. Levy-Hussen, 2.

21. Sharpe, *In the Wake*, 18.

22. Hersey, in e-mail communication with the author, November 2, 2018.

23. J. Morgan, "Moving Towards a Black Feminist Politics of Pleasure," 36.

24. May, "Belonging from Afar," 411.

25. May, 411.

26. Levy-Hussen, *How to Read African American Literature*, 2.

27. Routledge, *Nostalgia*, 4.

28. Illbruck, *Nostalgia*, 3.

29. J. Wilson, *Nostalgia*, 21.

30. Kline, "The Migratory Impulse vs. the Love of Home," 43.

31. Torrey, *A Portraiture of Domestic Slavery*, 71.

32. Jefferson, *Notes on the State of Virginia*, 139.

33. Torrey, *A Portraiture of Domestic Slavery*, 71.

34. Commander, *Afro-Atlantic Flight*, 3.

35. Snyder, "Suicide, Slavery, and Memory in North America," 50 (emphasis added).

36. Snyder, 51.

37. Sampson, *Slavery in the United States*, 70.

38. Sampson, 69.

39. Sampson, 68.

40. Silva, "Nostalgia and the Good Life."

41. Torrey, *A Portraiture of Domestic Slavery*, 9.

42. H. Wilson, *Medical Apartheid*.

43. Hunt, "Dr. Cartwright on Drapetomania," 439.

44. Matt, *Homesickness*, 110.

45. Bynum, "Discarded Diagnoses," 2176.

46. Routledge, *Nostalgia*, 5.

47. Hutcheon, "Irony, Nostalgia, and the Postmodern," 194.

48. Routledge, *Nostalgia*, 6.

49. Garrido, "The Influence of Personality and Coping Style," 263.

50. May, "Belonging from Afar," 404.

51. Boyd, *Jim Crow Nostalgia*, 158.

52. Murray, "Time of Breach," 12.

53. Boyd, *Jim Crow Nostalgia*, xv.

54. Johnson, *Hunting in Harlem*, 43.

55. Johnson, 14–15.

56. Margalit, "Nostalgia," 280.

57. Wanzo, *The Suffering Will Not Be Televised*, 3.

58. Baker, "Critical Memory and the Black Public Sphere," 3.

59. Baker, 4.

60. M. Neal, *Soul Babies*, 21.

61. Margalit, "Nostalgia," 280.

62. Hutcheon and Valdés, "Irony, Nostalgia, and the Postmodern," 21.

63. Metzl, *Dying of Whiteness*, 3.

64. Metzl, 5.

65. Sedikides et al., "Nostalgia Fosters Self-Continuity," 534.

66. Batcho and Shikh, "Anticipatory Nostalgia," 75.

67. Garrido, "The Influence of Personality and Coping Style," 259.

68. Hutcheon, "Irony, Nostalgia, and the Postmodern," 195.

69. Redmond, *Anthem*, 4.

70. *Oxford English Dictionary*, s.v. "regeneration, *n.*," accessed June 1, 2020, https://www.oed.com/.

71. Issues concerning health and African American communities have been well-documented in both scholarly and popular circles. Sonya A. Grier and Shiriki K. Kumanyika's essay "The Context for Choice" and Byron Hurt's documentary *Soul Food Junkies* are good places to start.

72. Gallop, "The Ethics of Reading."

73. Pickering, *Research Methods for Cultural Studies*, 1.

1. (Nostalgic) RETRIBUTION

1. Melville, *Great Short Works of Herman Melville*, 309.

2. Grandin, "Who Ain't a Slave?"

3. *Oxford English Dictionary*, s.v. "nostalgia," accessed June 6, 2020, https://www.oed.com/.

4. Hartman, "Venus in Two Acts," 3.

5. Hartman, 4.

6. Hartman, 9.

7. Keizer, *Black Subjects*, 8, 9.

8. Bell, *The Afro-American Novel and Its Tradition*, 289.

9. Rushdy, *Neo-Slave Narratives*, 7.

10. Rushdy, 3.

11. Keizer, *Black Subjects*, 3.

12. Keizer, 20.

13. Hirsch, *The Generation of Postmemory*, 5.

14. Dubey, "Speculative Fictions of Slavery," 781.

15. Levy-Hussen, *How to Read African American Literature*, 11.

16. Rody, *The Daughter's Return*, 18.

17. Rody, 8.

18. Brand, *A Map to the Door of No Return*, 22.

19. Brand, 22.

20. Mitchell, *The Freedom to Remember*, 4.

21. Mitchell, 4.

22. Tillet, *Sites of Slavery*, 137.

23. Tavia Nyong'o takes up this phenomenon masterfully in *Afro-Fabulations*. He references "queer fabulousness and black shade" as more than merely "ephemeral resistance and vain complicity" (17).

24. H. Elam and M. Elam, "Blood Debt," 103.

25. N'yongo, *Afro-Fabulations*, 44.

26. Boym, *The Future of Nostalgia*, xviii. I discuss white nostalgia more fully in the next chapter.

27. Levy-Hussen, *How to Read African American Literature*, 19.

28. Levy-Hussen, 18.

29. S. A. Williams, *Dessa Rose*, 20.

30. S. A. Williams, 30.

31. Ganeshram's response has been removed from the Scholastic website, but the publisher's defense of the title can be found on its website: Scholastic, "Response on *A Birthday Cake for George Washington.*"

32. The controversy around Ganeshram's book inspired the hashtag #slaverywithasmile.

33. Lenhart, "Hercules."

34. Azie Dungey, "About Azie," *Ask a Slave*: The Web Series (website), accessed March 11, 2019, http://www.askaslave.com/about-azie.html.

35. Dungey, "About Azie."

36. Woolfork, *Embodying Slavery*, 163.

37. Dungey, "'Ask a Slave' and Interpreting Race," 54.

38. Dungey, 58.

39. Dungey, 51.

40. Dungey, 49.

41. Dungey, 47.

42. Azie Dungey, "Lizzie Mae," *Ask a Slave*: The Web Series (website), accessed March 11, 2019, http://www.askaslave.com/lizzie-mae.html.

43. Dungey, "Lizzie Mae."

44. Colbert, "Reconstruction, Fugitive Intimacy, and Holding History," 503.

45. Whitehead, *Underground Railroad*, 110.

46. Dickson-Carr, *African American Satire*, 20.

47. Dungey, *Ask a Slave*, season 1, episode 5, "Two Sides to Every Coin," aired September 21, 2013.

48. See Freud, "Humor."

49. Dungey, *Ask a Slave*, season 1, episode 3, "You Can't Make This Stuff Up," aired September 8, 2013.

50. Christian, "The Race for Theory," 52.

51. Ernest, *Chaotic Justice*, 28.

52. Ernest, 64.

53. Dungey, *Ask a Slave*, season 1, episode 3, "You Can't Make This Stuff Up," aired September 8, 2013.

54. Finley, "Black Women's Satire," 252.

55. Dungey, *Ask a Slave*, season 1, episode 3, "You Can't Make This Stuff Up," aired September 8, 2013.

56. Finley, "Black Women's Satire," 256.

57. Woolfork, *Embodying Slavery*, 162.

58. Dungey, "'Ask a Slave' and Interpreting Race," 38.

59. Woolfork, *Embodying Slavery*, 183.

60. Woolfork, 186.

61. Woolfork, 185.

62. With my reference to "white fragility," I am invoking Robin D'Angelo's argument about the "racial comfort" that white people in the United States generally experience and, more importantly, have come to expect: "White people in North America live in a social environment that protects and insulates them from race-based stress" ("White Fragility," 55).

63. E. Jones, *The Known World*, 4.

64. E. Jones, 12.

65. E. Jones, 13.

66. "It was often the case that Alice, the Night Walker, would be standing just inside her door when Moses opened it each morning, dressed and ready to work, as if she had been standing at the door waiting for him all night" (E. Jones, 61).

67. E. Jones, 297.

68. Cervenak, *Wandering*, 23.

69. E. Jones, *The Known World*, 384.

70. E. Jones, 386.

71. Seger, "Ekphrasis and the Postmodern Slave Narrative," 1189.

72. Mutter, "Such a Poor Word."

73. E. Jones, *The Known World*, 385.

74. E. Jones, 385.

75. E. Jones, 174.

76. Mutter, "Such a Poor Word," 142.

77. Bassard, "Imagining Other Worlds," 418.

78. Bradley, "Re-Imagining Slavery in the Hip-Hop Imagination," 18.

79. E. Jones, *The Known World*, 68.

80. E. Jones, 68.

81. Currie, *About Time*, 33.

82. E. Jones, *The Known World*, 205.

83. E. Jones, 180.

84. Thoreau, "A Plea for Captain John Brown," 272.

85. Massaquoi, "Mystery of Malcolm X," 38.

86. Griffin, "John Brown's 'Madness,'" 370.

87. McBride, *The Good Lord Bird*, 2–3, 1.

88. McBride, 1–2.

89. Hutcheon, *A Poetics of Postmodernism*, 126.

90. McBride, *The Good Lord Bird*, 1.
91. McBride, 10–11.
92. McBride, 24.
93. McBride, 35.
94. McBride, 45.
95. McBride, 87.
96. McBride, 159.
97. McBride, 179.
98. T. Smith, *Weird John Brown*, 74.
99. T. Smith, 75.
100. McBride, *The Good Lord Bird*, 274.
101. Sedikides and Wildschut, "Past Forward," 319.

2. (Nostalgic) RESTORATION

1. The concept of white nostalgia has been heavily discussed in popular news media outlets, especially in response to the candidacy and presidency of Donald Trump. In "Trump's Rhetoric of White Nostalgia," Ronald Brownstein writes that during his 2016 presidential campaign Trump defined himself as "a candidate of cultural restoration."
2. Boym, *The Future of Nostalgia*, 41.
3. N'yongo, *Afro-Fabulations*, 44.
4. See Baker, "Critical Memory and the Black Public Sphere."
5. I use the term *new* here not to refer to an original phenomenon but rather to that which is, as Jacqui Alexander puts it, "structured through the 'old' scrambled, palimpsestic character of time [that] both jettisons the truncated distance of linear time and dislodges the impulse for incommensurability" (*Pedagogies of Crossing*, 190).
6. Redmond, *Anthem*, 5.
7. Redmond, 264.
8. J. D. Hall, "The Civil Rights Movement," 1235.
9. Wall, "For the Very Existence of Civilization," 862.
10. K. Smith, "Mere Nostalgia," 515–16.
11. K. Smith, 515.
12. "Founded in 1991 by the African People's Socialist Party, InPDUM is the leading organization in the struggle for Bread, Peace and Black Power in the 21st Century." InPDUM, "About AnPDUM," The International People's Democratic Uhuru Movement, accessed May 10, 2020, https://inpdum.org/about-inpdum/.
13. J. Jackson, *Real Black*, 176.
14. Iton, *In Search of the Black Fantastic*, 160.
15. Bowman, *Soulsville, U.S.A.*, 291.
16. Lierow, "The 'Black Man's Vision of the World.'"
17. Bowman, *Soulsville, U.S.A.*, 268.
18. McMay, *The Pop Festival*, 65.

19. Quoted in Bowman, *Soulsville, U.S.A.*, 292.

20. L. Neal, "The Black Arts Movement," 29.

21. Lierow, "The 'Black Man's Vision of the World,'" 7.

22. Lierow, 10.

23. Lierow, 11.

24. Bowman, *Soulsville, U.S.A.*, 268.

25. L. Williams, "Wattstax Concert at Coliseum," G8.

26. Quoted in Arnold, "As Real as Real Can Get," 69.

27. Arnold, "As Real as Real Can Get," 69.

28. M. Neal, *Soul Babies*, 3.

29. Baker and Baker, "Uptown Where We Belong," 219.

30. Haggins, *Laughing Mad*, 178–79.

31. M. Neal, *Soul Babies*, 102.

32. Davis, "Afro Images," 39.

33. Davis, 37.

34. Okeowo, "The Provocateur behind Beyoncé, Rihanna, and Issa Rae."

35. Okeowo.

36. Chokshi, "Rudy Giuliani."

37. E. Morgan, "Media Culture and the Public Memory of the Black Panther Party," 336.

38. Mann, "Why Does Country Music Sound So White?," 75.

39. Mann, 91.

40. Mowitt, *Percussion*, 57.

41. Arzumanova, "The Culture Industry and Beyoncé's Proprietary Blackness," 422.

42. Kornhaber, "What Beyoncé's 'Daddy's Lessons' Had to Teach." Also see Pecknold, *The Selling Sound*.

43. Lindsay-Habermann, "Till Victory Is Won."

44. Reslen, "Beyoncé Reveals the Deeply Personal Story."

45. Reslen.

46. Boym, *The Future of Nostalgia*, 43.

47. Brooks, "How #BlackLivesMatter Started a Musical Revolution."

48. Brooks.

49. Horowitz, "Kendrick Lamar Speaks on the Meaning behind 'HiiiPoWeR.'"

50. Levy-Hussen, *How to Read African American Literature*, 20.

3. (Nostalgic) REGENERATION

1. Gallop, "The Ethics of Reading," 10.

2. Trouillot, *Silencing the Past*, 17.

3. Elam, *The Past as Present in the Drama of August Wilson*, xi.

4. Mitchell, *The Freedom to Remember*, 4.

5. See Ron Eyerman's *Cultural Trauma*, Joy DeGruy's *Post-Traumatic Slave Syndrome*, and Sheldon George's *Trauma and Race*, to name a few.

6. Cvetkovich, "Depression Is Ordinary," 136.

7. *Oxford English Dictionary*, s.v. "regenerate," accessed October 12, 2016, https://www.oed.com/.

8. Harry J. Elam Jr. refers to August Wilson's drama cycle as invested in "regenerative models of healing," noting that it "integrates the political, the historical, and the spiritual in ways that push the realms of conventional realism and evoke a spirit that is both timeless and timely" (*The Past as Present*, xiv). Though Elam does not invoke the concept of nostalgia, it hovers over Wilson's oeuvre in ways that are similar to what is described in this chapter.

9. Copeland, *Bound to Appear*, 9.

10. Copeland, 10.

11. April Banks, "Bio," April Banks (artist's website), accessed April 30, 2019, http://www.aprilbanks.com/bio/.

12. Krista Franklin, "Artist Statement," *Milk* (website), accessed August 11, 2016, http://209.172.130.121/kristafrank6.html.

13. Franklin, "Artist Statement."

14. Sharpe, *In the Wake*, 116.

15. Sharpe, 116.

16. Wright, *Physics of Blackness*, 46.

17. Wright, "Pale by Comparison," 267–68.

18. AncestryDNA, "DNA," Ancestry.com, accessed April 30, 2019, https://www.ancestry.com/dna/.

19. Nelson, *The Social Life of DNA*, 5.

20. Banks, personal interview, June 22, 2015.

21. Hurston, "How It Feels to Be Colored Me."

22. Allen, "New Blanc Chicago Gallery Amanda Williams Art Exhibit."

23. Banks, personal interview, June 22, 2015.

24. April Banks, *Possession Is Nine Tenths*, April Banks (artist's website), accessed March 1, 2015, http://www.aprilbanks.com/possession-is-910ths.

25. Faber, *Stradivari's Genius*, 228.

26. Derrida, *Archive Fever*, 3.

27. April Banks, *Make. Believe.*, April Banks (artist's website), accessed March 1, 2015, http://www.aprilbanks.com/make-believe/.

28. Gates, *Finding Your Roots*, "Family Reunions."

29. Lambert-Beatty, "Make Believe," 66.

30. Lambert-Beatty, 70.

31. Wright, *Physics of Blackness*, 35.

32. Krista Franklin, "About," Krista Franklin (artist's website), accessed October 6, 2016, http://www.kristafranklin.com/about/.

33. Miller, "Afrosurreal Manifesto."

34. Miller.

35. Césaire, "The Domain of the Marvelous."

36. Cvetkovich, *An Archive of Feelings*, 7.

37. Bianca Williams, *The Pursuit of Happiness*, 6.
38. Carland and Cvetkovich, "Sharing an Archive of Feelings."
39. Miller, "Black to the Future Series."
40. Miller.
41. Schapiro and Meyer, "Femmage," 68.
42. Cooks, "Romare Bearden," 210.
43. Raaberg, "Beyond Fragmentation," 161.
44. For a discussion of feminism and love, see Nash, "Practicing Love," 3.
45. Braidotti, *Transpositions*, 230.
46. The phrase "black boy joy" was popularized as a hashtag by Chance the Rapper in August 2016. Chance's use of the hashtag inspired thousands of social-media posts with images of smiling, carefree black boys (and men). The images and the hashtag were deemed as both a welcome "break" from the persistent news stories of black death and a counternarrative to dominant representations of black masculinity as criminal, dangerous, or devoid of positive emotions.
47. Krista Franklin, "Artist Statement," Krista Franklin (artist's website), accessed December 20, 2016, http://www.kristafranklin.com/about/.
48. Goff et al., "The Essence of Innocence," 526.
49. Hunt, "Dr. Cartwright on Drapetomania," 439.
50. Hunt, 440.
51. Braidotti, *Transpositions*, 5.
52. Boniface and Cooper, *Worldwide Destinations*, 4.
53. Franklin, "Manifesto, or Ars Poetica #2."
54. Césaire, "Surrealism and Us," 37.
55. Miller, "AfroSurreal Generation."
56. Césaire, "Surrealism and Us," 38.
57. Edwards, "The Ethnics of Surrealism," 132.
58. Iton, *In Search of the Black Fantastic*, 16.
59. Rhonda Wheatley, "Hybrid Devices," Rhonda Wheatley (artist's website), accessed May 16, 2020, https://www.rhondawheatley.com/hybrid-devices-1/.
60. Steele, *We Heal from Memory*, 11.
61. Wheatley, *Post-Traumatic Soul Restoration and Brain Rewiring Device*, object label. *A Modern Day Shaman's Hybrid Devices, Power Objects, and Cure Books* (exhibit), Hyde Park Art Center (HPAC), 2017.
62. It is nearly impossible not to touch the sculptures, to engage with them, and when we visited it was apparent that some viewers/users had done just that. Wheatley repeatedly expressed her discontent that people had "messed with" the objects. However, her concern seemed to stem not from the fact that the objects had been touched but from the fact that they had not been properly replaced.
63. Meek, "One Last Thing before I Go."
64. Hester, "The Phone Booth for Japanese Mourners."
65. Brown, "Thing Theory," 5.
66. Pérez, "The Surrealist Collection of Objects," 114.

67. Wheatley, *Guidance Counselor*, object label. *A Modern Day Shaman's Hybrid Devices, Power Objects, and Cure Books* (exhibit), Hyde Park Art Center (HPAC), 2017.

68. Wheatley, *Life Review Device*, object label. *A Modern Day Shaman's Hybrid Devices, Power Objects, and Cure Books* (exhibit), Hyde Park Art Center (HPAC), 2017.

4. (Nostalgic) RECLAMATION

1. Lessing, *Lesser Beasts*, 49.

2. Muhammad, *How to Eat to Live*, Book 1, 72.

3. Wallach, "How to Eat to Live," section 5.

4. The wealth of blogs, websites, and cookbooks dedicated to creating authentic meals from the historical past is clear evidence of a general popular interest (and, perhaps, investment) in capturing the nostalgic past through the consumption of certain foodstuffs. Ivan Day's blog *Food History Jottings*, for example, describes the painstaking process of re-creating meals from the medieval period.

5. Twitty, *The Cooking Gene*, xiv.

6. Crawford, *Black Post-Blackness*, 3.

7. Tompkins, *Racial Indigestion*, 3–4.

8. Muhammad, *How to Eat to Live*, Book 1, 105.

9. Crawford, *Black Post-Blackness*, 17.

10. C. Hall, *Carla Hall's Soul Food*; Guy, *Black Girl Baking*; W. Jones, *The New Soul Food Cookbook*; Randall and Williams, *Soul Food Love*; Richards, *Soul*.

11. Wallach, "How to Eat to Live," section 1.

12. Muhammad, *How to Eat to Live*, Book 1, 2.

13. Muhammad, Book 1, 61.

14. Muhammad, Book 1, 86.

15. The NOI's legacy of anti-Semitism is one that appears to have crystallized in the rhetoric of Louis Farrakhan rather than the earlier works of Elijah Muhammad. Frederick M. Schweitzer and Marvin Perry dedicate a full chapter of their book *Anti-Semitism* to the NOI and its charges of anti-Semitism.

16. Muhammad, *How to Eat to Live*, Book 1, 1.

17. Muhammad, Book 1, 11.

18. Doris Witt's *Black Hunger* and Frederick Douglass Opie's *Hog and Hominy* offer incisive analyses of the radical food programs and politics of the NOI.

19. Curtis, *Black Muslim Religion in the Nation of Islam*, 172.

20. Curtis, 169.

21. Curtis, 180.

22. Quoted in Curtis, 180.

23. Curtis, 180.

24. Holbrook, "Good to Eat," 198.

25. Holbrook, 199.

26. Holbrook, 209.

27. Taylor, *Black Nationalism in the United States*, 2.
28. Muhammad, *How to Eat to Live*, Book 2, 95.
29. Muhammad, Book 1, 5.
30. Muhammad, Book 1, 35.
31. Muhammad, Book 1, 106.
32. Muhammad, Book 2, 82.
33. Muhammad, Book 1, 5.
34. Sula, "Bean Pie, My Brother?"
35. Sula.
36. Sula.

37. Laretta Henderson's article "*Ebony Jr!* and 'Soul Food'" identifies this trend in the 1970s publications of *Ebony Jr.* magazine, though *Ebony* magazine published a number of articles encouraging healthy food options for its adult readers. The most cited of these is Althea Smith's article "A Farewell to Chitterlings," which was printed in the September 1974 issue. Smith notes that black celebrities like Dick Gregory, Johnny Nash, Cicely Tyson, and some members of Earth, Wind & Fire were among those partaking in the new health trend. There were also a number of cookbooks that advanced the conceptual link between racial pride, race consciousness, and dietary choices. Among them were Vertamae Smart-Grosvenor's *Vibration Cooking* (1970), Helen Mendes's *The African Heritage Cookbook* (1971), and Norma Jean Darden and Carole Darden's *Spoonbread and Strawberry Wine* (1978).

38. Henderson, "*Ebony Jr!* and 'Soul Food,'" 82.
39. Henderson, 81–82.

40. Henderson, 95. Freda DeKnight's *The Ebony Cookbook* (1962) serves as an excellent example of the way that a major black publication tapped into the nouveau middle-class lifestyle of African Americans. The cookbook opens with a chapter entitled "A Guide for the Housewife." The ideas of "housewives" and cooking for leisure reflect fairly new ways of being and ways of living for a population that is distinctly understood in relationship to labor markets. The idea of a black leisure class is one that coincides with African American integration into corporate and institutional structures following affirmative action and the Civil Rights Act of 1964.

41. Jackson and Wishart, *The Integrated Cookbook*, 1.
42. Jackson and Wishart, 3.
43. Jackson and Wishart, 3.
44. Jackson and Wishart, 2.
45. Jackson and Wishart, 3.
46. Gregory, *Dick Gregory's Natural Diet*, 15.

47. Frederick Douglass Opie offers a short but informative video about the life and influence of Alvenia Fulton (Opie, "Lenten Season Part 4"). He is one of a few scholars who are invested in preserving and highlighting her legacy to the healthful food movement on the South Side of Chicago.

48. Efforts like this new Fultonia are part of a larger project to revitalize the Englewood community in Chicago. On March 20, 2014, the City of Chicago Plan Commission approved Green Healthy Neighborhoods, an initiative that is designed to "target public and private investments in the most efficient and effective way." One of the investors, Urban Juncture, is "leading a project to create a unique produce market, dining destination, and culinary incubator celebrating the cuisines, cultures, and communities of peoples of African descent" (Chicago Metropolitan Agency for Planning, "Planning for Green and Healthy Chicago Neighborhoods").

49. Gregory, *Dick Gregory's Natural Diet*, 25.

50. Gregory, 64.

51. Gregory, 78.

52. Gregory, 81.

53. Gregory, 156.

54. Wallach, "How to Eat to Live," section 4.

55. Terry, *Afro-Vegan*, 1; Samuelsson, *Yes, Chef*, 263.

56. Terry, "Try These Tasty Dishes."

57. Probyn, *Carnal Appetites*, 17. Stuart Hall refers to articulation as a "complex structure" in which "things are related, as much through their differences as through their similarities" (quoted in Slack, "The Theory and Method of Articulation in Cultural Studies," 116).

58. *Oxford English Dictionary*, s.v. "remix, *n.*," accessed June 7, 2020, https://www.oed.com/.

59. Terry, "Interview with Bryant Terry."

60. Quoted in Heynen, "Bending the Bars of Empire," 407.

61. Heynen, "Bending the Bars of Empire," 420.

62. Terry, "Interview with Bryant Terry."

63. Terry, *Afro-Vegan*, 2.

64. Terry, 2.

65. Terry, 3.

66. Freeman, "The Unbearable Whiteness of Milk," 1274.

67. The concept of "conscious capitalism" was popularized by Whole Foods CEO John Mackey in his book *Conscious Capitalism* (2013). In it, Mackey explains the method behind "creating both wealth and well-being" for businesses, so that they can help create a "world of compassion, freedom, and prosperity" (8–9).

68. Slocum, "Whiteness, Space and Alternative Food Practice," 526.

69. Terry, "The Problem with 'Thug' Cuisine."

70. Bad Manners (formerly Thug Kitchen), "Black Lives Matter," Bad Manners (website), accessed June 23, 2020, https://www.thugkitchen.com/protests. In June 2020, a few weeks after their release of this statement, the Thug Kitchen team announced that they would be rebranding as Bad Manners (Gilliver, "'Thug Kitchen' to Change Its Name").

71. Terry, *Afro-Vegan*, 1–2.

72. Guerrero, "B(l)ack in the Kitchen," 311.

73. Guerrero, 311–12.

74. Dickson, "Thug Kitchen."

75. Freeman, "The Unbearable Whiteness of Milk," 1275.

76. Freeman, 1276.

77. On March 12, 2014, Zagat.com featured the article "10 Southern Chefs to Watch." Curiously, none of them are black (Dobkin, "10 Southern Chefs").

78. Terry, *Afro-Vegan*, 2.

79. Hing, "Six Books That Shaped 'Afro-Vegan' Author Bryant Terry."

80. Terry, "Interview with Bryant Terry."

81. Terry, *Afro-Vegan*, 160.

82. During his performance at the Essence Festival in New Orleans on July 4, 2015, singer/performer Usher Raymond wore a white T-shirt on which the words "July Fourth" were crossed out, and the word "Juneteenth" appeared below, in bold letters. The T-shirt created a firestorm on Twitter, where he was applauded by some and derided by others for being too "political." In conversation with *Essence*, Usher explained his decision to wear the shirt: "We must know who we are in order be [*sic*] our best selves" (Lewis, "Usher Explains His Juneteenth Shirt").

83. Boym, *The Future of Nostalgia*, 354.

84. Quoted in Clark, "Scott Joplin Ragtime Gets Its Dues."

85. Ogunnaike, "The New Harlem Renaissance."

86. Golden, *Freestyle*, 14.

87. John Bankston, one of the artists featured in this exhibition, noted that his work acknowledges the persistence of race in American culture, in particular, but said that he also attempts to "complicate that reading by layering it with so many things—issues of gender, high/low culture, painterliness, color/absence of color, drawing/painting" (quoted in Byrd, "Is There a 'Post-Black' Art?," 38).

88. I write this with the understanding that even though the Black Arts/Black Power movement has generally been regarded as "complicit in denying the full range of black identities," the arbiters of that period as well as proponents of black respectability, as Mark Anthony Neal points out, engaged in a rather willful erasure of black identities deemed "detrimental" to the political and social advancement of "the race" (*Soul Babies*, 8). However, I want to make clear that the historical and critical "distance" to which I refer doesn't necessarily point to the evolution of "new" black identities; rather, it refers to the illusion of homogenous and monolithic notions of blackness made prevalent in earlier black historical moments.

89. Ogunnaike, "The New Harlem Renaissance."

90. Ogunnaike.

91. Wright, *Physics of Blackness*, 7.

92. Wright, 17.

93. Janer, "(In)Edible Nature," 391.

94. Janer, 392.

95. Samuelsson, *Yes, Chef*, 243.

96. Samuelsson, 266.

97. Samuelsson, 4.

98. Samuelsson, 7.

99. Eoyang, "Beyond Visual and Aural Criteria," 105.

100. Samuelsson notes that if he had "been interested only in delivering authentic, traditional dishes, [he] would have left that to the existing African restaurants, the ones that are cordoned off into ethnic enclaves, down a few flights of steps from the street, serving to expat cabdrivers and budget-conscious but adventurous college students" (*Yes, Chef*, 263).

101. Bryden, "An Aroma of Spices," 24.

102. Eoyang, "Beyond Visual and Aural Criteria," 101.

103. Eoyang, 104.

104. Samuelsson, *Yes, Chef*, 36.

105. Samuelsson, "Marcus Samuelsson on Cooking and Controversy."

106. Samuelsson, *Yes, Chef*, 39.

107. Bauerlein, "Marcus Samuelsson's Harlem Renaissance."

108. Samuelsson, *Yes, Chef*, 315.

109. Sifton, "Red Rooster Harlem."

110. "Philip Maysles' New Art at Red Rooster," Marcus Samuelsson (chef's website), posted October 20, 2011, https://marcussamuelsson.com/ (removed from website as of June 2020).

111. "Philip Maysles: The Comfort of Enlightenment," Monte Vista Projects (website of artists' collective), January 10, 2009, http://www.montevistaprojects.com/.

112. Baldwin, "Stranger in the Village."

113. Samuelsson, *Yes, Chef*, 312.

114. Samuelsson, "Moving to Harlem with Marcus Samuelsson."

115. Samuelsson, *Yes, Chef*, 283.

116. Huang, "Marcus Samuelsson's Overcooked Memoir."

117. Park, "Marcus Samuelsson's Unorthodox *Red Rooster Cookbook*."

118. Sifton, "Red Rooster Harlem."

119. Arena, *Driven from New Orleans*; Boyd, *Jim Crow Nostalgia*; Pattillo, *Black on the Block*; Brett Williams, "Gentrifying Water and Selling Jim Crow."

120. Samuelsson, *The Red Rooster Cookbook*, 16.

121. Spitznagel, "Sylvia Woods."

122. Wright, *Physics of Blackness*, 172.

123. Weiss, *Feast and Folly*, 86.

124. Weiss, 8–9.

125. Weiss, 85.

126. *Oxford English Dictionary*, s.v. "flavor, *n.*," accessed June 7, 2020, https://www.oed.com/ (emphasis added).

127. Eoyang, "Beyond Visual and Aural Criteria," 100.

Postscript: A Future for Black Nostalgia

1. *Los Angeles Times* film critic Sheila Benson called the film a "plentiful waste of time and money," and Vincent Canby from the *New York Times* wrote that the screenplay "seems to have escaped its doctors before it was entirely well." See Benson, "Spare Fare in Eddie Murphy's 'America'"; Canby, "An African Prince in Queens."
2. Robbins, "Michael Jackson Video Greatest Hits."
3. Amisu, *The Dangerous Philosophies of Michael Jackson*, 92.
4. Blight, *Race and Reunion*, 322.
5. Blight, 323.
6. Louise-Julie, "The Leader of the Pack."
7. Commander, *Afro-Atlantic Flight*, 3.
8. Commander, 15.
9. Okorafor, "In Conversation."
10. Okorafor, "Africanfuturism Defined."
11. Illbruck, *Nostalgia*, 233.
12. Nietzsche spells out his philosophy of free-spiritedness in *All Too Human* (1878): "You had to become master over yourself, master of your own good qualities. Formerly they were your masters: but they should be merely your tools along with other tools. You had to acquire power over your aye and no and learn to hold and withhold them in accordance with your higher aims" (4).
13. Blickle, *Heimat*, 28.
14. Blickle, 28.
15. Wood, *Hegel's Ethical Thought*, 51.
16. Lund, "Introducing the Sensational Black Panther!"
17. Lund.
18. Opam, "Wakanda Reborn," slide 18 of 61.
19. Opam, slide 21 of 61.
20. Coates, *Black Panther*, Book 1, n.p.
21. Coates, Book 1, n.p.
22. Coates, Book 1, n.p.
23. Coates, Book 2, n.p.
24. Tillet, "'Black Panther' Brings Hope, Hype and Pride."
25. Jefferson, *Notes on the State of Virginia*, 264.
26. Parks, "An Equation for Black People Onstage," 19.

Bibliography

Ahmed, Sara. *The Cultural Politics of Emotion*. New York: Routledge, 2014.

Alexander, Jacqui. *Pedagogies of Crossing: Meditations on Feminism, Sexual Politics, Memory, and the Sacred*. Durham, NC: Duke University Press, 2005.

Allen, Mark. "New Blanc Chicago Gallery Amanda Williams Art Exhibit Starts February 25th." *And the Ordinary People Said* (blog). *Chicago Now*, February 25, 2011. http://www.chicagonow.com/and-the-ordinary-people-said/.

Amisu, Elizabeth. *The Dangerous Philosophies of Michael Jackson*. New York: Praeger, 2016.

Araujo, Ana Lucia. *Shadows of the Slave Past: Memory, Heritage, and Slavery*. New York: Routledge, 2014.

Arena, John. *Driven from New Orleans: How Nonprofits Betray Public Housing and Promote Privatization*. Minneapolis: University of Minnesota Press, 2012.

Arnold, Gina. "'As Real as Real Can Get': Race, Representation, and Rhetoric at *Wattstax*, 1972." In *The Pop Festival: History, Music, Media, and Culture*, edited by George McKay, 61–74. New York: Bloomsbury, 2015.

Arzumanova, Inna. "The Culture Industry and Beyoncé's Proprietary Blackness." *Celebrity Studies* 7, no. 3 (2016): 421–24.

Atias, Nadia, and Jeremy Davies. "Nostalgia and the Shapes of History." *Memory Studies* 3, no. 3 (June 2010): 181–86.

Baker, Houston A., Jr. "Critical Memory and the Black Public Sphere." *Public Culture* 7, no. 1 (1994): 3–33.

Baker, Mark Frederick, and Houston A. Baker Jr. "Uptown Where We Belong: Space, Captivity, and the Documentary of Black Community." In *Struggles for Representation: African American Documentary Film and Video*, edited by Phyllis Rauch Klotman and Janet K. Cutler, 211–49. Bloomington: Indiana University Press, 2000.

Baldwin, James. "Stranger in the Village." *Harper's Magazine*, October 1953. https://harpers.org/.

Baldwin, Matthew, Monica Biernat, and Mark J. Landau. "Remembering the Real Me: Nostalgia Offers a Window to the Intrinsic Self." *Journal of Personality and Social Psychology* 108, no. 1 (2015): 128–47. http://dx.doi.org/10.1037/a0038033.

Bassard, Katherine Clay. "Imagining Other Worlds: Race, Gender, and the 'Power Line' in Edward P. Jones's *The Known World.*" *African American Review* 42, no. 3–4 (Fall–Winter 2008): 407–19.

Batcho, Krystine Irene, and Simran Shikh. "Anticipatory Nostalgia: Missing the Present before It's Gone." *Personality and Individual Differences* 98 (2016): 75–84.

Batiste, Stephanie. *Darkening Mirrors: Imperial Representation in Depression-Era African American Performance.* Durham, NC: Duke University Press, 2012.

Bauerlein, Monika. "Marcus Samuelsson's Harlem Renaissance." *Mother Jones*, August 10, 2012. https://www.motherjones.com/.

Bell, Bernard. *The Afro-American Novel and Its Tradition.* Amherst: University of Massachusetts Press, 1987.

Bennett, Jane. *Vibrant Matter: A Political Ecology of Things.* Durham, NC: Duke University Press, 2010.

Benson, Sheila. "Spare Fare in Eddie Murphy's 'America.'" *Los Angeles Times*, June 29, 1988. https://www.latimes.com/archives/.

Berlant, Lauren. *Cruel Optimism.* Durham, NC: Duke University Press, 2011.

Best, Stephen. *None Like Us: Blackness, Belonging, Aesthetic Life.* Durham, NC: Duke University Press, 2018.

Blickle, Peter. *Heimat: A Critical Theory of the German Idea of Homeland.* Rochester, NY: Camden House, 2002.

Blight, David. *Race and Reunion: The Civil War in American Memory.* Cambridge, MA: Harvard University Press, 2001.

Boniface, Brian, and Chris Cooper. *Worldwide Destinations: The Geography of Travel and Tourism.* Oxford: Elsevier, 2009.

Bonnett, Alastair. *Left in the Past: Radicalism and the Politics of Nostalgia.* New York: Continuum Books, 2010.

Bowman, Rob. *Soulsville, U.S.A.: The Story of Stax Records.* New York: Schimer Trade Books, 2003.

Boyd, Michelle. *Jim Crow Nostalgia: Reconstructing Race in Bronzeville.* Minneapolis: University of Minnesota Press, 2008.

Boym, Svetlana. *The Future of Nostalgia.* New York: Basic Books, 2001.

Bradley, Regina. "Re-Imagining Slavery in the Hip-Hop Imagination." *South* 49, no. 1 (Fall 2016): 3–24.

Braidotti, Rosi. *Transpositions: On Nomadic Ethics.* Cambridge: Polity Press, 2006.

Brand, Dionne. *A Map to the Door of No Return: Notes to Belonging.* Toronto: Vintage Canada, 2001.

Brooks, Daphne A. "How #BlackLivesMatter Started a Musical Revolution." *Guardian*, March 13, 2016. https://www.theguardian.com/.

Brown, Bill. "Thing Theory." *Critical Inquiry* 28, no. 1 (2001): 1–22.

Brownstein, Ronald. "Trump's Rhetoric of White Nostalgia." *Atlantic*, June 2, 2016. https://www.theatlantic.com/.

Bryden, Inga. "'An Aroma of Spices . . . Magnified the Sense of What It Meant to Live in England': Travel, 'Real' Food, and 'Misshapen' Identity." In *Mapping Appetite: Essays on Food, Fiction and Culture*, edited by Jopi Nyman and Pere Gallardo-Torrano, 8–27. New Castle: Cambridge Scholars, 2007.

Byerman, Keith. *Remembering the Past in Contemporary African American Fiction*. Chapel Hill: University of North Carolina Press, 2006.

Bynum, Bill. "Discarded Diagnoses." *Lancet* 358, no. 9299 (December 22, 2001): 2176.

Byrd, Cathy. "Is There a 'Post-Black' Art? Investigating the Legacy of the 'Freestyle' Show." *Art Papers* 26, no. 6 (2002): 34–39.

Canby, Vincent. "An African Prince in Queens." *New York Times*, June 29, 1988. https://www.nytimes.com/.

Carland, Tammy Rae, and Ann Cvetkovich. "Sharing an Archive of Feelings: A Conversation." *Art Journal* 72, no. 2 (2013). http://artjournal.collegeart.org/?p=3960.

Cervenak, Sarah. *Wandering: Philosophical Performances of Racial and Sexual Freedom*. Durham, NC: Duke University Press, 2014.

Césaire, Suzanne. "The Domain of the Marvelous" (excerpt from "The Esthetics of Alain"). In *Surrealist Painters and Poets: An Anthology*, edited by Mary Ann Caws, 157–58. Cambridge, MA: MIT Press, 2001.

———. "Surrealism and Us: 1943." In *The Great Camouflage: Writings of Dissent (1941–1945)*, edited by Daniel Maximen, translated by Keith L. Walker, 34–38. Middletown, CT: Wesleyan University Press, 2012.

Chambers-Letson, Joshua. *After the Party: A Manifesto for Queer of Color Life*. New York: New York University Press, 2018.

Chicago Metropolitan Agency for Planning (CMAP). "Planning for Green and Healthy Chicago Neighborhoods." Updated March 20, 2014. https://www.cmap.illinois.gov/programs/lta/ghn-chicago.

Chokshi, Niraj. "Rudy Giuliani: Beyoncé's Halftime Show Was an 'Outrageous' Affront to Police." *Washington Post*, February 8, 2016. https://www.washingtonpost.com/.

Christian, Barbara. "The Race for Theory." *Cultural Critique* 6 (Spring 1987): 51–63.

Clark, Philip. "Scott Joplin Ragtime Gets Its Dues." *Guardian*, January 22, 2014. https://www.theguardian.com/.

Coates, Ta-Nehisi. *Black Panther: A Nation under Our Feet*. Book 1. New York: Marvel, 2016.

———. *Black Panther: A Nation under Our Feet*. Book 2. New York: Marvel, 2017.

Colbert, Soyica. "Reconstruction, Fugitive Intimacy, and Holding History." *Modern Drama* 62, no. 4 (Winter 2019): 502–16.

Commander, Michelle. *Afro-Atlantic Flight: Speculative Returns and the Black Fantastic*. Durham, NC: Duke University Press, 2017.

Cooks, Bridget R. "Romare Bearden: On View." *Studies in the History of Art* 71 (2011): 207–19.

Copeland, Huey. *Bound to Appear: Art, Slavery, and the Site of Blackness in Multicultural America*. Chicago: University of Chicago Press, 2013.

Crawford, Margo Natalie. *Black Post-Blackness: The Black Arts Movement and Twenty-First-Century Aesthetics*. Urbana: University of Illinois Press, 2017.

Currie, Mark. *About Time: Narrative, Fiction and the Philosophy of Time*. Edinburgh: Edinburgh University Press, 2006.

Curtis, Edward E., IV. *Black Muslim Religion in the Nation of Islam, 1960–1975*. Chapel Hill: University of North Carolina Press, 2006.

Cvetkovich, Ann. "Affect." In *Keywords for American Cultural Studies*, edited by Bruce Burgett and Glenn Hendler, 13–16. New York: New York University Press, 2014.

———. *An Archive of Feelings: Trauma, Sexuality, and Lesbian Public Cultures*. Durham, NC: Duke University Press, 2003.

———. "Depression Is Ordinary: Public Feelings and Saidiya Hartman's *Lose Your Mother*." *Feminist Theory* 13, no. 2 (2012): 131–46.

D'Angelo, Robin. "White Fragility." *International Journal of Critical Pedagogy* 3, no. 3 (2011): 54–70.

Darden, Norma Jean, and Carole Darden. *Spoonbread and Strawberry Wine: Remembrances of a Family*. Garden City, NY: Anchor Press, 1978.

Davis, Angela. "Afro Images: Politics, Fashion, and Nostalgia." *Critical Inquiry* 21, no. 1 (Autumn 1994): 37–45.

Day, Ivan. *Food History Jottings* (blog). http://foodhistorjottings.blogspot.com/.

DeGruy, Joy. *Post-Traumatic Slave Syndrome*. New York: Amistad Press, 2005.

DeKnight, Freda. *The Ebony Cookbook: A Date with a Dish*. Chicago: Johnson, 1962.

Derrida, Jacques. *Archive Fever: A Freudian Impression*. Translated by Eric Prenowitz. Chicago: University of Chicago Press, 1996.

Dickson, Akeya. "Thug Kitchen: A Recipe in Blackface." *Root*, September 30, 2014. https://www.theroot.com/.

Dickson-Carr, Darryl. *African American Satire: The Sacredly Profane Novel*. Columbia: University of Missouri Press, 2001.

Dobkin, Kelly. "10 Southern Chefs to Watch." Zagat.com, March 12, 2014. https://www.zagat.com/b/10-southern-chefs-to-watch.

Drumming, Neil. "We Are in the Future." *This American Life*, NPR podcast, August 18, 2017. https://www.thisamericanlife.org/radio-archives/episode/623/transcript.

Dubey, Madhu. "Speculative Fictions of Slavery." *American Literature* 82, no. 4 (December 2010): 779–805.

Dungey, Azie Mira. "'Ask a Slave' and Interpreting Race on Public History's Front Line: Interview with Azie Mira Dungey." By Amy M. Tyson. *Public Historian* 36, no. 1 (February 2014): 36–60.

Edwards, Brent Hayes. "The Ethnics of Surrealism." *Transition* 78 (1998): 84–135.

———. *The Practice of Diaspora: Literature, Translation, and the Rise of Black Internationalism.* Cambridge, MA: Harvard University Press, 2003.

Elam, Harry J., Jr. *The Past as Present in the Drama of August Wilson.* Ann Arbor: University of Michigan Press, 2009.

Elam, Harry J., Jr., and Michele Elam. "Blood Debt: Reparations in Langston Hughes's *Mulatto*." *Theatre Journal* 61, no. 1 (March 2009): 85–103.

Eoyang, Eugene. "Beyond Visual and Aural Criteria: The Importance of Flavor in Chinese Literary Criticism." *Critical Inquiry* 6, no. 1 (1979): 99–106.

Ernest, John. *Chaotic Justice: Rethinking African American Literary History.* Chapel Hill: University of North Carolina Press, 2009.

Eyerman, Ron. *Cultural Trauma: Slavery and the Formation of African American Identity.* New York: Cambridge University Press, 2002.

Faber, Tony. *Stradivari's Genius: Five Violins, One Cello, and Three Centuries of Enduring Perfection.* New York: Random House, 2006.

Fauset, Jessie. "Nostalgia." *Crisis* 22, no. 4 (August 1921): 154–57.

Finley, Jessyka. "Black Women's Satire as (Black) Postmodern Performance." *Studies in American Humor* 4, no. 2 (November 2016): 236–65.

Franklin, Krista. "Black to the Future Series: An Interview with Krista Franklin." By Tempestt Hazel. *The Chicago Arts Archive: A Sixty Inches from Center Project*, May 28, 2013. http://sixtyinchesfromcenter.org/archive/?p=15558.

———. "Manifesto, or Ars Poetica #2. *Poetry*, April 2015. https://www.poetryfoundation.org/.

Freeman, Andrea. "The Unbearable Whiteness of Milk: Food Oppression and the USDA." *UC Irvine Law Review* 3 (2013): 1251–77.

Freud, Sigmund. "Humor." *International Journal of Psychoanalysis* 9 (1928): 1–6.

Gallop, Jane. "The Ethics of Reading: Close Encounters." *Journal of Curriculum Theorizing* 16, no. 3 (Fall 2000): 7–17.

Garrido, Sandra. "The Influence of Personality and Coping Style on the Affective Outcomes of Nostalgia: Is Nostalgia a Healthy Coping Mechanism or Rumination?" *Personality and Individual Differences* 120 (2018): 259–64.

Gates, Henry Louis, Jr., host. *Finding Your Roots.* Season 3, episode 7, "Family Reunions." Aired February 16, 2016, on PBS. https://www.pbs.org/weta/finding-your-roots/.

George, Sheldon. *Trauma and Race: A Lacanian Study of African American Racial Identity.* Waco, TX: Baylor University Press, 2016.

Gilliver, Liam. "'Thug Kitchen' to Change Its Name Following Accusations of 'Digital Blackface.'" *Plant-Based News*, June 21, 2020. https://www.plantbasednews.org/.

Goff, Phillip Atiba, Matthew Christian Jackson, Brooke Allison Lewis Di Leone, Carmen Marie Culotta, and Natalie Ann DiTomasso. "The Essence of Innocence: Consequences of Dehumanizing Black Children." *Journal of Personality and Social Psychology* 106 (2014): 526–45.

Golden, Thelma. *Freestyle.* Exhibition catalog. New York: Studio Museum in Harlem, 2001.

Grandin, Greg. "Who Ain't a Slave? Historical Fact and the Fiction of 'Benito Cereno.'" *Chronicle of Higher Education*, December 16, 2013. https://www.chronicle.com/.

Gregory, Dick. *Dick Gregory's Natural Diet for Folks Who Eat: Cookin' with Mother Nature.* New York: Harper and Row, 1973.

Greyser, Naomi. *On Sympathetic Grounds: Race, Gender, and Affective Geographies in Nineteenth-Century North America.* New York: Oxford University Press, 2017.

Grier, Sonya A., and Shiriki K. Kumanyika. "The Context for Choice: Health Implications of Targeted Food and Beverage Marketing to African Americans." *American Journal of Public Health* 98, no. 9 (September 2008): 1616–29.

Griffin, Charles J. G. "John Brown's 'Madness.'" *Rhetoric and Public Affairs* 12, no. 3 (2009): 369–88.

Guerrero, Lisa. "B(l)ack in the Kitchen: Food Network." In *African Americans on Television: Race-ing for Ratings*, edited by David J. Leonard and Lisa Guerrero, 299–313. Westport, CT: Praeger, 2013.

Gumbs, Alexis Pauline. *Spill: Scenes of Black Feminist Fugitivity.* Durham, NC: Duke University Press, 2016.

Guy, Jerrelle. *Black Girl Baking: Wholesome Recipes Inspired by a Soulful Upbringing.* Salem, MA: Page Street, 2018.

Haggins, Bambi. *Laughing Mad: The Black Comic Persona in Post-Soul America.* New Brunswick: Rutgers University Press, 2007.

Hall, Carla. *Carla Hall's Soul Food: Everyday and Celebration.* New York: Harper Wave, 2018.

Hall, Jacquelyn Dowd. "The Civil Rights Movement and the Political Uses of the Past." *Journal of American History* 91, no. 4 (2005): 1233–63.

Harding, Susan, and Daniel Rosenberg, eds. *Histories of the Future.* Durham, NC: Duke University Press, 2005.

Hartman, Saidiya. *Scenes of Subjection: Terror, Slavery, and Self-Making in Nineteenth-Century America.* New York: Oxford University Press, 1997.

———. "Venus in Two Acts." *Small Axe* 26 (June 2008): 1–14.

Henderson, Laretta. "*Ebony Jr!* and 'Soul Food': The Construction of an Ethnic Identity through the Use of Food." *MELUS* 32, no. 4 (Winter 2007): 81–97.

Hester, Jessica Leigh. "The Phone Booth for Japanese Mourners." *Citylab*, January 10, 2017. http://www.citylab.com/.

Heynen, Nik. "Bending the Bars of Empire from Every Ghetto for Survival: The Black Panther Party's Radical Anti-Hunger Politics of Social Reproduction and Scale." *Annals of the Association of American Geographers* 99, no. 2 (May 2009): 406–22.

Hing, Julianne. "Six Books That Shaped 'Afro-Vegan' Author Bryant Terry." *ColorLines*, April 8, 2014. https://www.colorlines.com/.

Hirsch, Marianne. *The Generation of Postmemory: Writing and Visual Culture after the Holocaust*. New York: Columbia University Press, 2012.

Holbrook, Kate. "Good to Eat: Culinary Priorities in the Nation of Islam and the Church of Jesus Christ of Latter-Day Saints." In *Religion, Food, and Eating in North America*, edited by Benjamin E. Zeller, Marie W. Dallam, Reid L. Neilson, and Nora L. Rubel, 195–213. New York: Columbia University Press, 2014.

Horowitz, Steven. "Kendrick Lamar Speaks on the Meaning behind 'HiiiPoWeR,' Working with J. Cole." *HipHopDX*, July 1, 2011. https://hiphopdx.com.

Huang, Eddie. "Marcus Samuelsson's Overcooked Memoir Makes His Pricey Harlem Discomfort Food Hard to Swallow: The Chickens Come Home to (Red) Roost." *Observer*, June 25, 2012. https://observer.com/.

Hunt, S. B. "Dr. Cartwright on Drapetomania." *Buffalo Medical Journal* 10 (1855): 438–42.

Hurston, Zora Neale. "How It Feels to Be Colored Me." *World Tomorrow* 11 (May 1928): 215–16. https://www.facinghistory.org/resource-library/how-it-feels-be-colored-me.

Hurt, Byron, dir. *Soul Food Junkies*. Fanwood, NJ: God Bless the Child Productions, 2013. Film, 64 min.

Hutcheon, Linda. "Irony, Nostalgia, and the Postmodern." *Studies in Comparative Literature* 30 (2000): 189–207.

———. *A Poetics of Postmodernism: History, Theory, Fiction*. New York: Routledge, 1988.

Hutcheon, Linda, and Mario J. Valdés. "Irony, Nostalgia and the Postmodern: A Dialogue." *Poligrafías* 3 (1998–2000): 18–41.

Illbruck, Helmut. *Nostalgia: Origins and Ends of an Unenlightened Disease*. Evanston, IL: Northwestern University Press, 2012.

Iton, Richard. *In Search of the Black Fantastic*. New York: Oxford University Press, 2008.

Jackson, John L., Jr. *Real Black: Adventures in Racial Sincerity*. Chicago: University of Chicago Press, 2005.

Jackson, Mary, and Lelia Wishart. *The Integrated Cookbook or the Soul of Good Cooking*. Chicago: Johnson, 1971.

Janer, Zilkia. "(In)Edible Nature: New World Food and Coloniality." *Cultural Studies* 21, no. 2–3 (2007): 385–405.

Jefferson, Thomas. *Notes on the State of Virginia*. London: printed for John Stockdale, 1787. Reprint, {PLACE: PUBLISHER OF REPRINT}, 1986.

Johnson, Mat. *Hunting in Harlem*. New York: Bloomsbury, 2003.

Jones, Edward P. *The Known World*. New York: Amistad Press, 2003.

Jones, Wilbert. *The New Soul Food Cookbook*. New York: Citadel, 2000.

Keizer, Arlene. *Black Subjects: Identity Formation in the Contemporary Narrative of Slavery*. Ithaca, NY: Cornell University Press, 2004.

Kline, Linus. "The Migratory Impulse vs. the Love of Home." *American Journal of Psychology* 10, no. 1 (October 1898): 1–81.

Kornhaber, Spencer. "What Beyoncé's 'Daddy's Lessons' Had to Teach." *Atlantic*, November 3, 2016. http://www.theatlantic.com/.

Lambert-Beatty, Carrie. "Make Believe: Parafiction and Plausibility." *October* 129 (Summer 2009): 51–84.

Lenhart, Chelsea. "Hercules." In *The Digital Encyclopedia of George Washington*, edited by James P. Ambuske. Mount Vernon, VA: Mount Vernon Ladies' Association, 2012–. http://www.mountvernon.org/digital-encyclopedia/article /hercules.

Lessing, Mark. *Lesser Beasts: A Snout-to-Tail History of the Humble Pig*. New York: Basic Books, 2015.

Levin, Kevin M. "The Case against Vandalizing Monuments." *Atlantic*, December 21, 2011. http://www.theatlantic.com/.

———. "Why I Changed My Mind about Confederate Monuments." *Atlantic*, August 19, 2017. https://www.theatlantic.com/.

Levins Morales, Aurora. *Remedios: Stories of Earth and Iron from the History of Puertorriqueñas*. Boston: Beacon Press, 1998.

Levy-Hussen, Aida. *How to Read African American Literature: Post–Civil Rights Fiction and the Task of Interpretation*. New York: New York University Press, 2016.

Lewis, Taylor. "Usher Explains His Juneteenth Shirt: 'Know What You're Celebrating.'" *Essence*, July 9, 2015. https://www.essence.com/.

Lierow, Lars. "The 'Black Man's Vision of the World': Rediscovering Black Arts Filmmaking and the Struggle for a Black Cinematic Aesthetic." *Black Camera* 4, no. 2 (Spring 2013): 3–21.

Lillvis, Kristen. *Posthuman Blackness and the Black Female Imagination*. Athens: University of Georgia Press, 2017.

Lindsay-Habermann, Claudette. "Till Victory Is Won: The Staying Power of 'Lift Every Voice and Sing.'" *Morning Edition*, NPR, August 16, 2018. https://www .npr.org/.

Louise-Julie, Paul. "The Leader of the Pack." Posted by Rich Johnston. *Bleeding Cool*, March 15, 2015. https://bleedingcool.com/comics/the-pack/.

Lund, Martin. "'Introducing the Sensational Black Panther!': *Fantastic Four* #52–53, the Cold War, and Marvel's Imagined Africa." *Comics Grid* 6, no. 1 (2016). https://www.comicsgrid.com/articles/10.16995/cg.80/.

Mackey, John. *Conscious Capitalism: Liberating the Heroic Spirit of Business*. Boston: Harvard Business Review Press, 2013.

Mann, Geoff. "Why Does Country Music Sound So White? Race and the Voice of Nostalgia." *Ethnic and Racial Studies* 31, no. 1 (2008): 73–100.

Margalit, Avishai. "Nostalgia." *Psychoanalytic Dialogues* 21, no. 3 (2011): 271–80.

Massaquoi, Hans. "Mystery of Malcolm X." *Ebony*, September 1993.

Matt, Susan J. *Homesickness: An American History*. New York: Oxford University Press, 2011.

Maus, Derek C., and James Donahue, eds. *Post-Soul Satire: Black Identity after Civil Rights*. Jackson: University of Mississippi Press, 2015.

May, Vanessa. "Belonging from Afar: Nostalgia, Time and Memory." *Sociological Review* 65, no. 2 (2017): 401–15.

McBride, James. *The Good Lord Bird*. New York: Penguin, 2013.

McMay, George. *The Pop Festival: History, Music, Media, Culture*. New York: Bloomsbury Academic, 2015.

Meek, Miki. "One Last Thing before I Go." *This American Life*, NPR podcast, episode 597, September 23, 2016. https://www.thisamericanlife.org/.

Melville, Herman. *Great Short Works of Herman Melville*. 1855. Reprint, New York: Harper Perennial Modern Classics, 2004.

Mendes, Helen. *The African Heritage Cookbook*. New York: Macmillan, 1971.

Metzl, Jonathan. *Dying of Whiteness: How the Politics of Racial Resentment Is Killing America's Heartland*. New York: Basic Books, 2019.

Miller, D. Scot. "Afrosurreal Manifesto: Black Is the New Black—A 21st Century Manifesto." *San Francisco Bay Guardian*, May 20, 2009. Republished, *D. Scot Miller: AfroSurreal Generation* (blog), May 20, 2009. http://dscotmiller.blogspot .com/2009/05/afrosurreal.html.

———. "Black to the Future Series: A Conversation with D. Scot Miller." By Tempestt Hazel. *The Chicago Arts Archive: A Sixty Inches from Center Project*, June 4, 2012. http://sixtyinchesfromcenter.org/archive/?p=15571.

Mitchell, Angelyn. *The Freedom to Remember: Narrative, Slavery, and Gender in Contemporary Black Women's Fiction*. New Brunswick, NJ: Rutgers University Press, 2002.

Morgan, Edward P. "Media Culture and the Public Memory of the Black Panther Party." In *In Search of the Black Panther Party: New Perspectives on a Revolutionary Movement*, edited by Jama Lazerow and Yohuru Williams, 324–74. Durham, NC: Duke University Press, 2006.

Morgan, Joan. "Moving Towards a Black Feminist Politics of Pleasure." *Black Scholar: Journal of Black Studies and Research* 45, no. 4 (October 2015): 36–46.

Mowitt, John. *Percussion: Drumming, Beating, Striking*. Durham, NC: Duke University Press, 2002.

Muhammad, Elijah. *How to Eat to Live*. Book 1. Phoenix, AZ: Secretarius MEMPS, 1967.

———. *How to Eat to Live*. Book 2. Phoenix, AZ: Secretarius MEMPS, 1972.

Muñoz, José. *Cruising Utopia: The Then and There of Queer Futurity*. New York: New York University Press, 2009.

Murray, Rolland. "Time of Breach: Class Division and the Contemporary African American Novel." *Novel* 43, no. 1 (2010): 11–17.

Mutter, Sarah Mahurin. "'Such a Poor Word for a Wondrous Thing': Thingness and the Recovery of the Human in *The Known World*." *Southern Literary Journal* 43, no. 2 (Spring 2011): 125–46.

Nash, Jennifer. "Practicing Love: Black Feminism, Love-Politics, and Post-Intersectionality." *Meridians* 11, no. 2 (2011): 1–24.

Neal, Larry. "The Black Arts Movement." *Drama Review: TDR* 12, no. 4 (Summer 1968): 28–39.

Neal, Mark Anthony. *Soul Babies: Black Popular Culture and the Post-Soul Aesthetic.* New York: Routledge, 2001.

Nelson, Alondra. *The Social Life of DNA.* Boston: Beacon Press, 2016.

Nietzsche, Friedrich. *All Too Human: A Book for Free Spirits.* 1878. Reprint, New York: Prometheus Books, 2008.

Nyong'o, Tavia. *Afro-Fabulations: The Queer Drama of Black Life.* New York: New York University Press, 2018.

Ogunnaike, Lola. "The New Harlem Renaissance." *Food and Wine,* November 2008. Updated March 31, 2015. https://www.foodandwine.com/.

Okeowo, Alexis. "The Provocateur behind Beyoncé, Rihanna, and Issa Rae." *New Yorker,* March 2, 2017. http://www.newyorker.com/.

Okorafor, Nnedi. "Africanfuturism Defined." *Nnedi's Wahala Zone Blog,* October 19, 2019. https://nnedi.blogspot.com/.

———. "In Conversation: Nnedi Okorafor on Venom, George R.R. Martin and Why Artists Can't Have Mentors." Interview by Abiola Oke. *OkayAfrica,* September 13, 2017. https://www.okayafrica.com/.

Opam, Kwame. "Wakanda Reborn: Tour Black Panther's Reimagined Homeland with Ta-Nehisi Coates." *Verge,* May 15, 2017. https://www.theverge.com/a/marvel-black-panther.

Opie, Frederick Douglass. *Hog and Hominy: Soul Food from Africa to America.* New York: Columbia University Press, 2010.

———. "Lenten Season Part 4: Fasting and Dr. Alvenia Fulton." Uploaded February 28, 2012. YouTube video, 3:43. https://www.youtube.com/watch?v=h6xbECJoNPo.

Park, Benjamin. "Marcus Samuelsson's Unorthodox *Red Rooster Cookbook* Is a Literary Love Letter to Harlem." *Vanity Fair,* October 28, 2016. https://www.vanityfair.com/.

Parks, Suzan-Lori. "An Equation for Black People Onstage." In *The America Play and Other Works,* 19–22. New York: Theater Communications Group, 1994.

Pattillo, Mary. *Black on the Block: The Politics of Race and Class in the City.* Chicago: University of Chicago Press, 2008.

Pecknold, Diane. *The Selling Sound: The Rise of the Country Music Industry.* Durham, NC: Duke University Press, 2007.

Pérez, Letitia. "The Surrealist Collection of Objects." *425°F: Electronic Journal of Theory of Literature and Comparative Literature* 2 (2010): 114–26.

Pickering, Michael. *Research Methods for Cultural Studies.* Edinburgh: Edinburgh University Press, 2008.

Probyn, Elspeth. *Carnal Appetites.* New York: Routledge, 2000.

Raaberg, Gwen. "Beyond Fragmentation: Collage as Feminist Strategy in the Arts." *Mosaic* 31, no. 3 (1998): 153–71.

Randall, Alice, and Caroline Randall Williams. *Soul Food Love: Healthy Recipes Inspired by One Hundred Years of Cooking in a Black Family*. New York: Clarkson Potter, 2015.

Redmond, Shana. *Anthem: Social Movements and the Sound of Solidarity in the African Diaspora*. New York: New York University Press, 2013.

Reslen, Eileen. "Beyoncé Reveals the Deeply Personal Story behind Her Black National Anthem Performance at Coachella." *Harper's Bazaar*, August 6, 2018. https://www.harpersbazaar.com/.

Richards, Todd. *Soul: A Chef's Culinary Evolution in 150 Recipes*. New York: Southern Living, 2018.

Robbins, Ira. "Michael Jackson Video Greatest Hits—HIStory." *Entertainment Weekly*, updated July 21, 1995. https://ew.com/.

Rody, Caroline. *The Daughter's Return: African-American and Caribbean Women's Fictions of History*. New York: Oxford University Press, 2010.

Routledge, Clay. *Nostalgia: A Psychological Resource*. New York: Routledge, 2015.

Routledge, Clay, Tim Wildschut, Constantine Sedikides, and Jacob Juhl. "Nostalgia as a Resource for Psychological Health and Well-Being." *Social and Personality Psychology Compass* 7, no. 11 (November 2013): 808–18.

Rushdy, Ashraf. *Neo-Slave Narratives: Studies in the Logic of a Literary Form*. New York: Oxford University Press, 1999.

Sampson, Marmaduke Blake. *Slavery in the United States: A Letter to the Hon. Daniel Webster*. London: S. Highly, 1845.

Samuelsson, Marcus. "Marcus Samuelsson on Cooking and Controversy." Interview by Tim Carman. *Washington Post*, August 10, 2012.

———. "Moving to Harlem with Marcus Samuelsson." Interview by Melissa Clark. *Splendid Table*, October 18, 2016. https://www.splendidtable.org/.

———. *The Red Rooster Cookbook: A Story of Food and Hustle and Harlem*. New York: Rux Martin/Houghton Mifflin Harcourt, 2016.

———. *The Soul of a New Cuisine: A Discovery of the Foods and Flavors of Africa*. Hoboken, NJ: John Wiley, 2006.

———. *Yes, Chef: A Memoir*. New York: Random House, 2012.

Schapiro, Miriam, and Melissa Meyer. "Femmage." *Heresies: Women's Traditional Arts: The Politics of Aesthetics*, Winter 1978.

Scholastic. "Response on *A Birthday Cake for George Washington*." *OOM: On Our Minds* (blog). Scholastic, January 15, 2016. http://oomscholasticblog.com/.

Schweitzer, Frederick M., and Marvin Perry. *Anti-Semitism: Myth and Hate from Antiquity to the Present*. New York: Palgrave, 2002.

Sedikides, Constantine, and Tim Wildschut. "Past Forward: Nostalgia as Motivational Force." *Trends in Cognitive Science* 20, no. 5 (May 2016): 319–21.

Sedikides, Constantine, Tim Wildschut, Wing-Yee Cheung, Clay Routledge, Erica G. Hepper, Jamie Arndt, Kenneth Vail, Xinyue Zhou, Kenny Brackstone, and

Ad J. J. M. Vingerhoets. "Nostalgia Fosters Self-Continuity: Uncovering the Mechanism (Social Connectedness) and Consequence (Eudaimonic Well-Being)." *Emotion* 16, no. 4 (June 2016): 524–39.

Seger, Maria. "Ekphrasis and the Postmodern Slave Narrative: Reading the Maps of Edward P. Jones's *The Known World*." *Callaloo* 37, no. 5 (Fall 2014): 1181–95.

Sharpe, Christina. *In the Wake: On Blackness and Being*. Durham, NC: Duke University Press, 2016.

Sifton, Sam. "Red Rooster Harlem." *New York Times*, March 8, 2011. https://www.nytimes.com/.

Silva, Cristobal. "Nostalgia and the Good Life." *Eighteenth Century* 55, no. 1 (2014): 123–28.

Slack, Jennifer Daryl. "The Theory and Method of Articulation in Cultural Studies." In *Stuart Hall: Critical Dialogues in Cultural Studies*, edited by David Morley and Kuan-Hsing Chen, 113–29. London: Routledge, 1996.

Slocum, Rachel. "Whiteness, Space and Alternative Food Practice." *Geoforum* 38 (2007): 520–33.

Smart-Grosvenor, Vertamae. *Vibration Cooking: Or the Travel Notes of a Geechee Girl*. New York: Doubleday, 1970.

Smith, Althea. "A Farewell to Chitterlings: Vegetarianism Is on the Rise among Diet-Conscious Blacks." *Ebony*, September 1974.

Smith, Kimberly K. "Mere Nostalgia: Notes on a Progressive Paratheory." *Rhetoric and Public Affairs* 3, no. 4 (Winter 2000): 505–27.

Smith, Ted. *Weird John Brown: Divine Violence and the Limit of Ethics*. Stanford, CA: Stanford University Press, 2014.

Smith, Zadie. "Novelist Zadie Smith on Historical Nostalgia and the Nature of Talent." Interview by Terry Gross. *Fresh Air*, NPR, November 21, 2016.

Snyder, Terri L. "Suicide, Slavery, and Memory in North America." *Journal of American History* 97, no. 1 (June 2010): 39–62.

Spitznagel, Eric. "Sylvia Woods: An Oral History." *New York Times Magazine*, January 30, 2012. http://archive.nytimes.com/www.nytimes.com/interactive/2012/12/30/magazine/the-lives-they-lived-2012.html.

Steele, Cassie Premo. *We Heal from Memory: Sexton, Corde, Anzaldua, and the Poetry of Witness*. London: Palgrave Macmillan, 2000.

Stewart, Kathleen. *Ordinary Affects*. Durham, NC: Duke University Press, 2007.

Sula, Mike. "Bean Pie, My Brother?" *Chicago Reader*, November 18, 2013.

Taylor, James. *Black Nationalism in the United States: From Malcolm X to Barack Obama*. Boulder: Lynne Rienner, 2014.

Terry, Bryant. *Afro-Vegan: Farm-Fresh African, Caribbean, and Southern Flavors Remixed*. Berkeley, CA: Ten Speed Press, 2014.

———. "Interview with Bryant Terry: Part 1." By Freedes. *Africa on the Blog*, September 4, 2014. https://www.africaontheblog.org/interview-bryant-terry-part-1/.

————. "The Problem with 'Thug' Cuisine." CNN, October 10, 2014. https://www
.cnn.com/.

————. "Try These Tasty Dishes from Bryant Terry's 'Afro-Vegan.'" Interview by
#teamEBONY. June 2014. Uploaded November 20, 2019. https://www.ebony
.com/.

Thompson, Krista. *Shine: The Visual Economy of Light in African Diasporic Aesthetic Practice.* Durham, NC: Duke University Press, 2015.

Thoreau, Henry D. "A Plea for Captain John Brown." 1859. In *The Essays of Henry D.
Thoreau,* edited by Lewis Hyde, 259–80. New York: North Point Press, 2002.

Tillet, Salamishah. "'Black Panther' Brings Hope, Hype and Pride." *New York
Times,* February 9, 2018. https://www.nytimes.com/.

————. *Sites of Slavery: Citizenship and Racial Democracy in the Post-Civil Rights
Imagination.* Durham, NC: Duke University Press, 2012.

Tompkins, Kyla Wazana. *Racial Indigestion: Eating Bodies in the 19th Century.*
New York: New York University Press, 2012.

Torrey, Jesse, Jr. *A Portraiture of Domestic Slavery in the United States: With
Reflections on Restoring the Moral Rights of the Slave, without Impairing the
Legal Privileges of the Possessor; and A Project of a Colonial Asylum for Free
Persons of Colour: Including Memoirs of Facts on the Interior Traffic in Slaves
and on KIDNAPPING.* Philadelphia: published by the author; John Bioren,
printer, 1817.

Trouillot, Michel-Rolph. *Silencing the Past: Power and the Production of History.*
Boston: Beacon Press, 1997.

Twitty, Michael. *The Cooking Gene: A Journey through African American Culinary
History in the Old South.* New York: Amistad, 2017.

Wall, Tyler. "'For the Very Existence of Civilization': The Police Dog and Racial
Terror." *American Quarterly* 68, no. 4 (December 2016): 861–82.

Wallach, Jennifer Jensen. *Every Nation Has Its Dish: Black Bodies and Black Food
in Twentieth-Century America.* Chapel Hill: University of North Carolina Press,
2018.

————. "How to Eat to Live: Black Nationalism and the Post-1964 Culinary Turn."
Study the South, July 2, 2014. http://southernstudies.olemiss.edu/study-the-
south/how-to-eat-to-live/.

Wanzo, Rebecca. *The Suffering Will Not Be Televised: African American Women
and Sentimental Political Storytelling.* Buffalo: State University of New York
Press, 2015.

Weiss, Allen. *Feast and Folly: Cuisine, Intoxication, and the Poetics of the Sublime.*
Buffalo: State University of New York Press, 2002.

Whitehead, Colson. *Underground Railroad.* New York: Doubleday, 2016.

Williams, Bianca. *The Pursuit of Happiness: Black Women, Diasporic Dreams,
and the Politics of Emotional Transnationalism.* Durham, NC: Duke University
Press, 2018.

Williams, Brett. "Gentrifying Water and Selling Jim Crow." *Urban Anthropology and Studies of Cultural Systems and World Economic Development* 31, no. 1 (2002): 93–121.

Williams, Lance A. "Wattstax Concert at Coliseum." *Los Angeles Times*, August 22, 1972.

Williams, Raymond. *Marxism and Literature*. New York: Oxford University Press, 1977.

Williams, Sherley Anne. *Dessa Rose*. New York: HarperCollins, 1986.

Wilson, Harriet. *Medical Apartheid: The Dark History of Medical Experimentation on Black Americans from Colonial Times to the Present*. Norwell, MA: Anchor Press, 2008.

Wilson, Janelle. *Nostalgia: Sanctuary of Meaning*. Lewisburg, PA: Bucknell University Press, 2005.

Witt, Doris. *Black Hunger: Soul Food and America*. Minneapolis: University of Minnesota Press, 2004.

Wood, Allen. *Hegel's Ethical Thought*. New York: Cambridge University Press, 1990.

Woolfork, Lisa. *Embodying Slavery in Contemporary Culture*. Urbana: University of Illinois Press, 2008.

Wright, Michelle. "Pale by Comparison: Black Liberal Humanism and the Postwar Era." In *Black Europe and the African Diaspora*, edited by Darlene Clark Hine, Steven Small, and Tricia Keaton, 260–76. Urbana: University of Illinois Press, 2009.

———. *Physics of Blackness: Beyond the Middle Passage Epistemology*. Minneapolis: University of Minnesota Press, 2015.

Index

Note: Page number for illustrations are indicated in **bold**.

Badia Ahad-Legardy is an associate professor in the Department of English and Vice Provost for Faculty Affairs at Loyola University Chicago. She is the author of *Freud Upside Down: African American Literature and Psychoanalytic Culture.*

THE NEW BLACK STUDIES SERIES

Beyond Bondage: Free Women of Color in the Americas
Edited by David Barry Gaspar and Darlene Clark Hine
The Early Black History Movement, Carter G. Woodson,
and Lorenzo Johnston Greene   *Pero Gaglo Dagbovie*
"Baad Bitches" and Sassy Supermamas: Black Power Action Films
Stephane Dunn
Black Maverick: T. R. M. Howard's Fight for Civil Rights and
Economic Power   *David T. Beito and Linda Royster Beito*
Beyond the Black Lady: Sexuality and the New
African American Middle Class   *Lisa B. Thompson*
Extending the Diaspora: New Histories of Black People
Dawne Y. Curry, Eric D. Duke, and Marshanda A. Smith
Activist Sentiments: Reading Black Women in
the Nineteenth Century   *P. Gabrielle Foreman*
Black Europe and the African Diaspora   *Edited by Darlene Clark Hine,
Trica Danielle Keaton, and Stephen Small*
Freeing Charles: The Struggle to Free a Slave on the Eve
of the Civil War   *Scott Christianson*
African American History Reconsidered   *Pero Gaglo Dagbovie*
Freud Upside Down: African American Literature
and Psychoanalytic Culture   *Badia Sahar Ahad*
A. Philip Randolph and the Struggle for Civil Rights   *Cornelius L. Bynum*
Queer Pollen: White Seduction, Black Male Homosexuality,
and the Cinematic   *David A. Gerstner*
The Rise of Chicago's Black Metropolis, 1920–1929   *Christopher Robert Reed*
The Muse Is Music: Jazz Poetry from the Harlem Renaissance
to Spoken Word   *Meta DuEwa Jones*
Living with Lynching: African American Lynching Plays, Performance,
and Citizenship, 1890–1930   *Koritha Mitchell*
Africans to Spanish America: Expanding the Diaspora   *Edited by
Sherwin K. Bryant, Rachel Sarah O'Toole, and Ben Vinson III*
Rebels and Runaways: Slave Resistance in Nineteenth-Century Florida
Larry Eugene Rivers
The Black Chicago Renaissance   *Edited by Darlene Clark Hine and
John McCluskey Jr.*
The Negro in Illinois: The WPA Papers   *Edited by Brian Dolinar*
Along the Streets of Bronzeville: Black Chicago's Literary Landscape
Elizabeth Schroeder Schlabach
Gendered Resistance: Women, Slavery, and the Legacy of Margaret Garner
Edited by Mary E. Frederickson and Delores M. Walters

The University of Illinois Press
is a founding member of the
Association of University Presses.

———————————————

Composed in 10.5/13 Minion Pro
with Anivers display
by Kirsten Dennison
at the University of Illinois Press
Manufactured by Sheridan Books, Inc.

University of Illinois Press
1325 South Oak Street
Champaign, IL 61820-6903
www.press.uillinois.edu